Turning Threaded Boxes

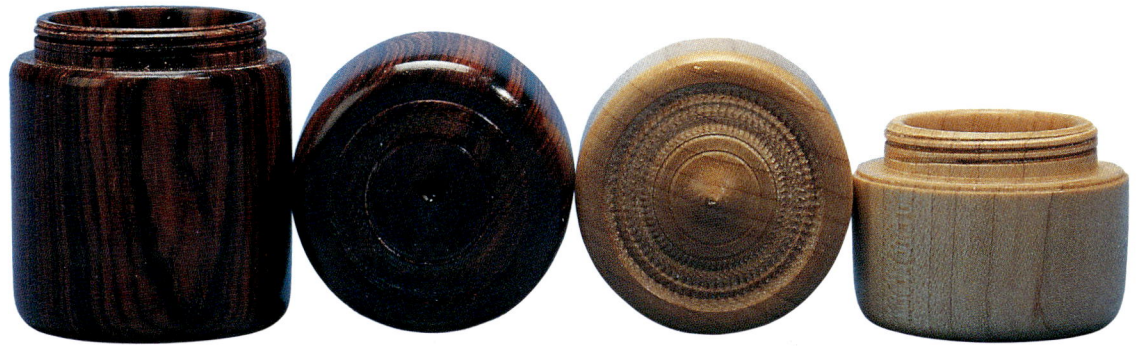

John Swanson

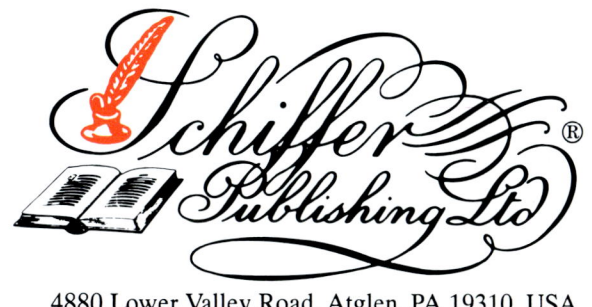

4880 Lower Valley Road, Atglen, PA 19310 USA

Dedication

To Bev, my dear wife, friend, helpmate, companion and critic. The one who gives me encouragement, ideas, advice, guidance, and great feedback.

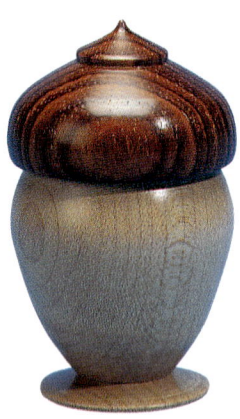

Designed by Randy L. Hensley
Type set in Americana Xbd BT/ZaphHumnst BT

ISBN: 0-7643-0743-6
Printed in China

Published by Schiffer Publishing Ltd.
4880 Lower Valley Road
Atglen, PA 19310
Phone: (610) 593-1777; Fax: (610) 593-2002
E-mail: Schifferbk@aol.com
Please visit our web site catalog at
www.schifferbooks.com
or write for a free catalog.
This book may be purchased from the publisher.
Please include $3.95 for shipping.

In Europe, Schiffer books are distributed by
Bushwood Books
6 Marksbury Rd.
Kew Gardens
Surrey TW9 4JF England
Phone: 44 (0)181 392-8585; Fax: 44 (0)181 392-9876
E-mail: Bushwd@aol.com

Please try your bookstore first.

We are interested in hearing from authors
with book ideas on related subjects.

Contents

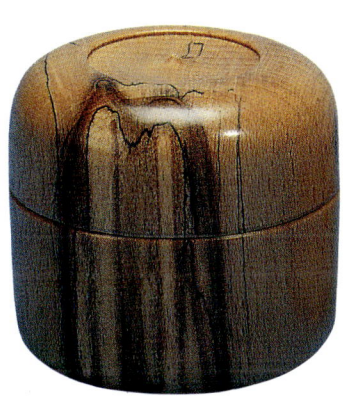
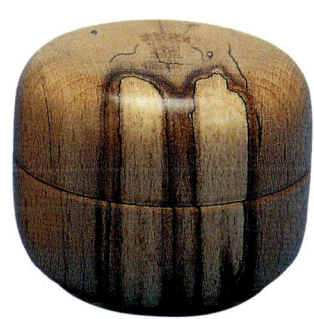

Acknowledgments

I would especially like to thank the following people: Bonnie Klein for designing an accurate and easy to use threading jig; Kip Christensen for teaching me basic wood turning skills; Dale Nish for motivating and sharing his vast knowledge of form, design and advanced turning techniques; and my many wood turning friends. To each and every one, a very hearty "Thank You and may you all have curly shavings!!"

I would also like to acknowledge a few of the sources of quality products that have been particularly helpful to me. They include: Craft Supplies USA, 1287 E.1120 S., Provo, Utah 84606, (800) 551-8876, (wood turning tools & training); Berea Hardwoods, 6367 Eastland Road, Brook Park OH 44142, (216) 234-7949, (wood and turning supplies); Bonham's Woodworking Supply, 1916 Morningside Drive, Garland TX 75042, (800) 266-4267, (lathes and turning tools); Klein Design Inc., 17910 SE 110th Street, Renton WA 98059, (425) 226-2756, (Mini-lathe and threading jig); and Woodcraft Supply Corp., 210 Wood County Industrial Park, Parkersburg WV 26102, (800) 225-1153, (wood turning tools and supplies). There are many other fine sources of useful products and instruction as well, too many to mention here.

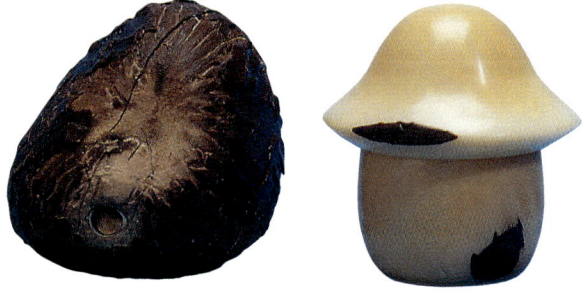

Preface

My life started on a farm in Iowa. My parents were share croppers, raising corn and soybeans. They instilled in their children a strong desire for education and constant learning. They also inbued us all with a desire to do the best in everything we do. If something is worth doing, it is worth doing right.

I left the farm and joined the US Navy. I applied myself and promotions were made quickly. I was awarded an academic scholarship to Purdue University, where I majored in electrical engineering, computer and naval systems. Following commissioning, I was sent to flight training. My first assignment, after getting my flight officer's wings in 1966, was as a bombardier/navigator on the A6 Intruder. My assignment after training was as an instructor on the A6. In SE Asia, I replaced a good friend who had been lost in combat. After two combat tours, I was reassigned to instructor duty. In July 1972, I was sent to SE Asia for another combat tour in the A6. That tour ended when my back was broken and I was subsequently hospitalized for spinal fusion. Upon recovery, it was back to instructor duty.

Prior to retiring from the US Navy in 1976, I purchased my first lathe. I carried it around for 15 years without using it. I had loaned it to my stepson but he didn't have room for it when he moved into a new house three years ago. When he asked if I wanted it back, my wife, Bev, said yes. I played with it a little and found it enjoyable. If I was going to master this tool, however, I realized I needed training. Bev encouraged me to take a basic turning course at the local Woodcraft Store. That started it all in the spring of 1995. Since then, my cabinet making and other wood working projects have decreased, replaced by wood turning.

Boeing, my last employer, was down sizing in the summer of 1995. So when the offer to retire early was presented, I gladly accepted. My years as a design engineer on the 777, a flight crew instructor and a systems test integration pilot all were very rewarding, the positions all were satisfying; however, retirement—with the time for mastering the lathe it presented—was an opportunity too good to past up.

I was determined to master the lathe and its associated tools. Since I believe in learning correctly from the best available source, I enrolled in a week long basic turning class. It was there that Kip Christensen taught me wood turning skills. I was sent home to practice, which I did. During the summer of 1997 I went back for the intermediate course with Dale Nish. It was there that my creative juices were stimulated.

In addition to those formal classes, I have had the privilege of attending various symposiums and turning work shops. My skills continued to improve and I have been asked to demonstrate box turning techniques to various chapters of the AAW (American Association of Woodturners, 3200 Lexington Avenue, Shoreview, MN 55126, 612-484-9094; fax: 612-484-1724). I was given much encouragement and was asked to do this book. I hope it is of assistance and beneficial to you. You are welcome to attempt to copy my methods; however, it is much easier to understand the concepts and principles, and then apply your own skills and methods to the job at hand. You will soon find what you like and what works best for you. With a small amount of material, you can turn a box that is a joy to make and a thrill to receive.

Introduction

My purpose is to take you step-by-step through the processes I use to make a box with a threaded lid. A box with a friction fit lid is nice; a box with a threaded lid is extra special.

Most of the tools I use are readily available but they aren't the only tools for the tasks. There are thousands of ways to do a thing, some are just easier and/or quicker than others. I firmly believe that if a method is easy to use, you will do it again. If it is too difficult, you will probably that technique aside.

I may show you a different method or two for doing the same procedure. If one method or tool doesn't work, maybe the other one will. I have made mistakes over the years and wish to share with you the methods that I have found to produce functional and useful boxes.

Box design is very subjective. The function of the box may dictate that you have a certain size or shape. The ratio of size between top and bottom that produces a well proportioned box is 2/5:3/5. I have included a layout chart using that ratio. Enter the chart at the length of your material and you will have the maximum length of the top. If you want the box shorter, just move up the chart. Allowances are included for the threaded spigot and the material lost in parting off.

To begin the project, first choose the material for your box. It is hard to beat hard maple for your first box. Its working characteristics are good, the threads are strong and it takes a good finish. It is also economical.

There are a number of ways to hold the material on the lathe. There are 3 and 4 jaw self-centering chucks, direct mounting on face plates or mounting on a face plate with a waste block. I usually mount my material via the last method. My reasoning is that with this method you can secure the bottom section of the box more tightly, hence with increased safety, when cutting the threads.

Another important decision to make is the choice of thread cutting methods. Threads can be cut by hand using thread chasers or with a mechanical threading jig. I use a threading jig.

Steps for Making a Box with a Threaded Lid

1. After the material is mounted, turn it to a cylinde The tools used can be a roughing gouge, spind gouge or skew. I usually finish with my friend, th half inch skew.
2. Mark and part off the lid. I refer to the layout char
3. Mount the lid so it can be hollowed. I normally use self-centering chuck as it is quick and centers th lid. True up the mating surface. Hollow out and shap the inside of the lid, ensuring the sides are perfect straight for the threads.
4. Cut a clearance for one thread. The threading jig ca not cut full length, so clearance is necessary.
5. Bevel surfaces for a smooth feel.
6. Sand and finish the interior of the lid. I don't recom mend wax on the interior surfaces of a box.
7. Mount the cutter and threading jig, then cut ver light threads. 4 or 5 threads are sufficient.
8. Apply thin cyanoacrylate (CA) glue to the thread are This strengthens the threads and reduces chipping
9. Cut threads to their full depth.
10. Lightly sand the threads. This removes any rough ness left by the cutter.
11. Remove the lid and remount the bottom on the headstock.
12. Measure the inside of the lid threads.
13. Add .05 inches to the measurement in Step #12. This is the rough diameter of the tenon for the bot tom.
14. Cut the tenon on the bottom.
15. Remove the interior waste from the bottom. En sure that the interior sides are parallel at the tenon.
16. Sand and finish the inside of the bottom.
17. Cut the tenon to its final length and diameter, the bevel. The length should be under 1/4 inch and the diameter should be .04 greater than the diameter of threads in the lid.

18. Mount the cutter and threading jig, then cut very light threads up to the shoulder of the tenon.
19. Flow thin CA glue into the threads.
20. Adjust the threading jig for deeper threads. Test fit the lid. Re-cut the threads deeper if necessary.
21. Remount the bottom on the headstock and lightly sand the threads.
22. Mount the lid onto the bottom and turn the lid to its final shape.
23. Adjust the length of the tenon to get the grain to match between the pieces.
24. Sand and finish the lid.
25. Remove the bottom from the waste block or chuck.
26. Make a jam fit chuck to hold the bottom of the box.
27. Shape the bottom of the box. Sand and finish.
28. Remove the bottom, fit the top.
29. Congratulations, you have made a box with a threaded lid!

Box Layout Table

(2/5 Top and 3/5 Bottom)
[1/4 tenon and 1/4 for parting]

Unit	Top	Bottom	Bottom & tenon	Parting cut	Material Length
1/8	1/4	3/8	5/8	1/4	1 1/8
3/16	3/8	9/16	13/16	1/4	1 7/16
1/4	1/2	3/4	1	1/4	1 3/4
5/16	5/8	15/16	1 3/16	1/4	2 1/16
3/8	3/4	1 1/8	1 3/8	1/4	2 3/8
7/16	7/8	1 5/16	1 9/16	1/4	2 11/16
1/2	1	1 1/2	1 3/4	1/4	3
9/16	1 1/8	1 11/16	1 15/16	1/4	3 5/16
5/8	1 1/4	1 7/8	2 1/8	1/4	3 5/8
11/16	1 3/8	2 1/16	2 5/16	1/4	3 15/16
3/4	1 1/2	2 1/4	2 1/2	1/4	4 1/4
13/16	1 5/8	2 7/16	2 11/16	1/4	4 9/16
7/8	1 3/4	2 5/8	2 7/8	1/4	4 7/8
15/16	1 7/8	2 13/16	3 1/16	1/4	5 3/16
1	2	3	3 1/4	1/4	5 1/2

Tools & Woods, An Introduction

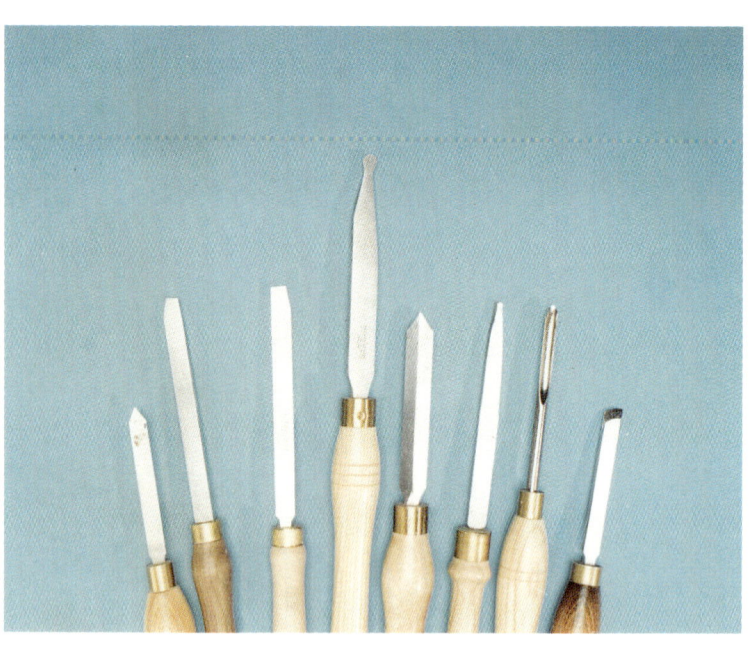

Some of the tools that I use for turning my boxes. They include (from left to right) parting tools, square ended scrapers, round nosed scrapers, and my two favorites, the 3/8" spindle gouge and 1/2" skew chisel.

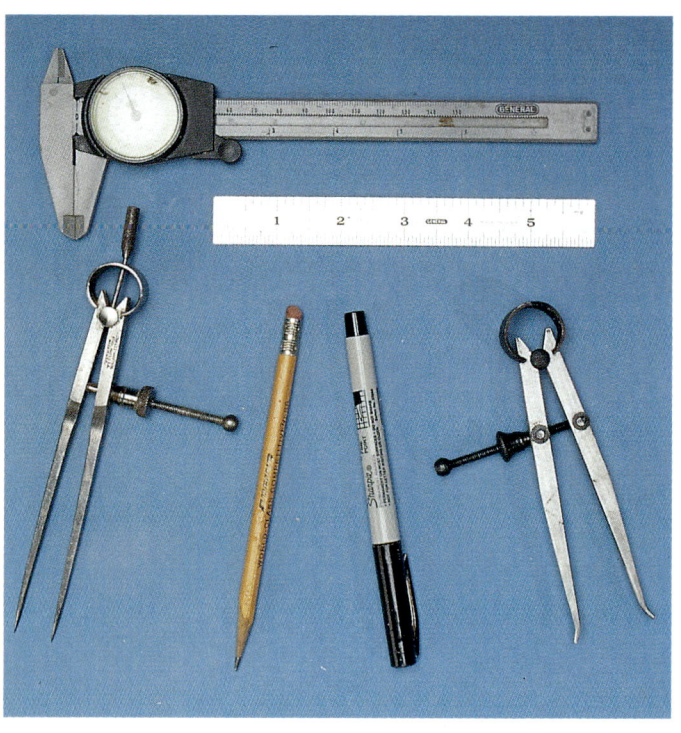

Measuring and layout tools that I use.

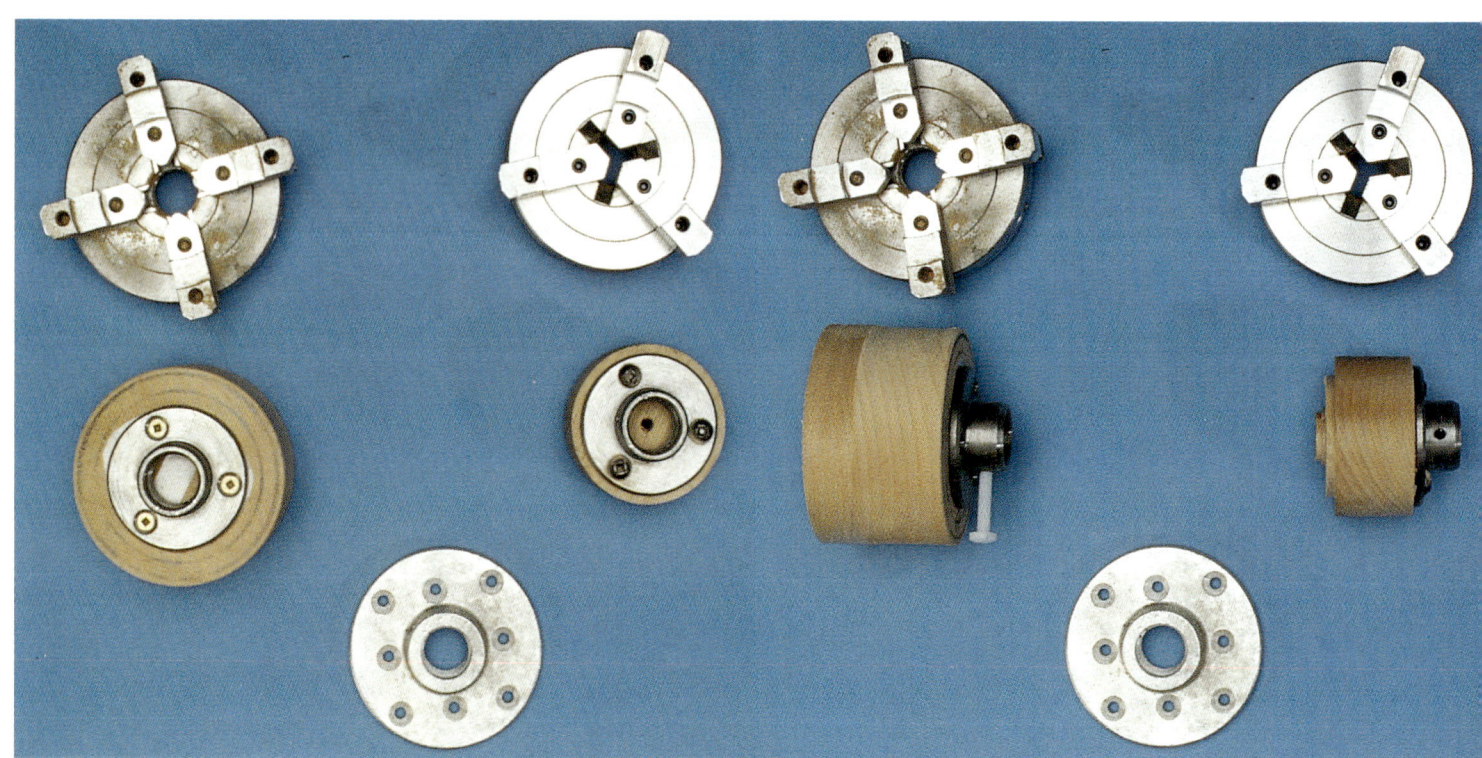

This is the equipment used to hold the material on the lathe. These objects include three and four jaw scroll chucks and face plates with waste blocks attached. The face plates are drilled and tapped for a 10/32" nylon screw.

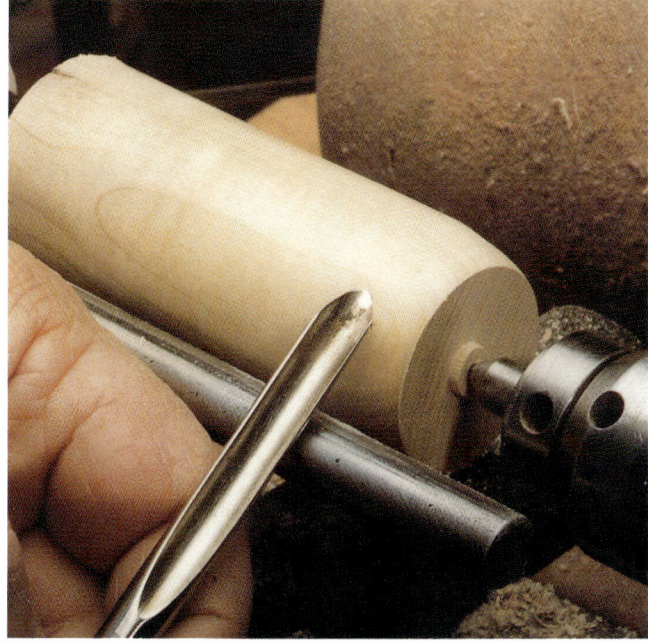

One of my workhorses, for all types of work, is the 3/8" spindle gouge. It is ground with a fingernail profile and must be kept sharp.

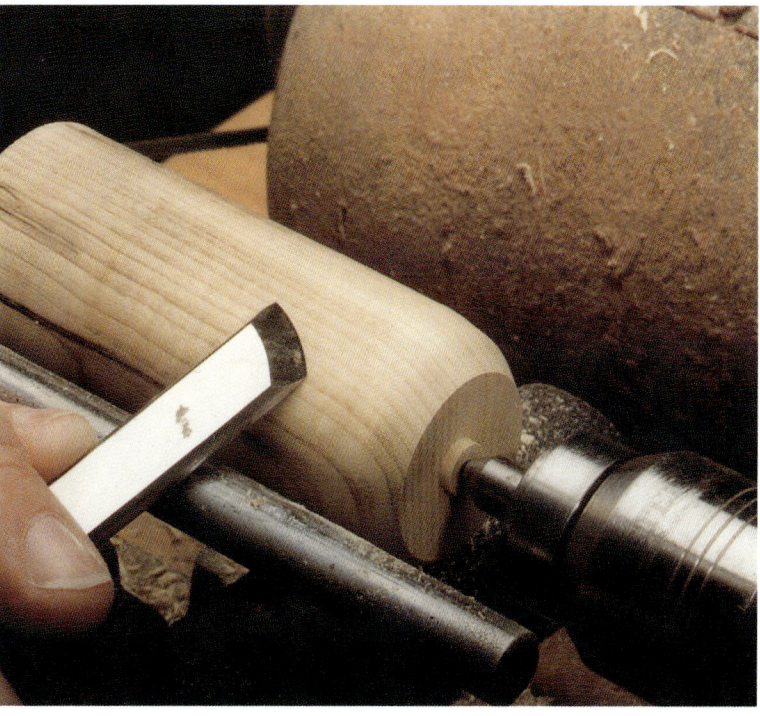

Another of my basic tools is the 1/2" skew chisel. It is ground with a Raffan style or curved edge. The toe starts off straight and becomes curved toward the heel.

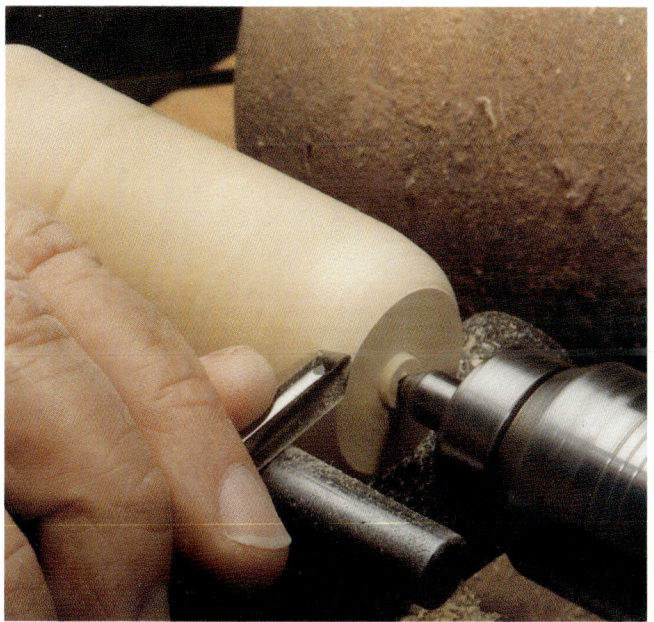

The spindle gouge is used for putting coves on the tops and bottoms of boxes and for rough hollowing.

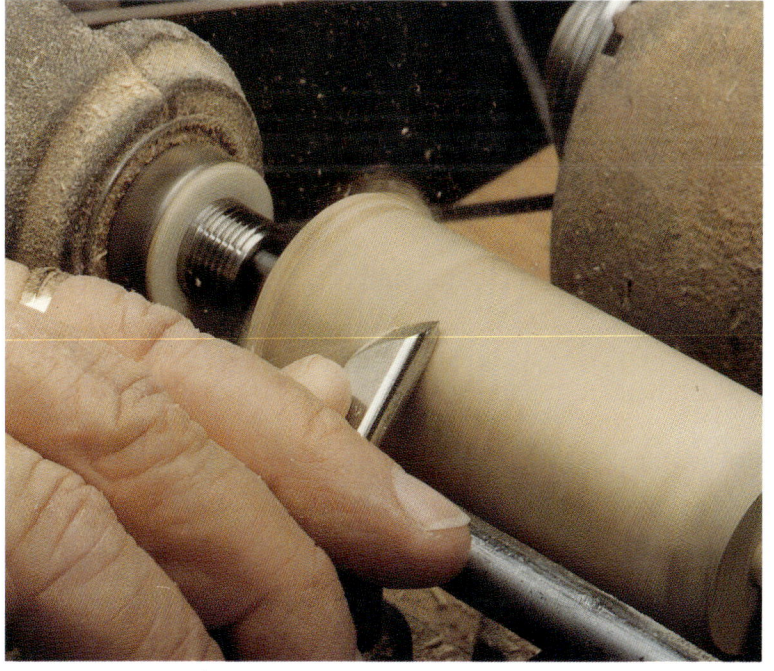

It is used for exterior shaping, end grain paring, and shear scraping. Exterior finish cuts are made with the heel leading.

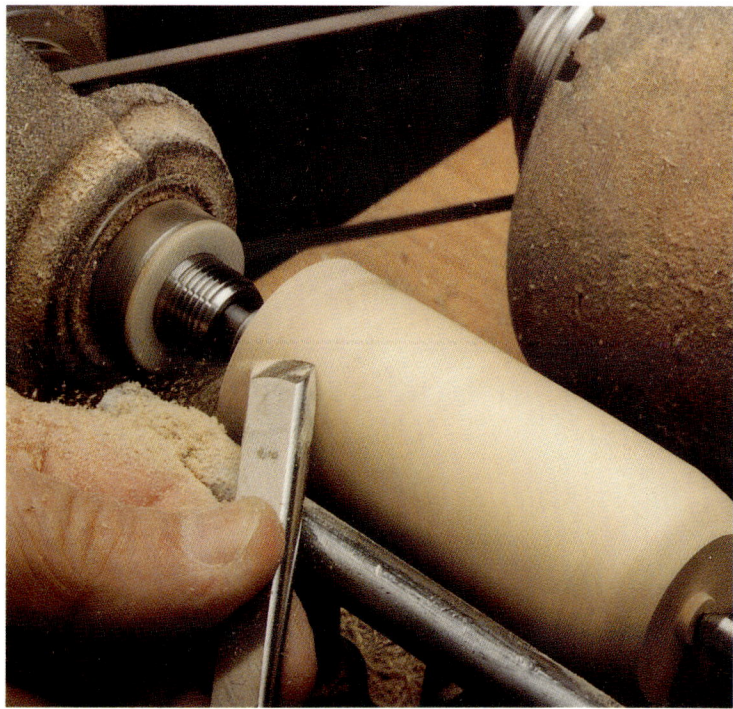

It can also be used with the toe leading.

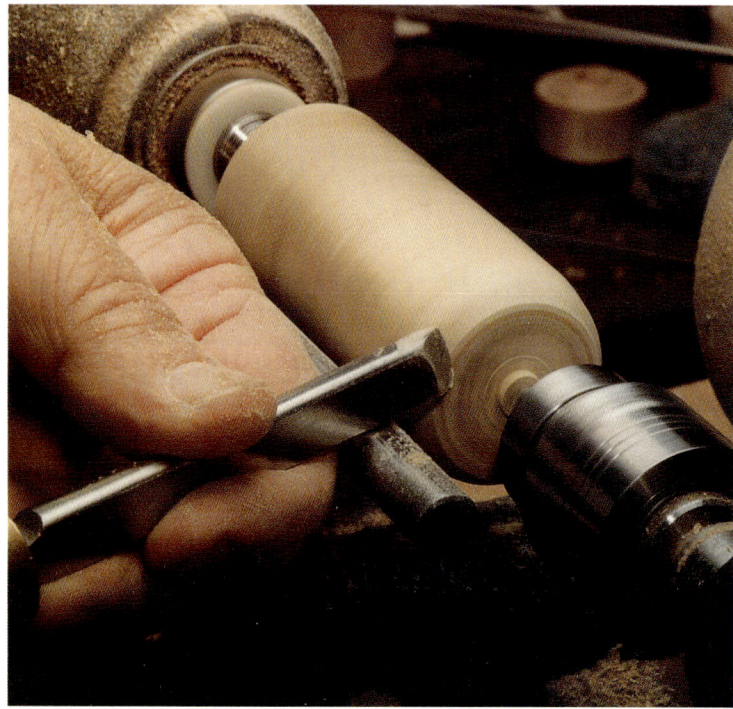

Nothing cuts across end grain better than an arcing cut with the toe of a skew.

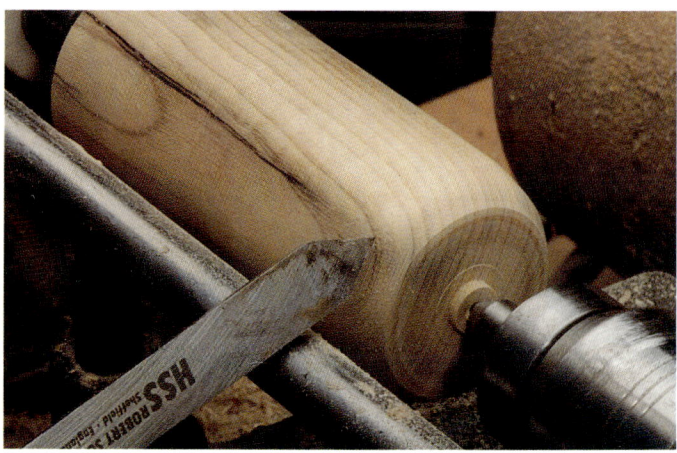

This is a 1/8" parting tool.

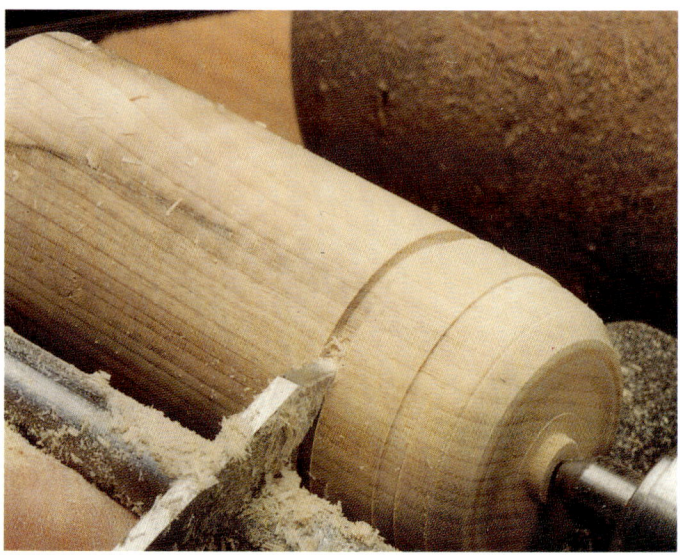

The parting tool is used for layout, smoothing, and parting off.

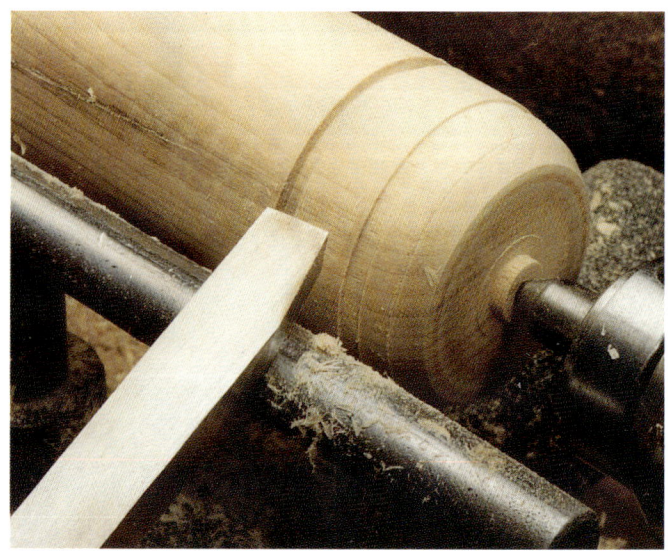

A 3/8" thick x 1/2" wide tool steel blank was ground into a square ended scraper. The angle is slightly less than 90 degrees. The cutting is done on the point at the right side.

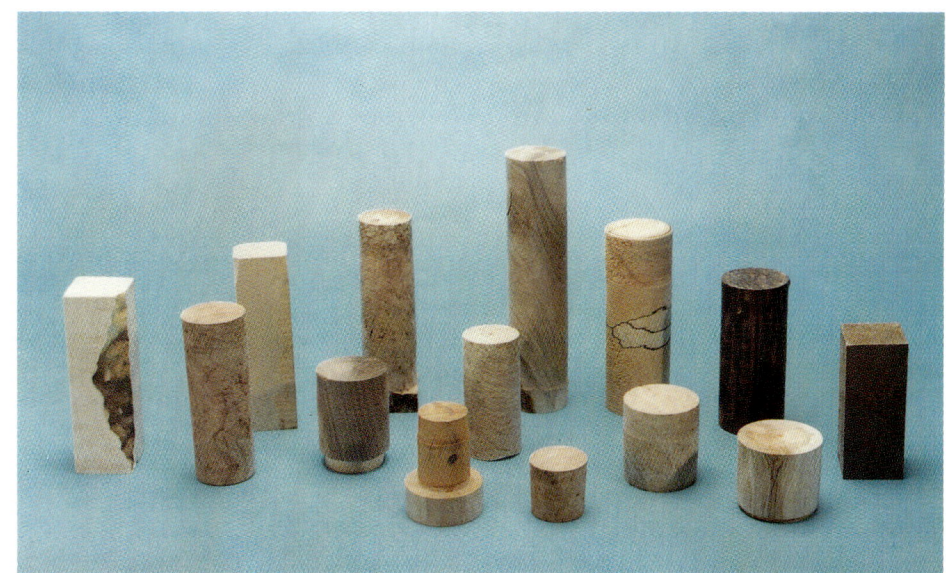

Similarly, a left hand scraper has been made. The handle of the scraper should be elevated above the cutting point to avoid dig ins. These scrapers will be used on the interior cuts for the boxes.

Here are samples of hardwoods that make excellent boxes. The species shown include curly maple, maple burl, redwood burl, walnut, cocobolo, osage orange, and apple. The second block from the left in the back row is Eastern hard maple, the wood used for the first project in this book.

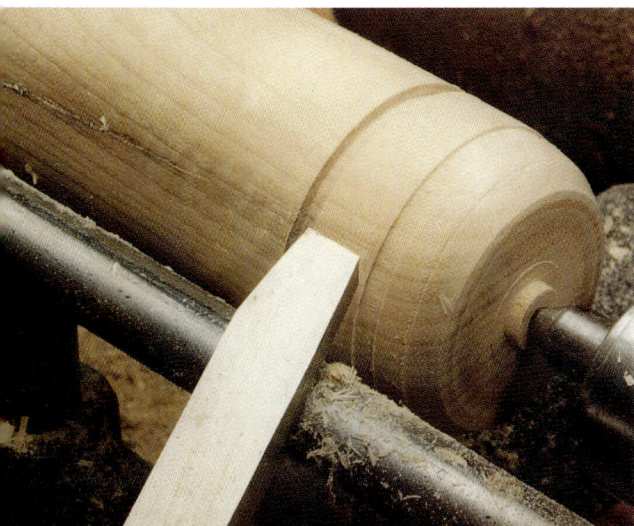

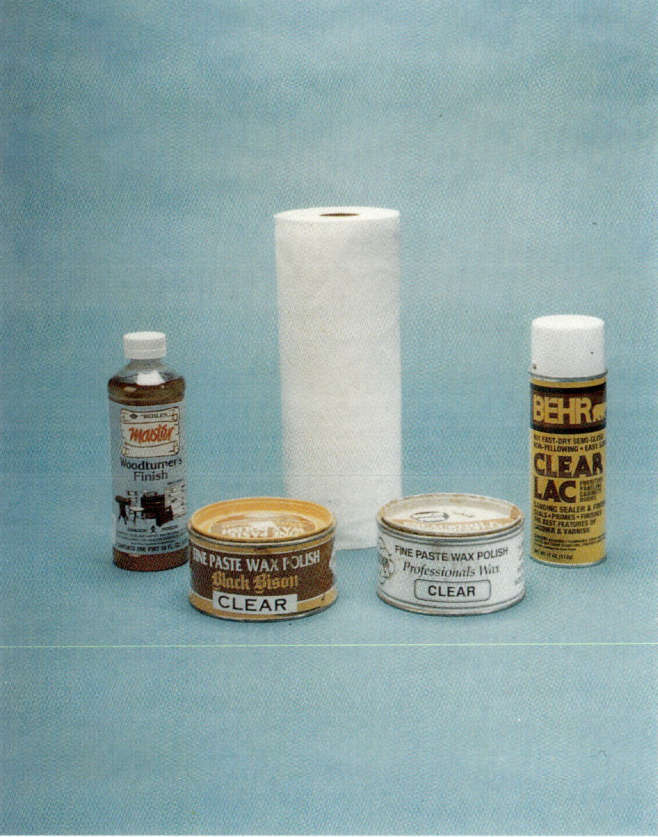

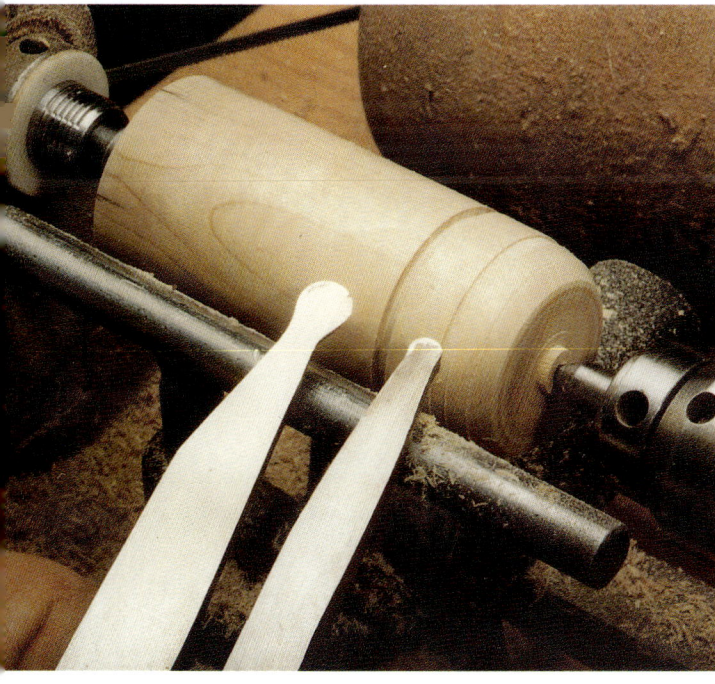

Some of the finishing supplies that I use. The paper towels I use are two ply, white, and soft. I do not use cloth as it can become entangled in the work.

Occasionally, round nosed scrapers are used in finishing off the tops and bottoms inside the boxes.

Project 1: A Threaded Box from a Maple Block

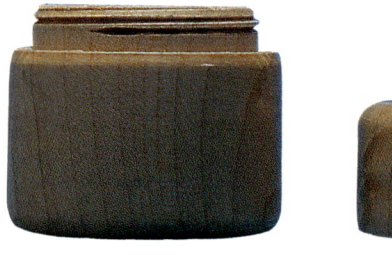
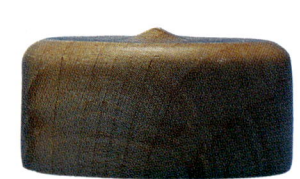

The first project.

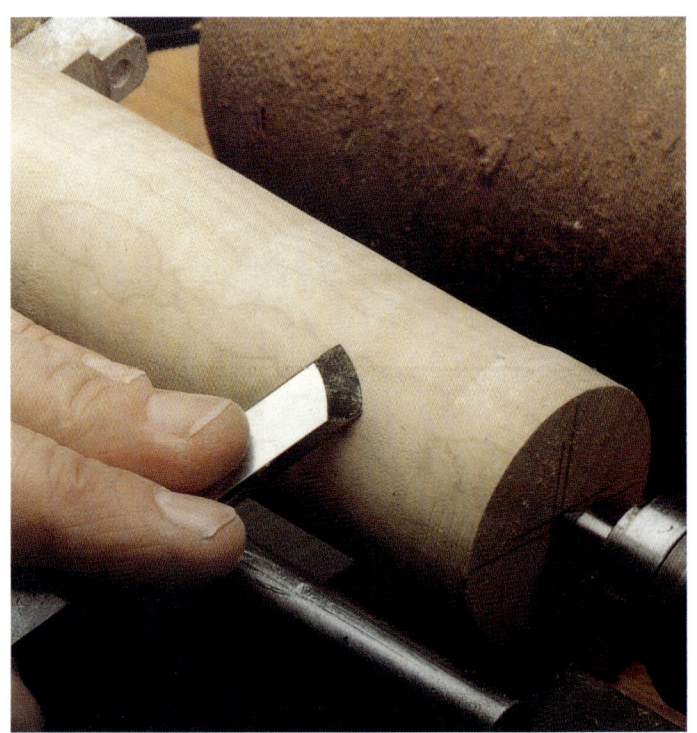

The final shaping is done with a 1/2" or 3/4" skew chisel.

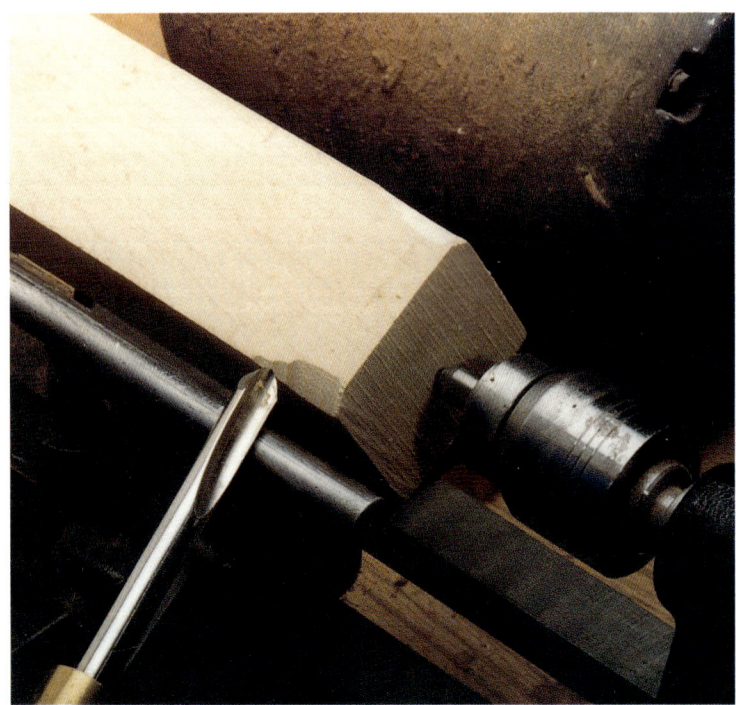

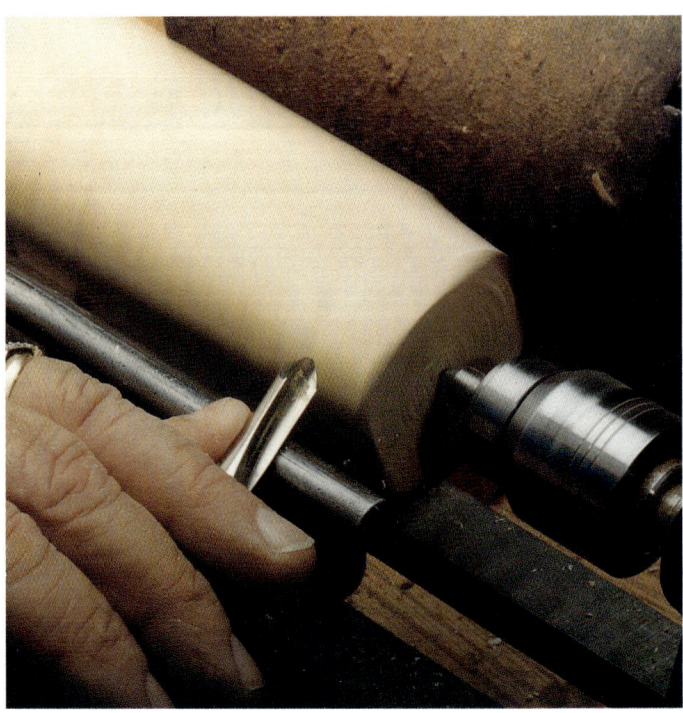

The primary tool I use for turning square wood to round is the
3/8" spindle gouge. Other tools that can be used include
roughing gouges, and skew chisels.

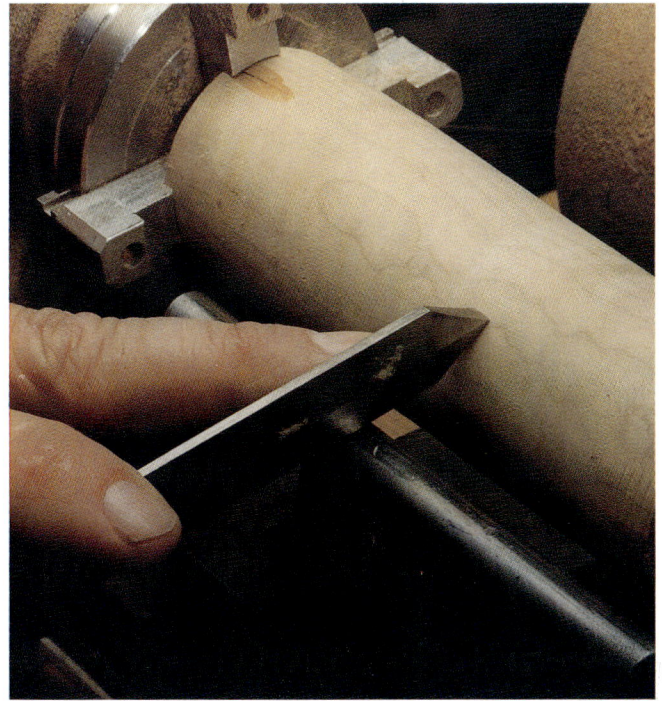

Next, use the parting tool to cut off the length of wood to be used to make the box.

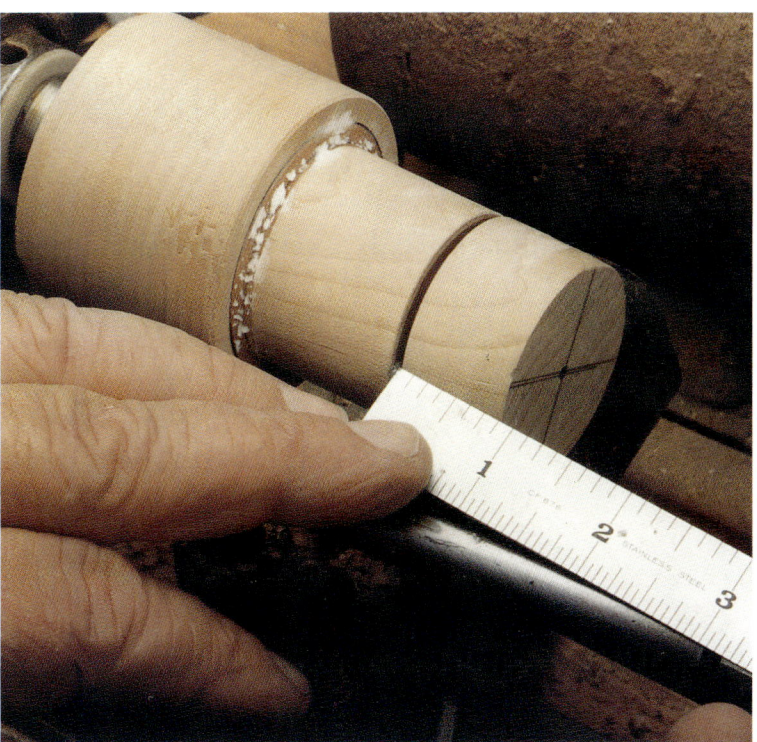

For a box of this length, we will turn a 7/8" top and a 1 1/4" bottom. The top is separated from the bottom with a parting tool.

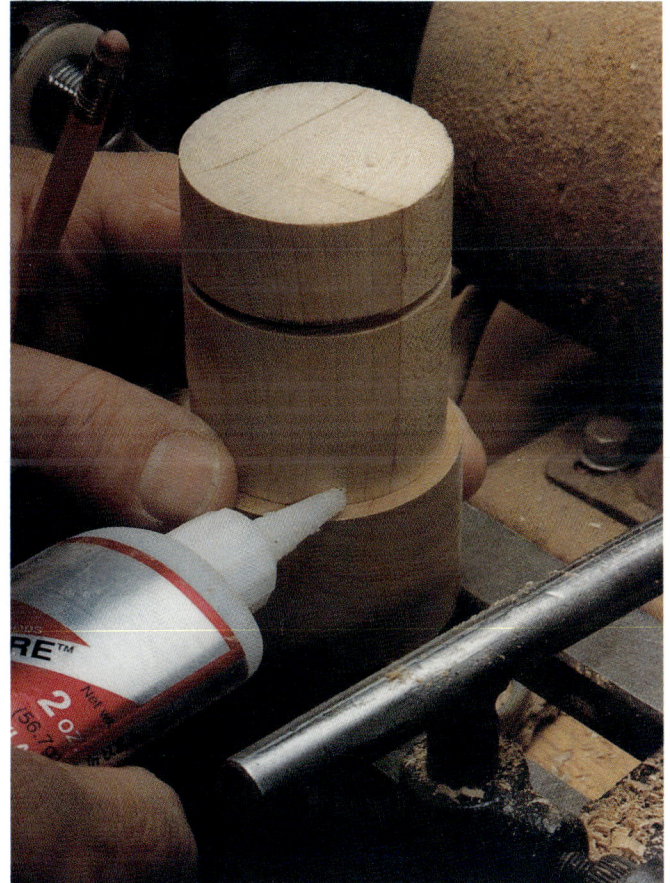

The blank is attached to a waste block which is screwed to a faceplate. An application of thick Super Glue is preferred for securing the blank to the waste block. Alternate methods include double stick tape, carpenters' glue and hot melt glue.

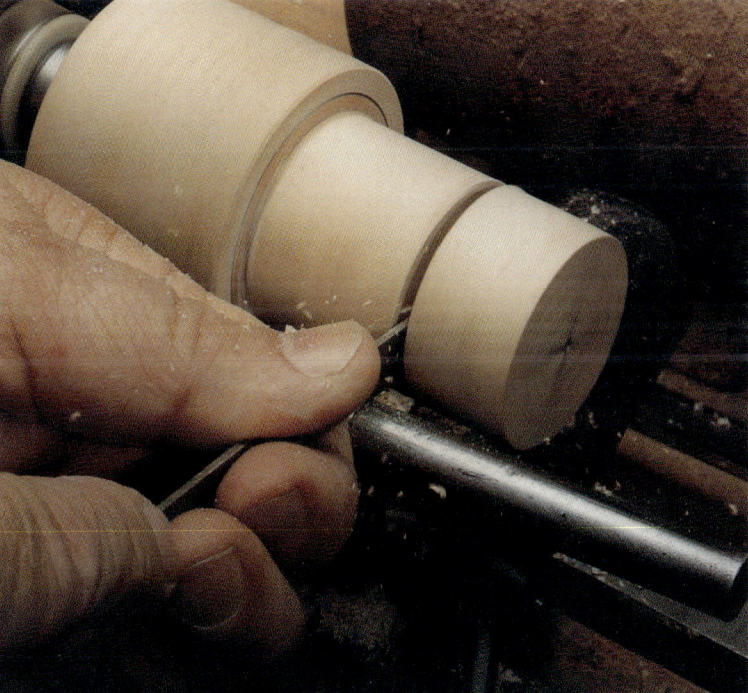

Parting the lid. The thinner the blade of the parting tool used now, the better the grain match will be later.

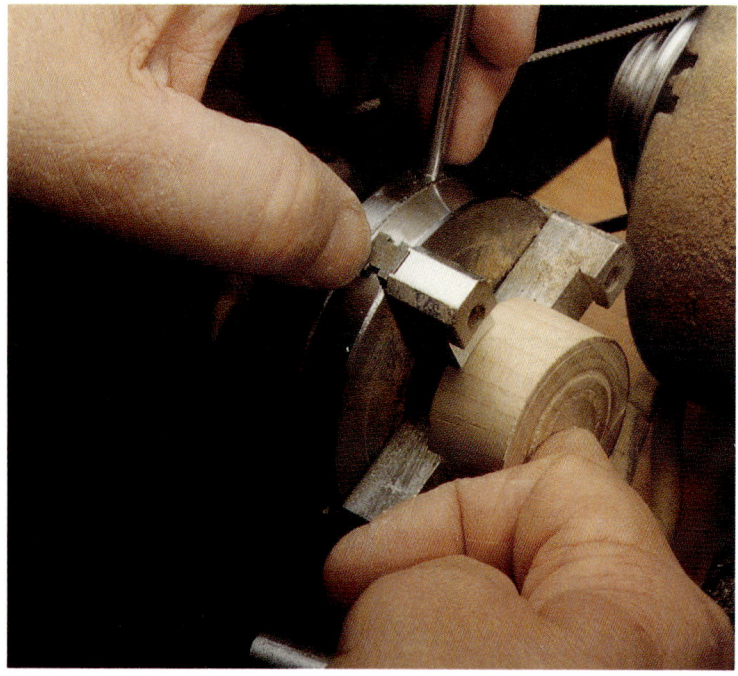

The top of the lid is held securely in a four jaw chuck. Other methods for holding the lid include a three jaw chuck or another face plate and waste block combination.

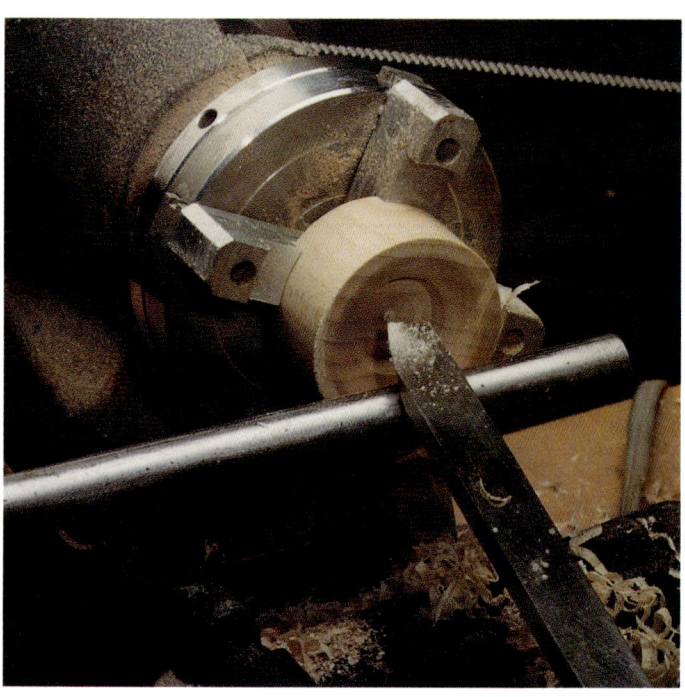

Final hollowing is accomplished using a square ended scraper. The angle between the two surfaces of the scraper should be slightly less than 90 degrees. The cutting is accomplished by the burr left when sharpening the square ended scraper.

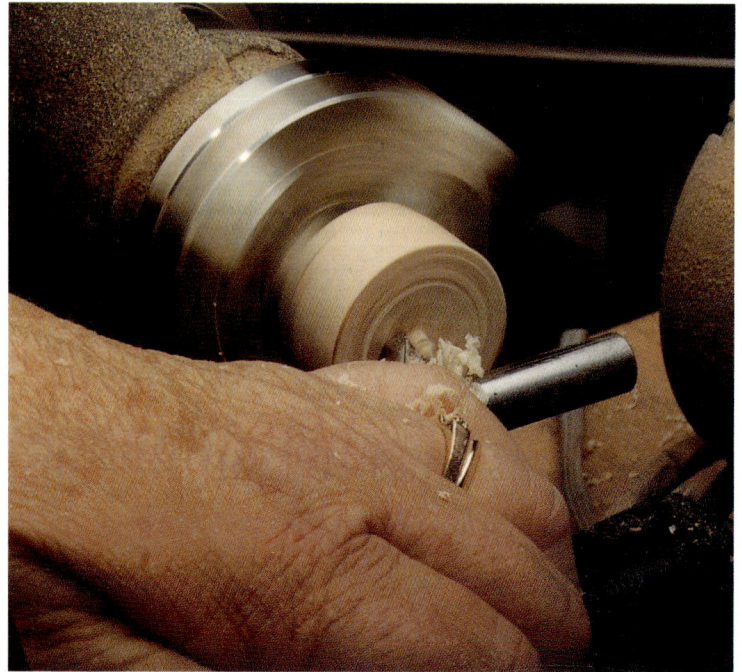

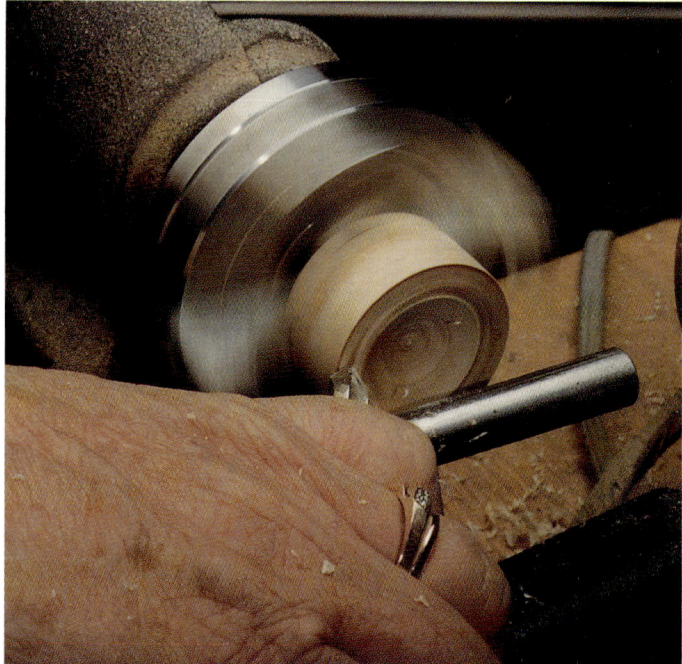

The lid can be hollowed out with a number of different tools. I use a 3/8" spindle gouge to ensure that the lip is smooth. The interior of the lid is hollowed to within one half inch of the top, and is usually left slightly concave.

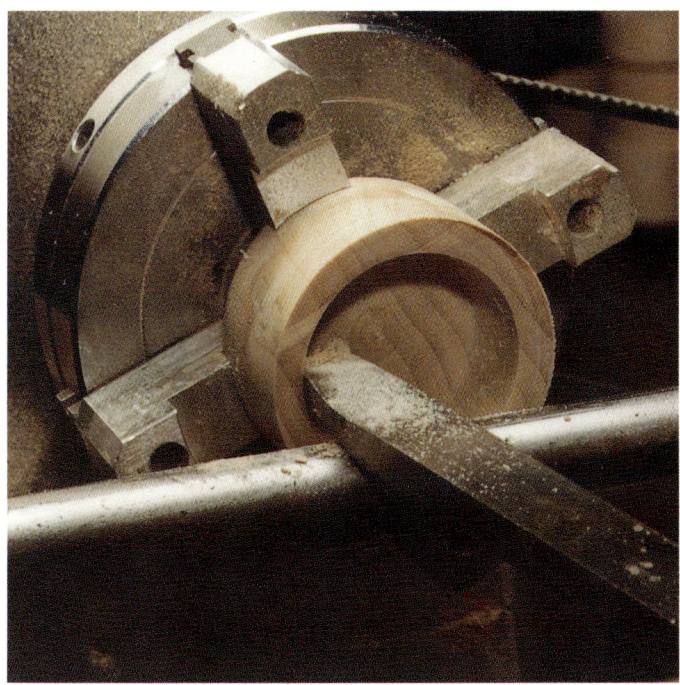

For the lid and bottom to fit together well, the hollowed out lid must have parallel sides.

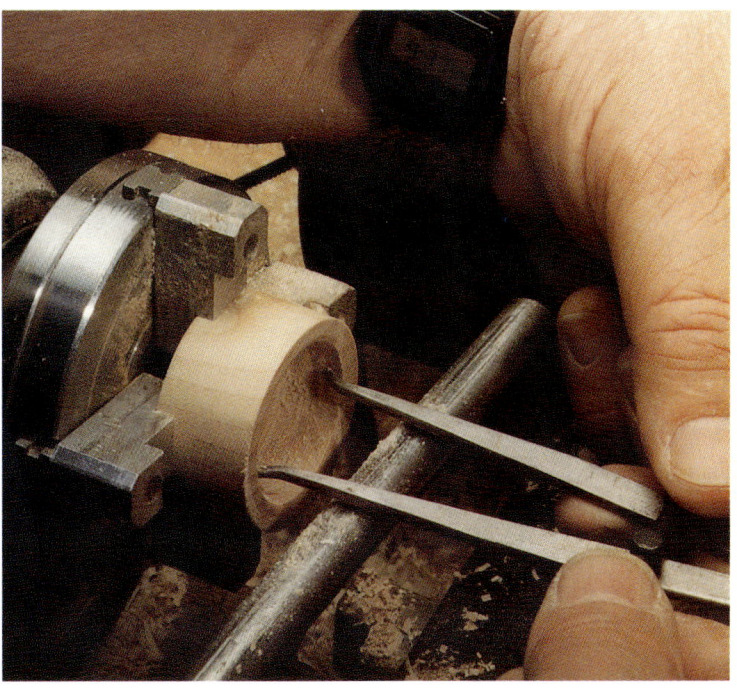

An alternate method involves using outside calipers to ensure that the walls are parallel.

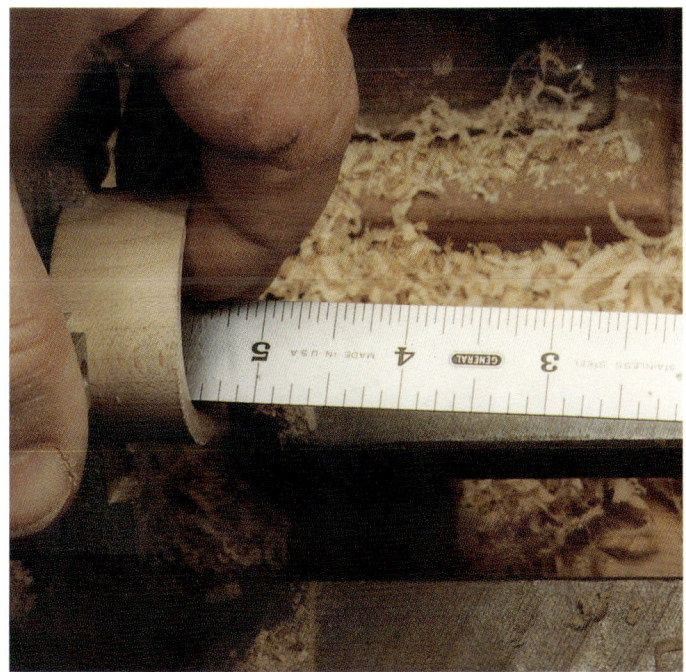

One method used to check whether the lid side walls are parallel is to place a ruler against the side wall of the lid to insure that it lines up to the ways of the lathe bed.

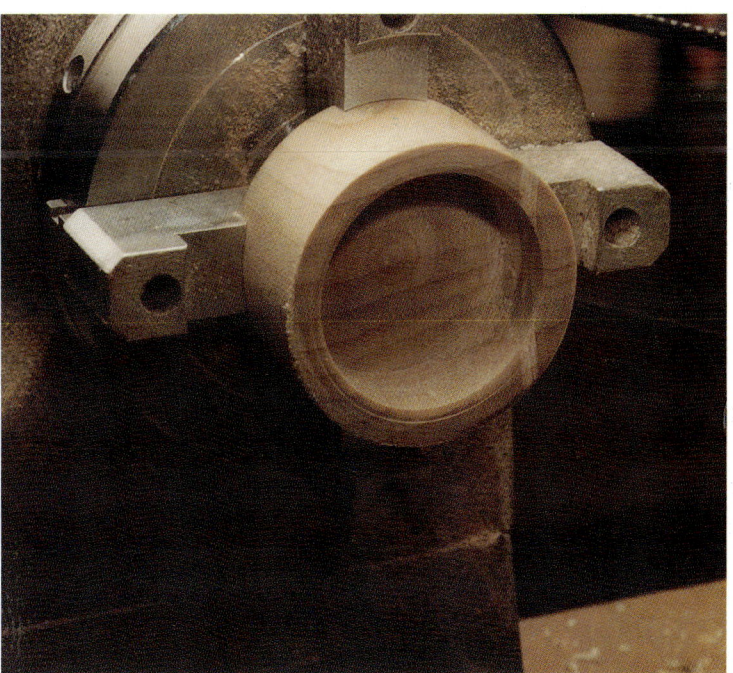

The inside of the lid is now ready for final sanding.

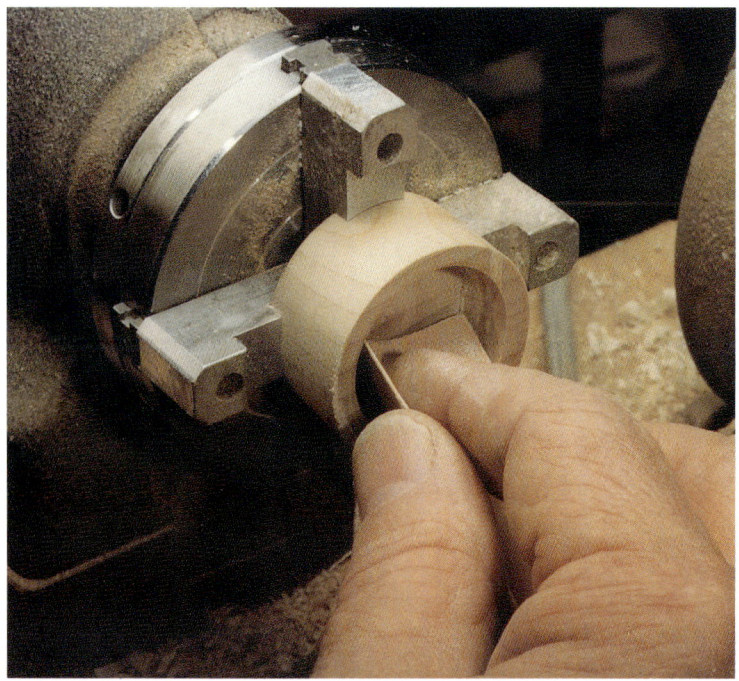

Sanding is done starting with 150 grit and working through 180, 220, 320, 400, and 600. Do not use wet/dry sandpaper on light colored woods. Wet/dry paper is black and may discolor the wood.

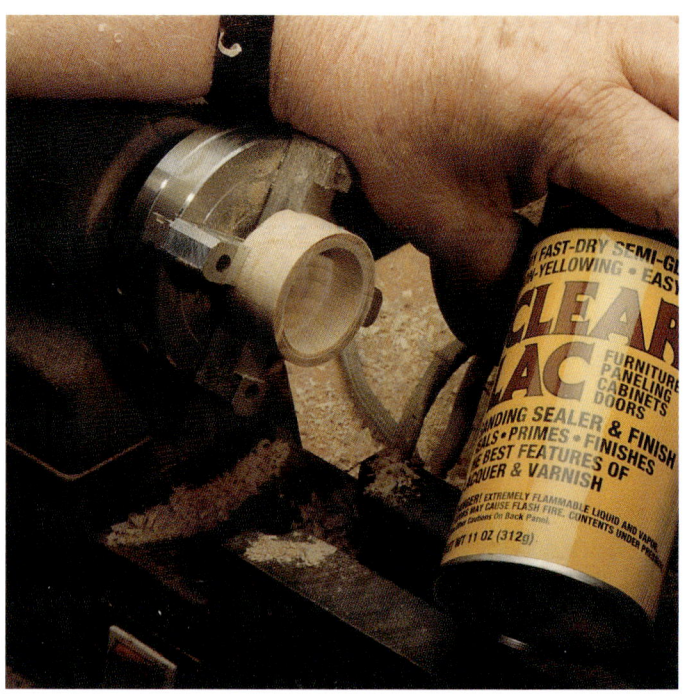

I use a lacquer based spray sanding sealer with the lathe stopped to finish the piece.

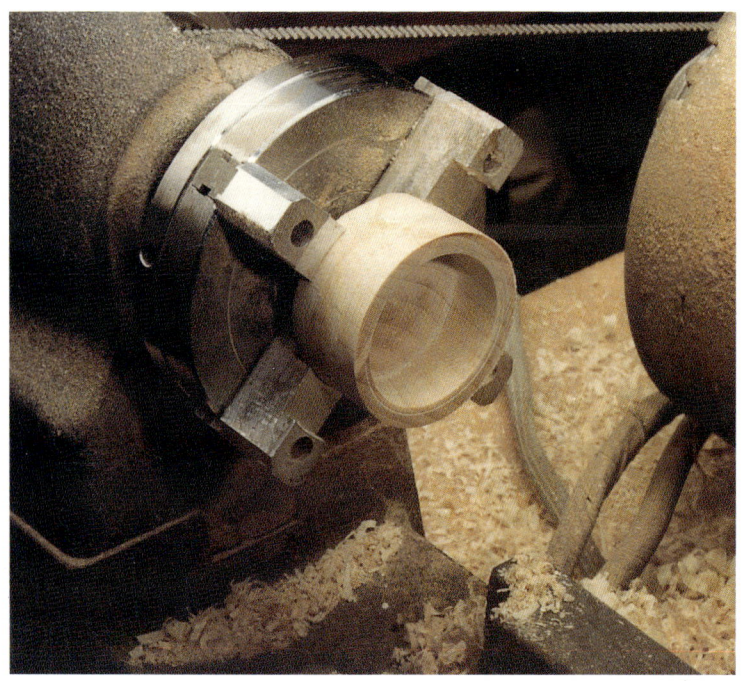

The lid is ready for final finishing.

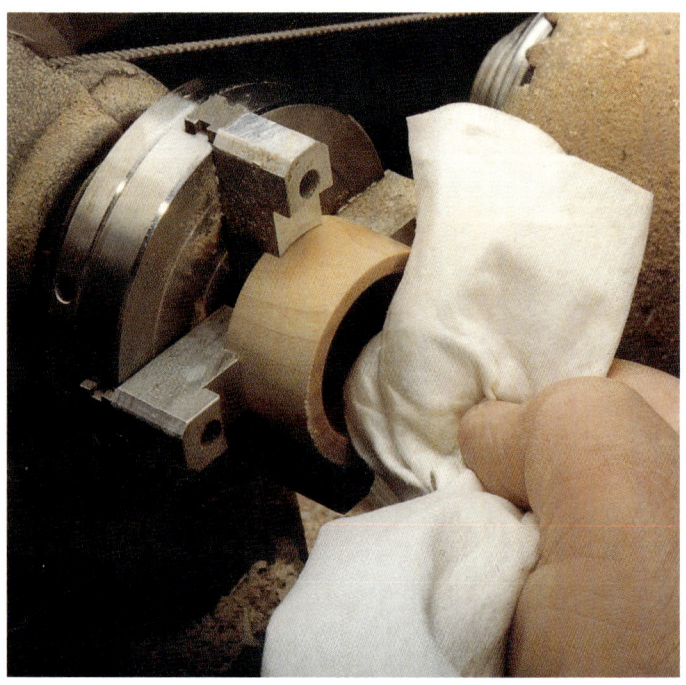

Flood the lid and wipe it dry with a paper towel. Cloth towels can wrap around your box and pull your hand into the lathe.

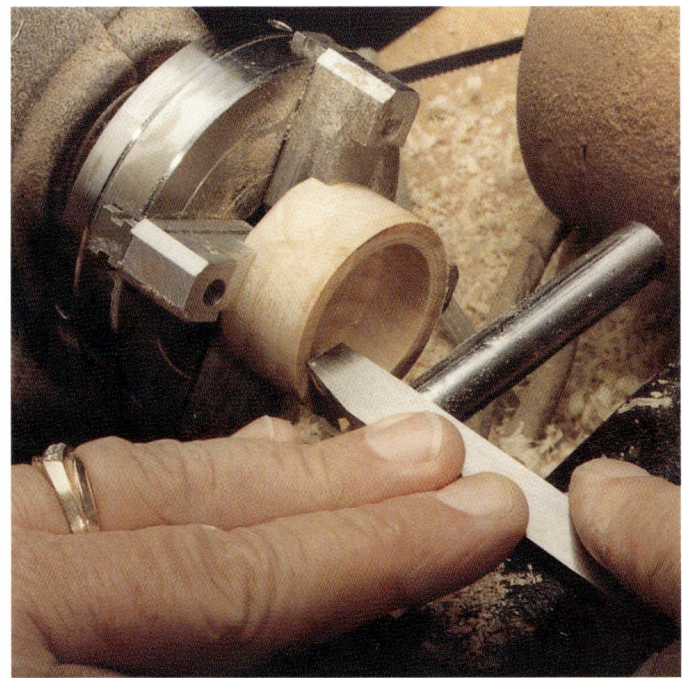

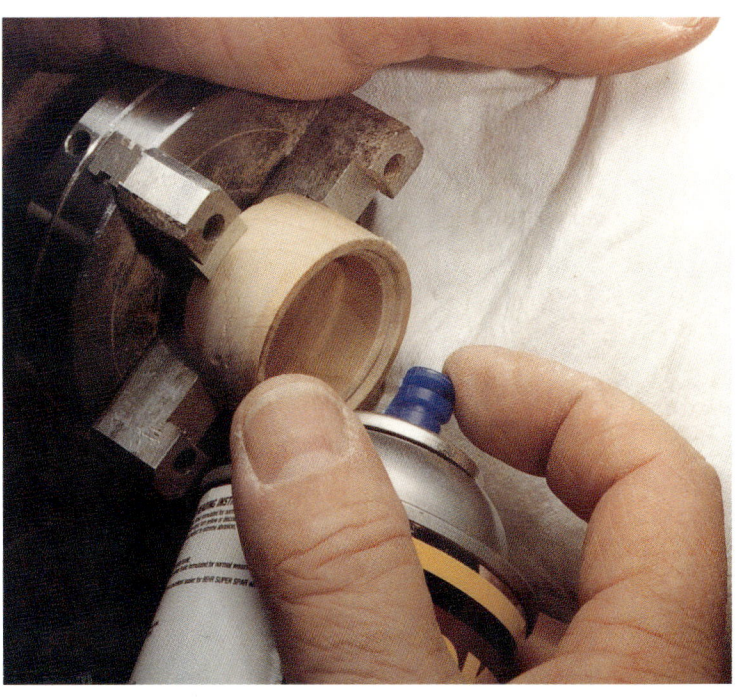

The final lid cut is made with a square ended scraper. Make a 1/16" x 1/16" recess in the lid edge. This allows for an area where threads can't be cut on the bottom spigot.

Sanding sealer is again applied to the inside of the lid. This ensures all surfaces are sealed.

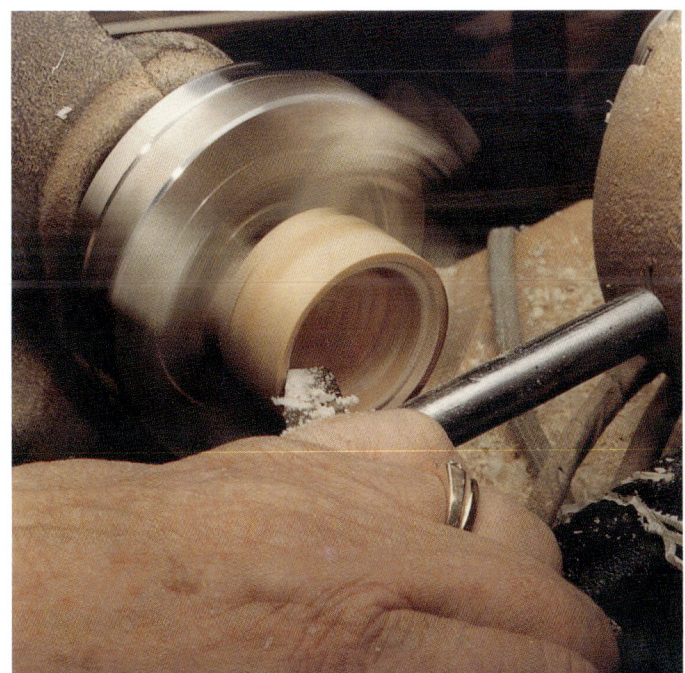

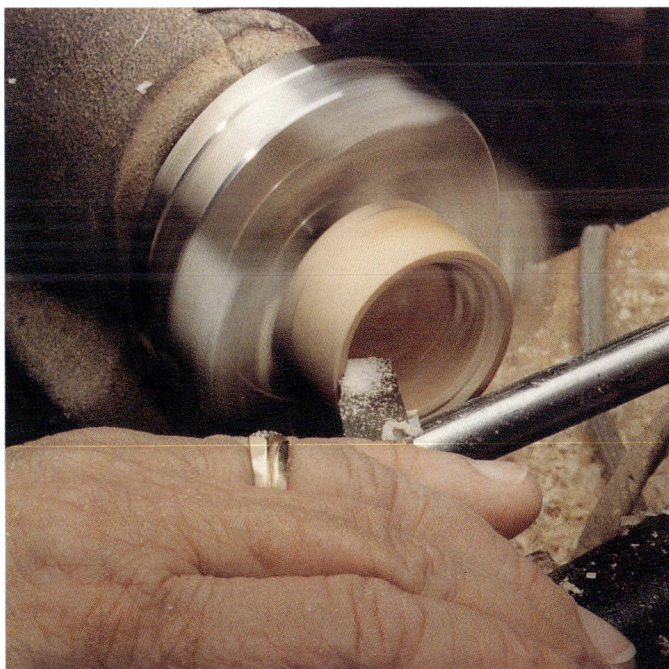

The lip of the lid is chamferred to soften the edge of the lid.

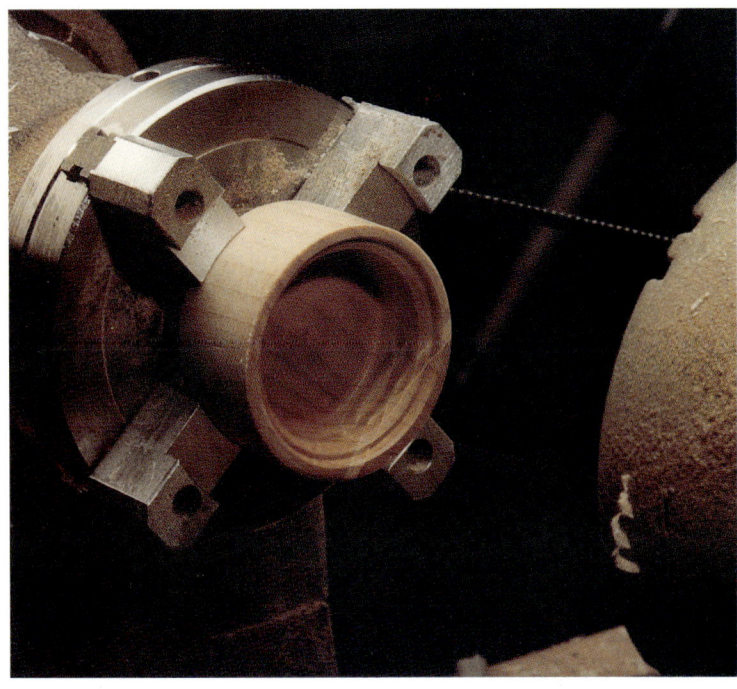

The lid is ready for threads.

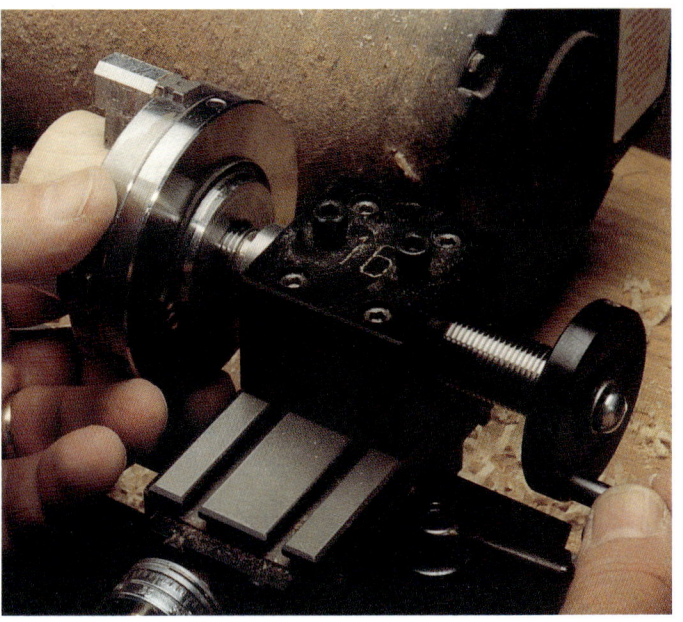

The lid is attached to the threadbox. I use the Klein Design threading jig that readily adapts to the Carbatec and Klein lathes.

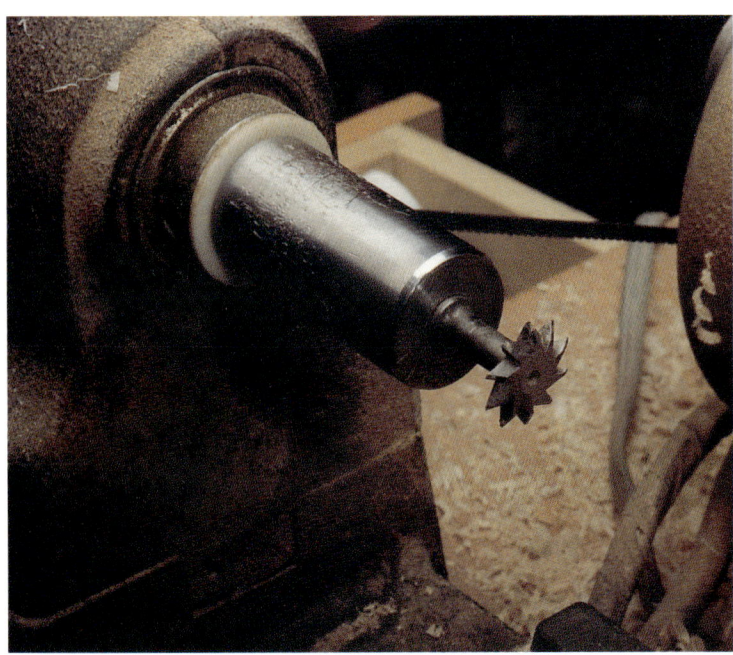

The cutter is attached to the head stock of the lathe.

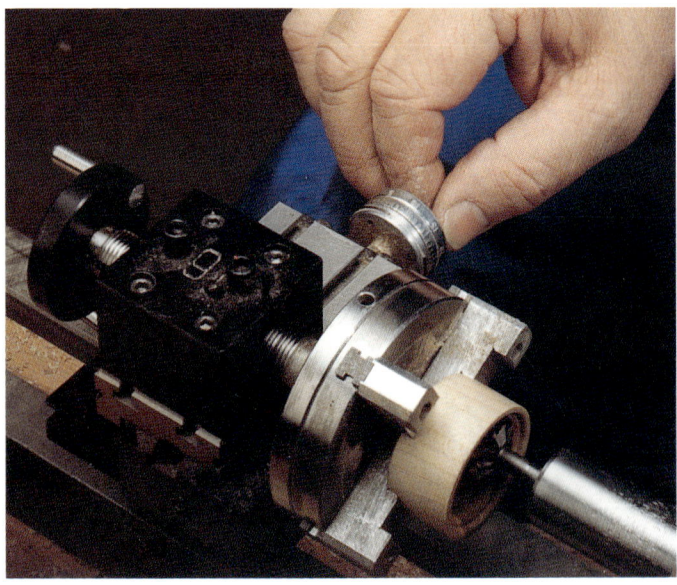

The cross vice is adjusted until the inside of the lid makes contact with the cutter.

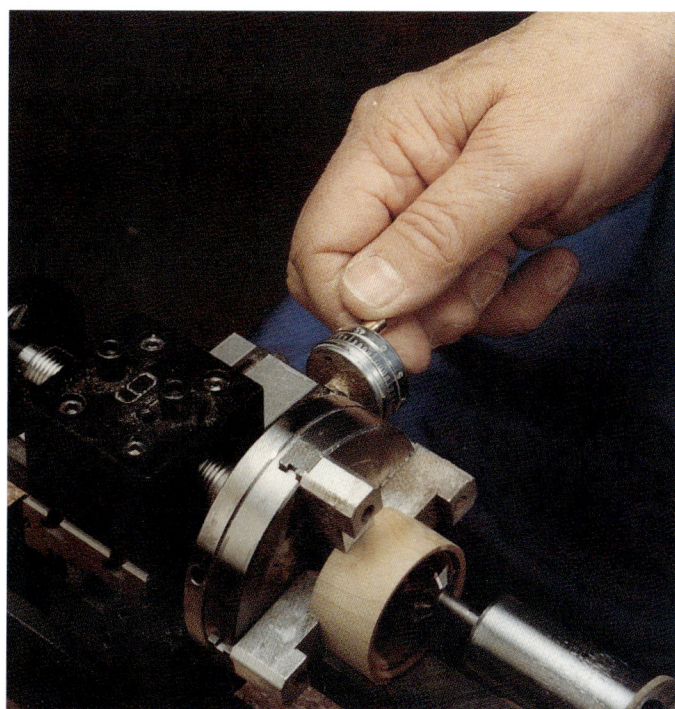

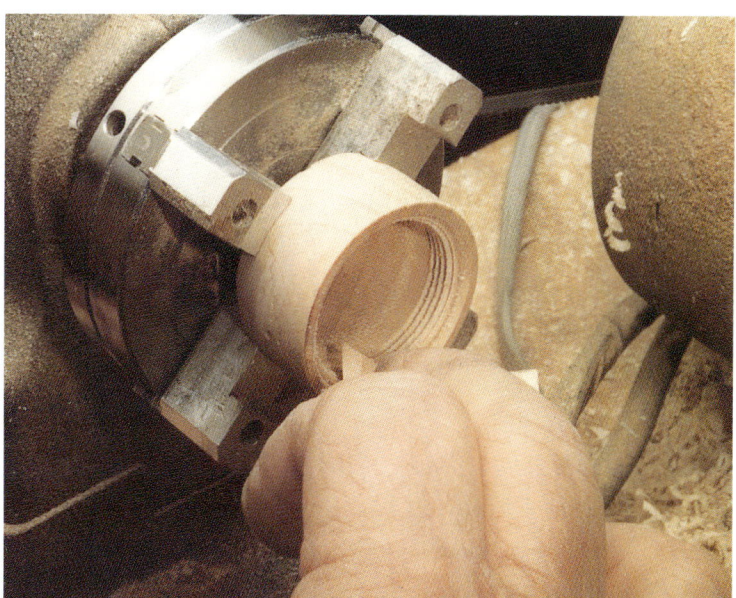

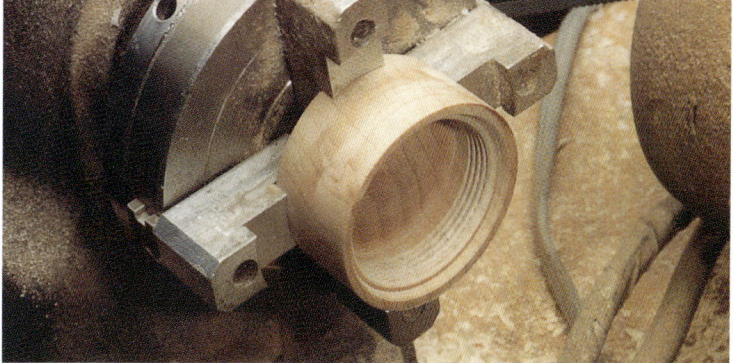

With the box backed off, the cross vice is advanced three quarters of a turn. This will produce threads that are approximately 40 thousandths of an inch deep.

Lightly sand the threads with 400 grit sandpaper to remove any burrs.

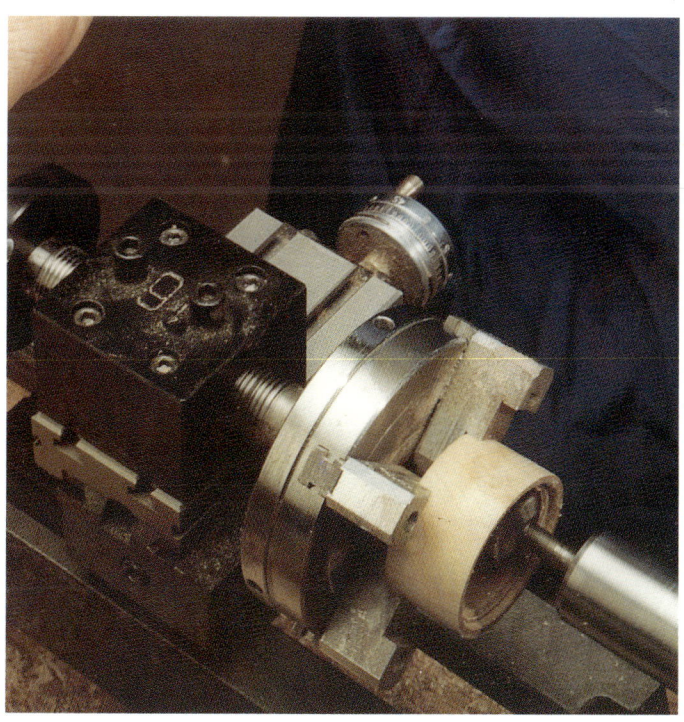

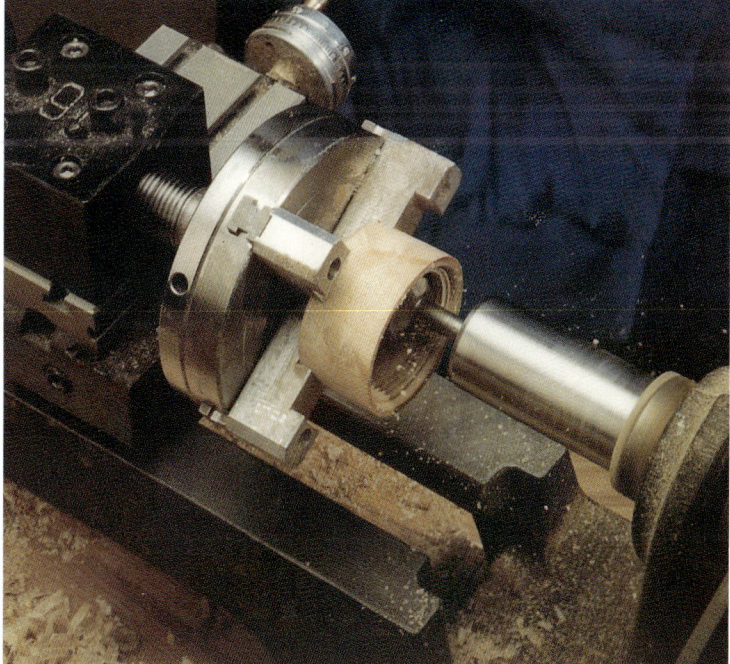

Cutting the threads. The threads should have sharp, crisp and pointed tops.

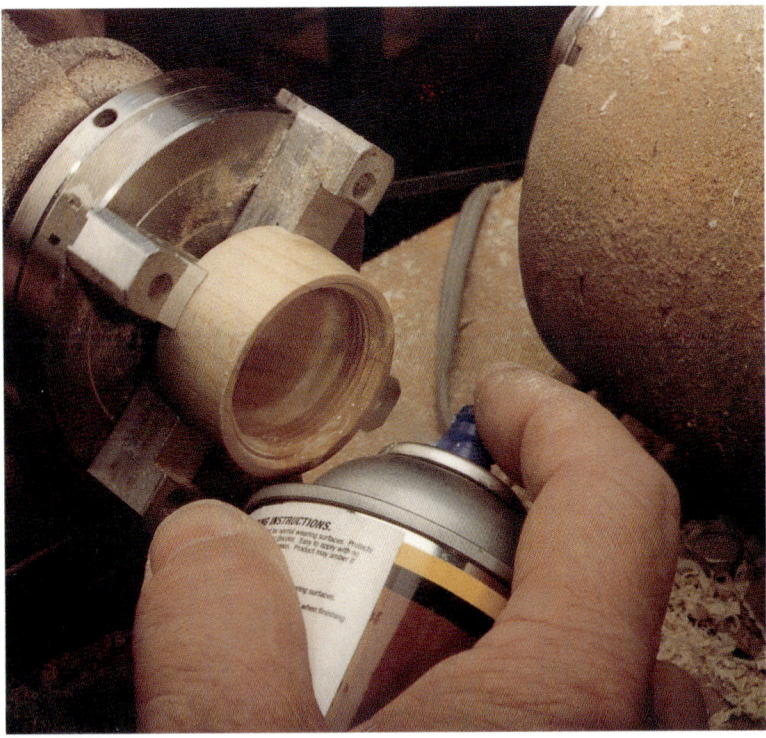

Add a final coat of sanding sealer. This keeps the entire lid uniform in appearance.

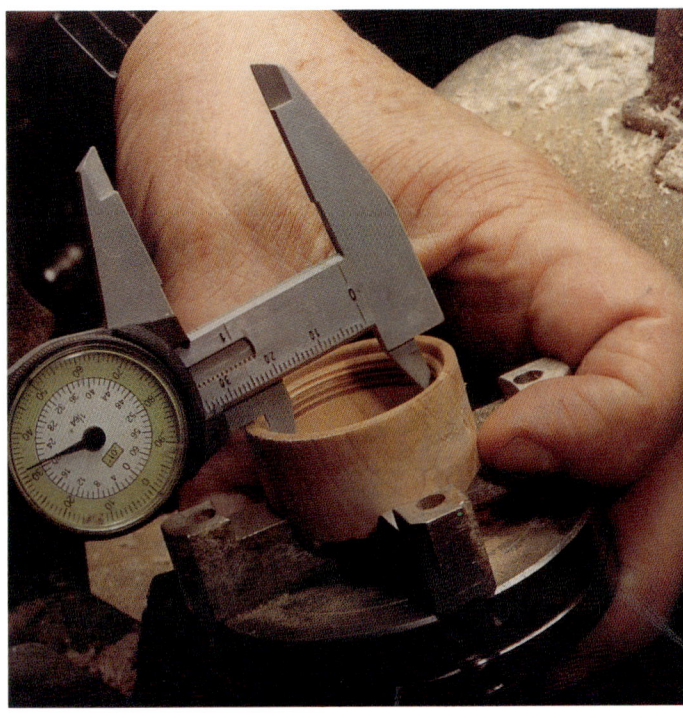

The diameter of the lid is measured so that the tenon diameter for the bottom of the box can be calculated. In our case, the measurement was 1.32".

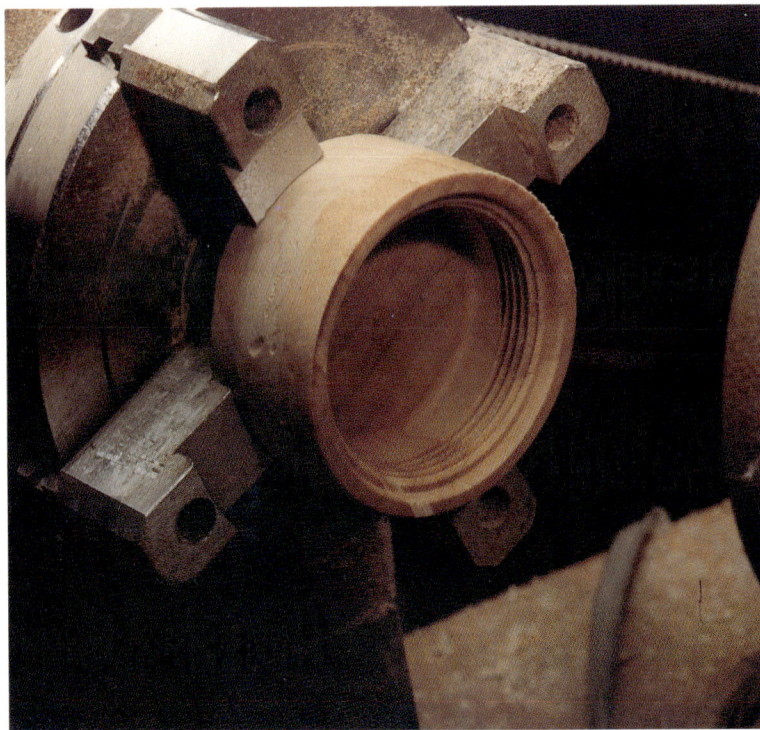

The inside of the lid is complete.

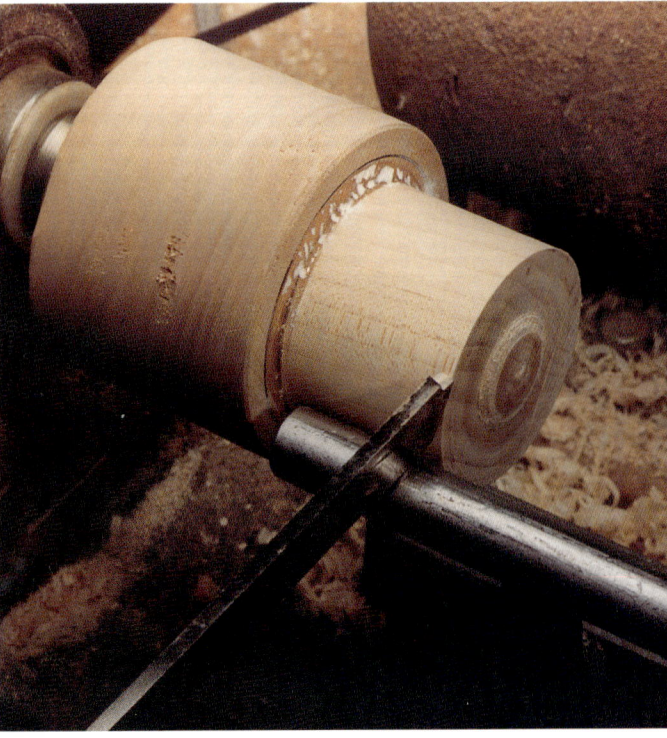

The bottom of the box is attached to the head stock.

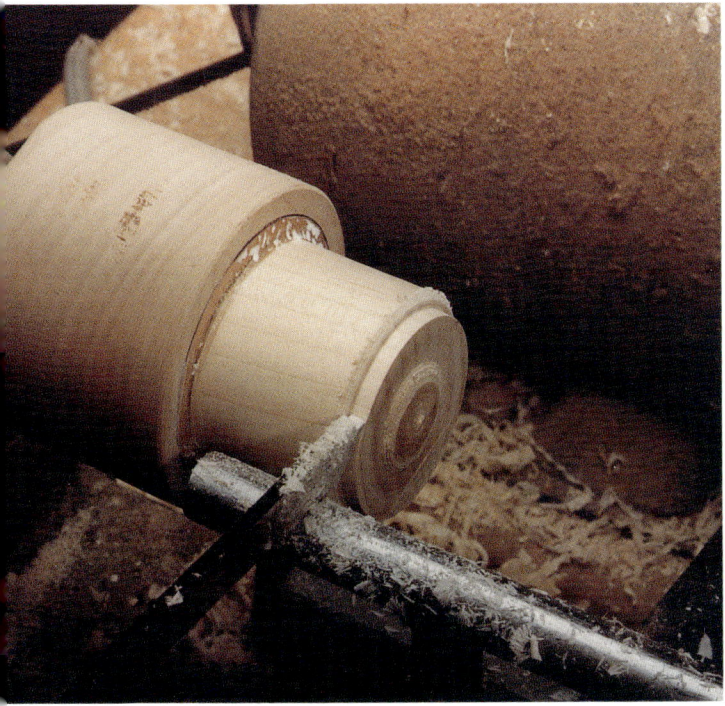

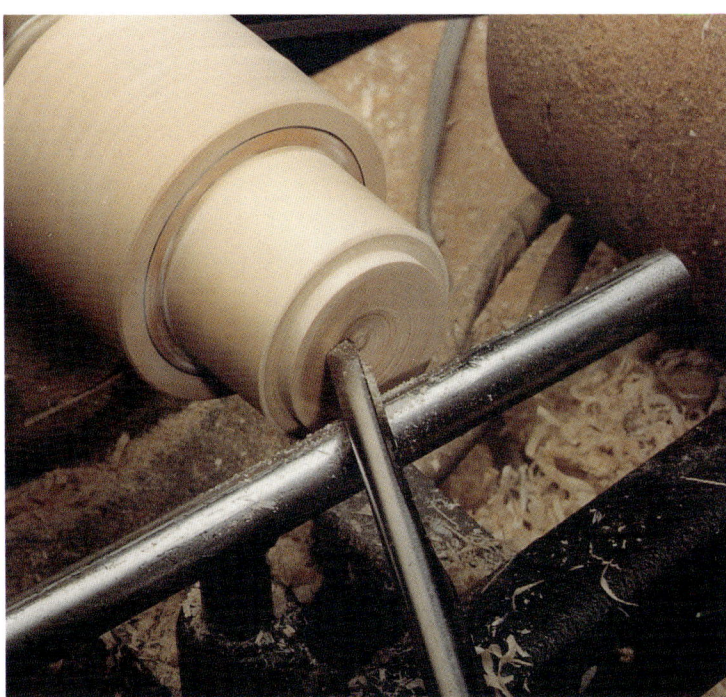

A short tenon is rough cut to 60 thousandths over the size of the inside diameter of the lid to allow for wood movement during hollowing. This measurement was 1.38" for this box.

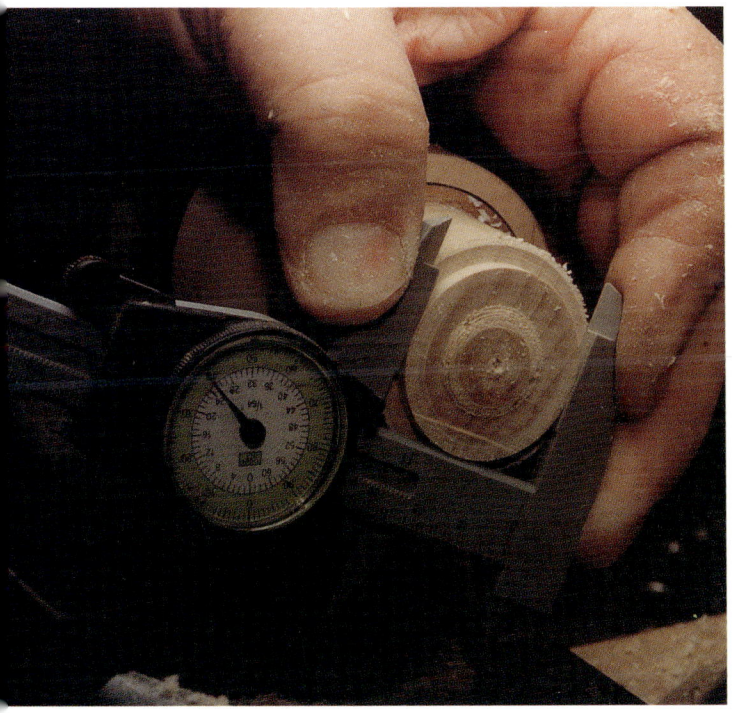

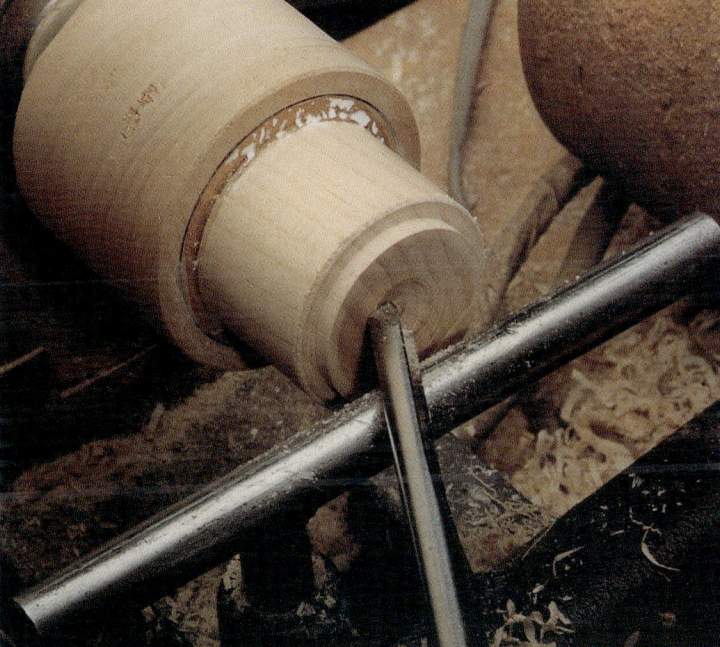

A recess is cut into the center of the box face, which becomes slightly concave and smooth.

This tenon allows you to see the final thickness of the box walls.

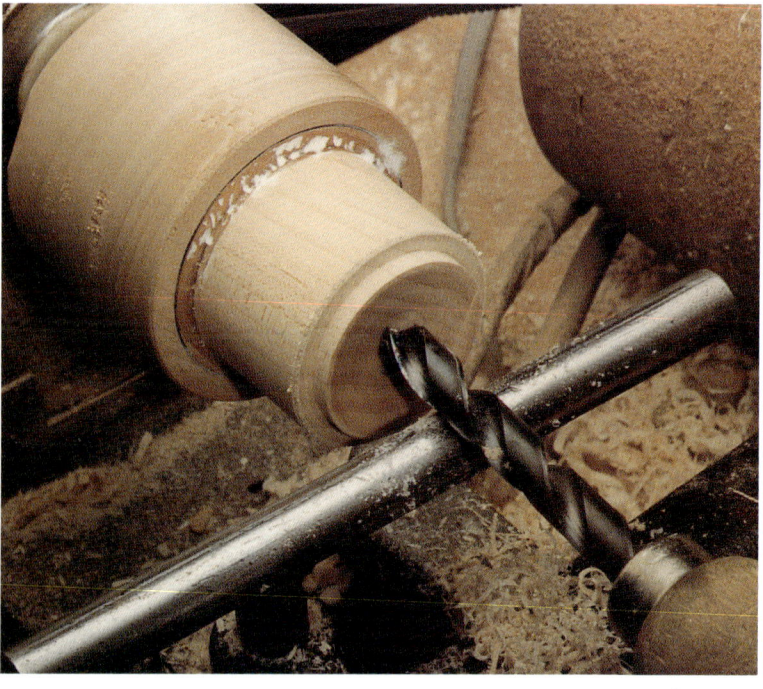

To aid in hollowing, a 3/8" hole is drilled into the box.

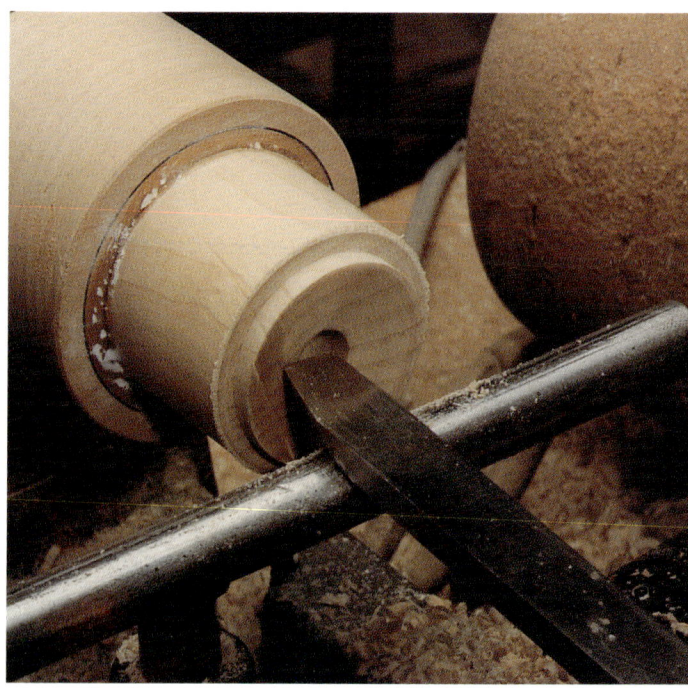

The interior is hollowed out using a square ended scraper.

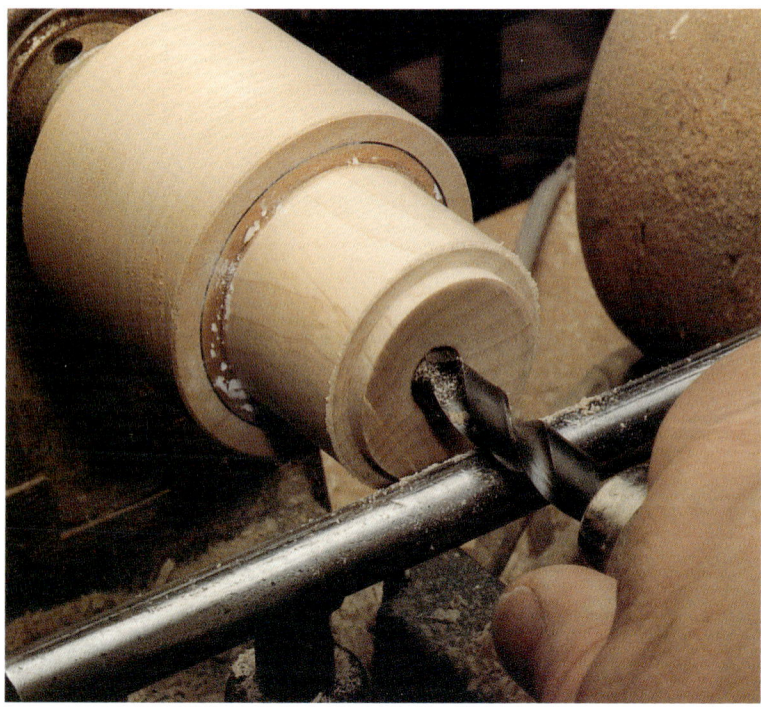

The hole is drilled to the desired depth. A depth of one-quarter inch from the bottom is recommended.

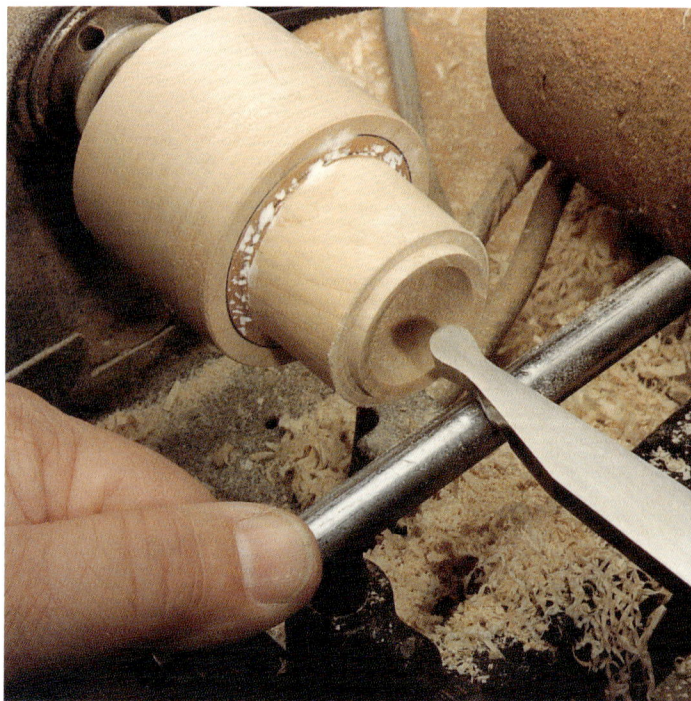

A round nosed scraper is used to soften the edges inside the bottom.

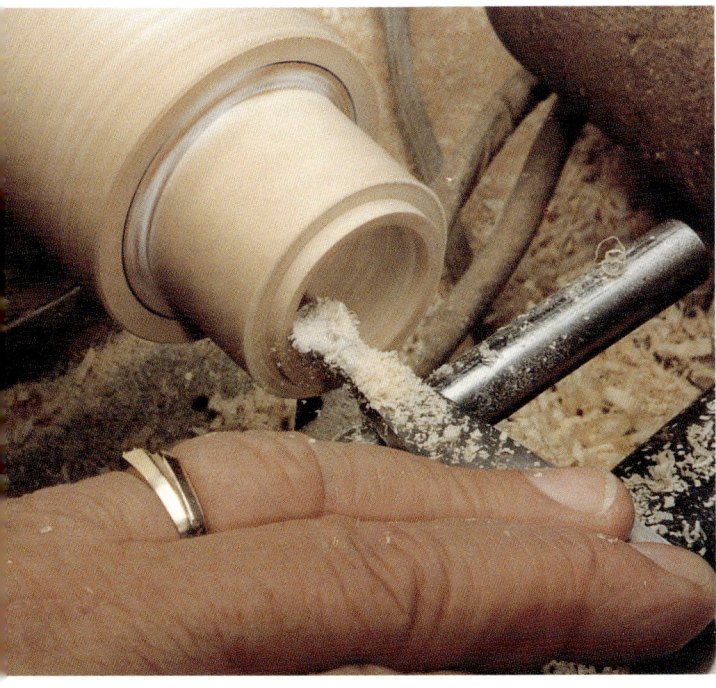

Using the round nosed scraper.

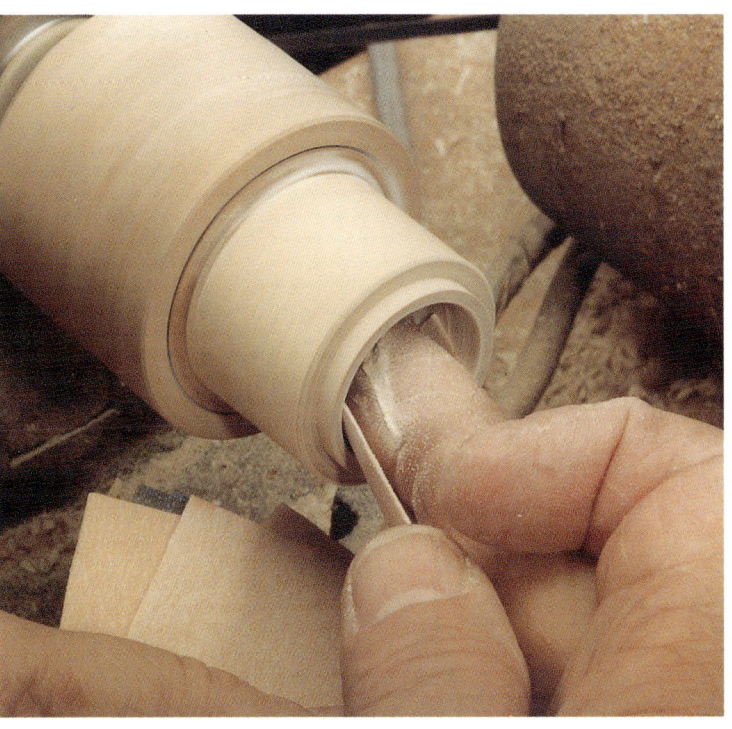

The inside of the box is ready for sanding. Starting with 180 grit paper, move up through 220 and 320, finishing with 400 grit paper.

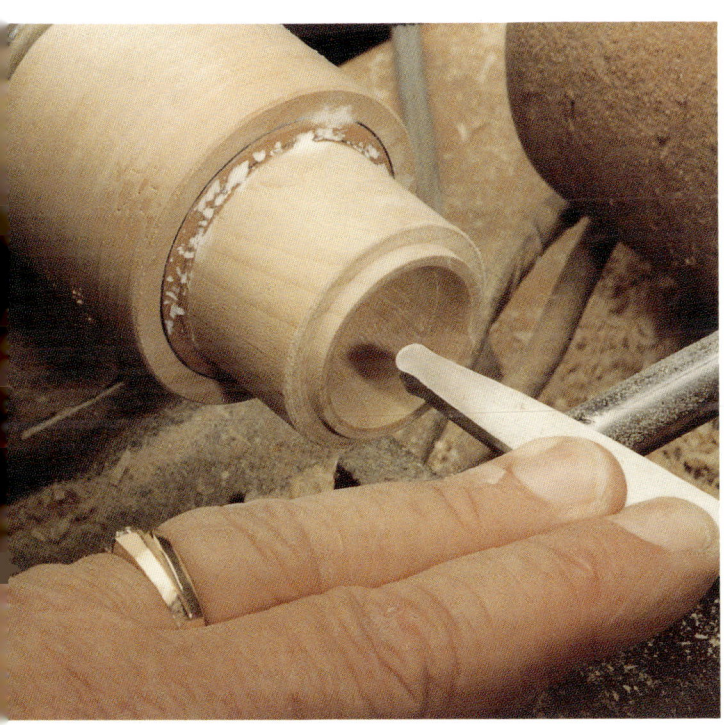

A small round nosed scraper is used for clean up when there are uneven edges in the bottom.

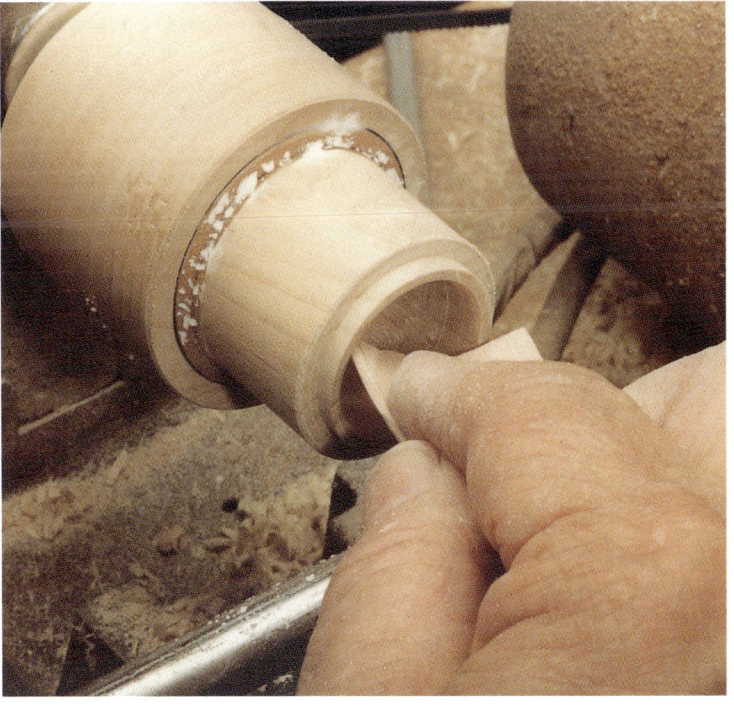

Once you have a satisfactory interior, perform a final sanding.

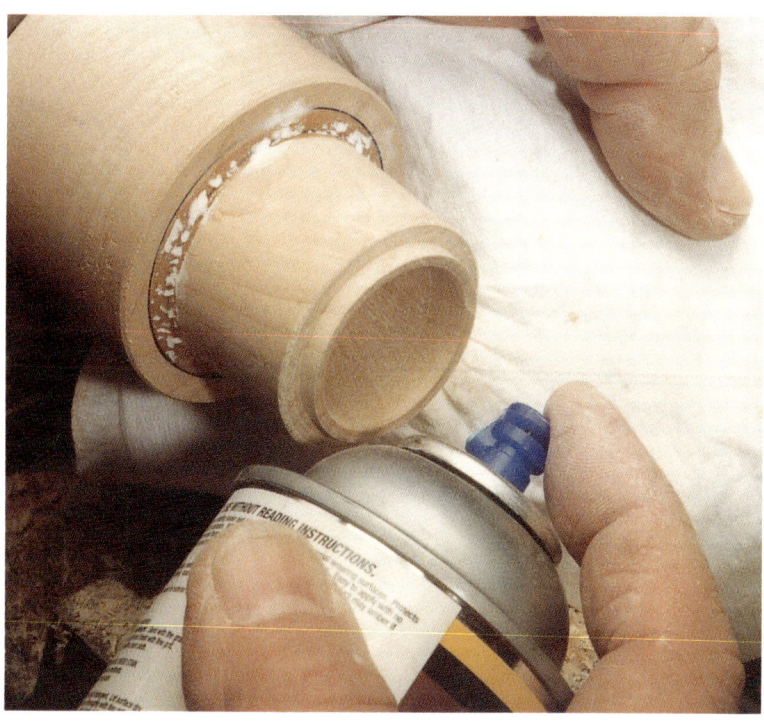

The inside of the bottom is sealed just like the top.

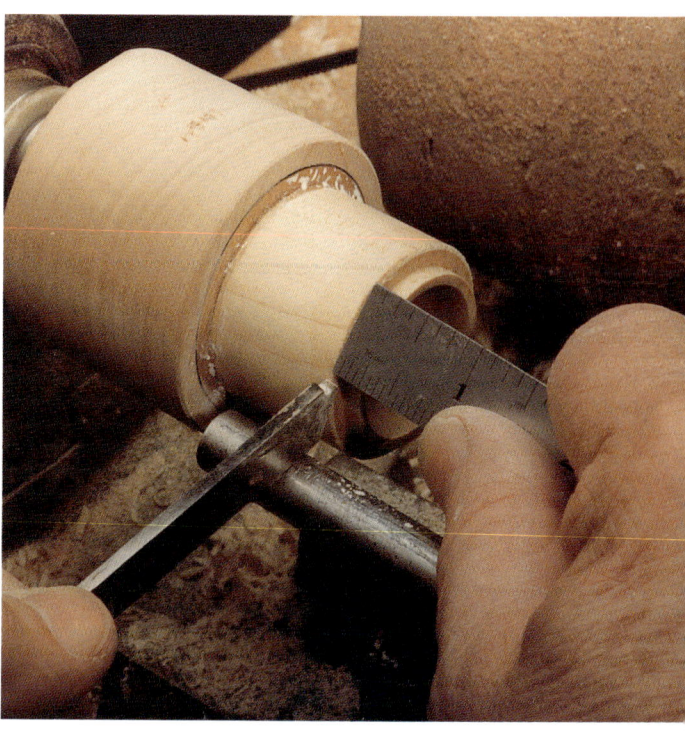

The length of the tenon is increased to 3/16". This will produce three threads when using the 16 threads per inch (tpi) threadbox.

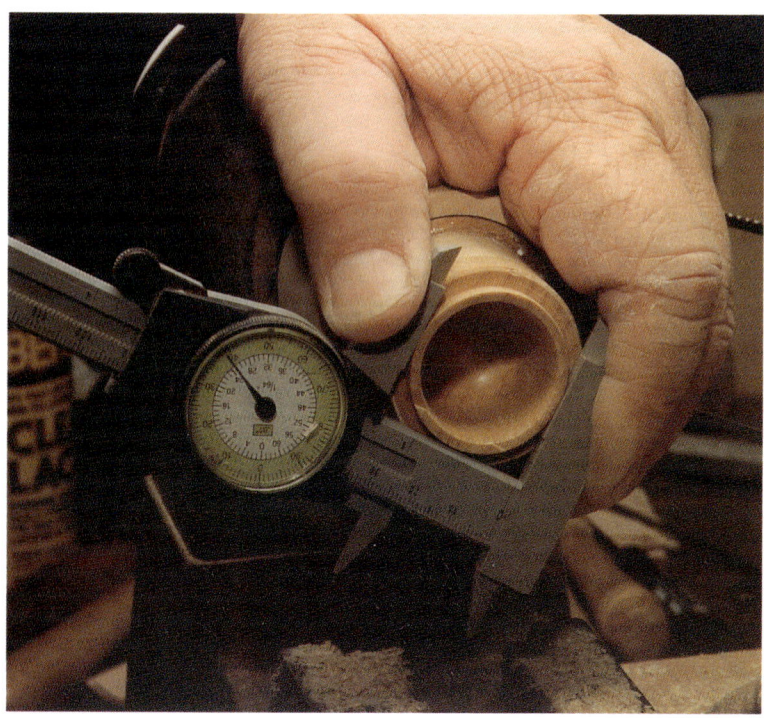

With the interior removed, the exterior may have changed slightly.

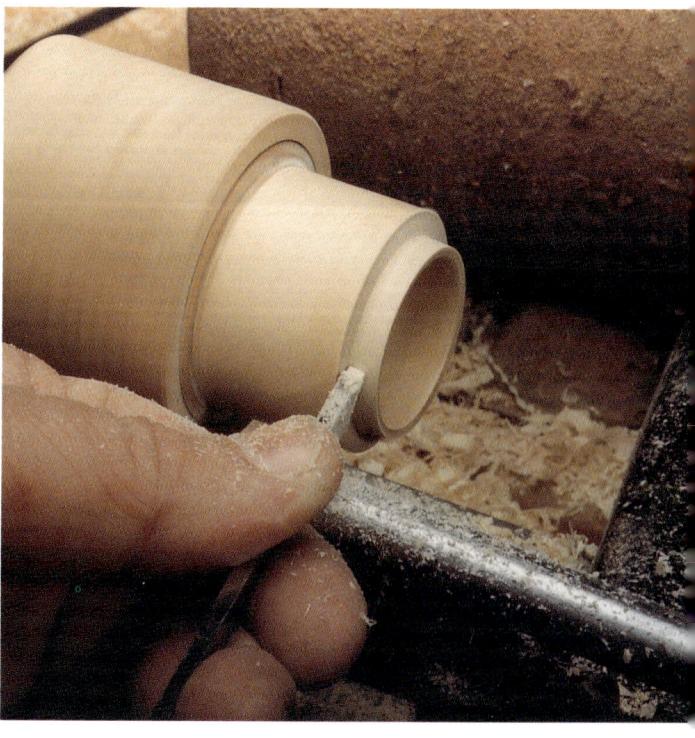

The tenon is made parallel to the ways of the bed.

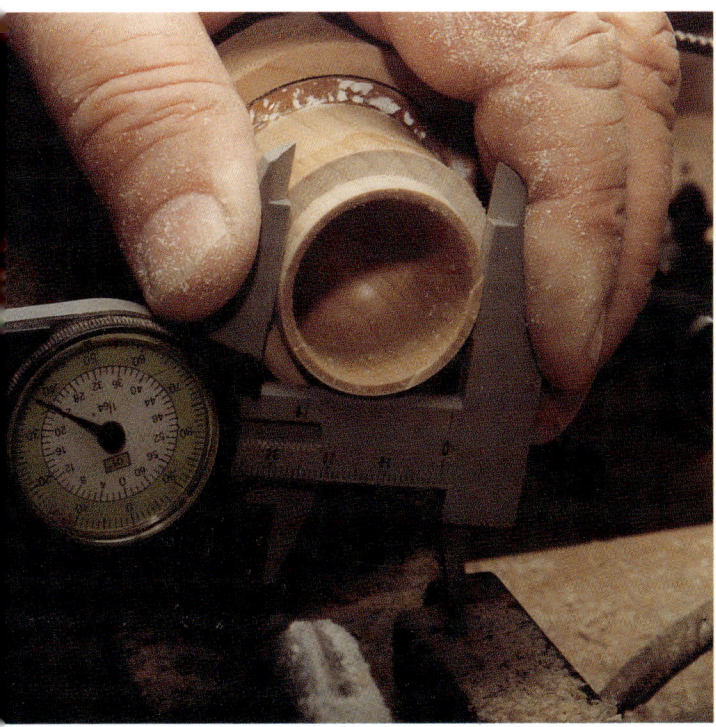

The tenon is reduced to a final diameter that is 40 to 50 thousandths greater than the lid threads. In our case, the tenon diameter is 1.37".

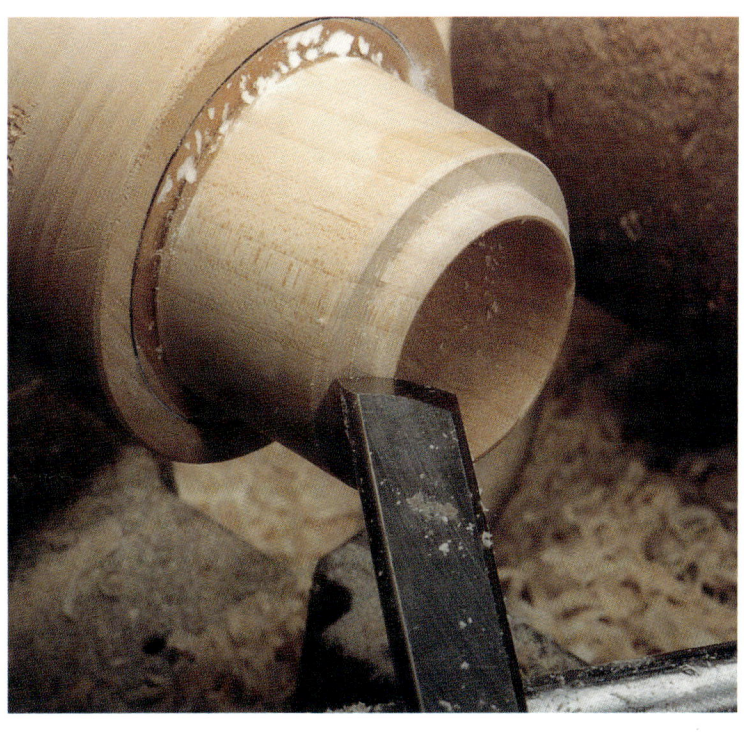

The chamfer is in place.

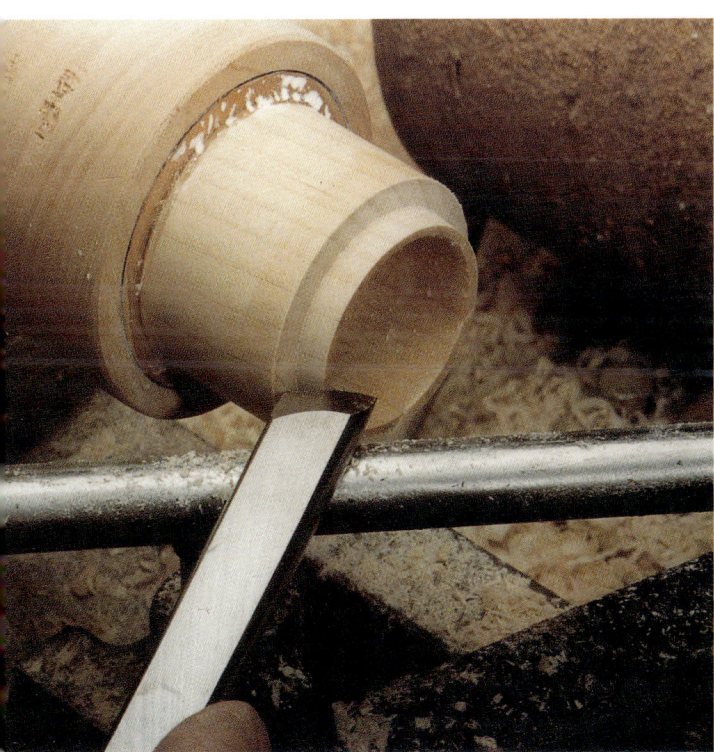

Before cutting the threads on the tenon, the last step is to put a slight chamfer on the outside edge with the skew chisel. This makes the first thread stronger.

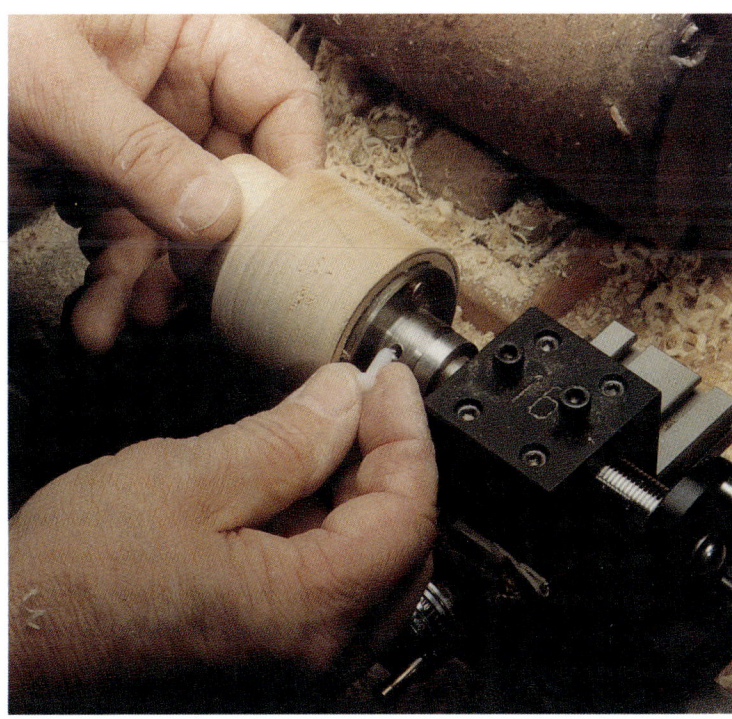

Since the lathe and the bottom will be rotating in the same direction, a nylon screw is inserted in the face plate to prevent it from unscrewing from the threadbox.

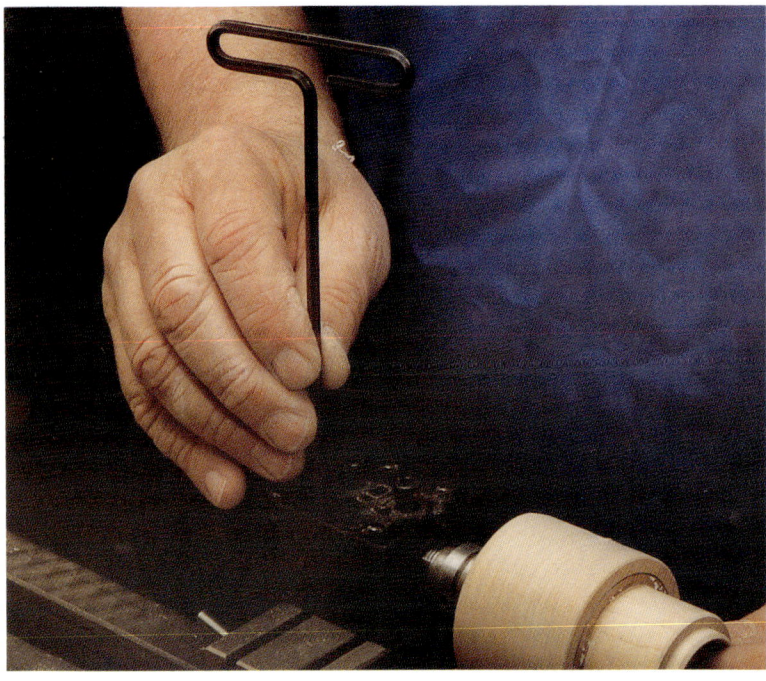

The four screws in the threadbox allow different sized boxes to be fitted to the jig. The minimum box diameter that can be accommodated is approximately one inch with the maximum being about 3 1/2".

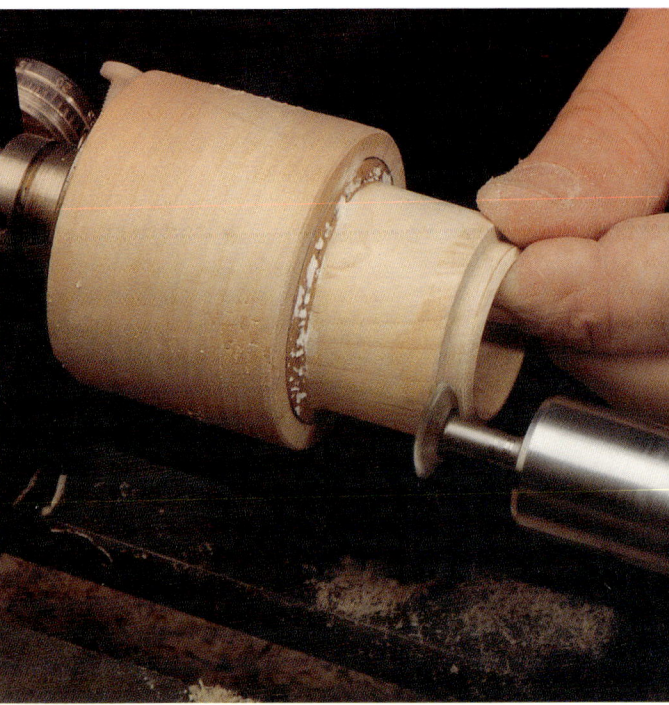

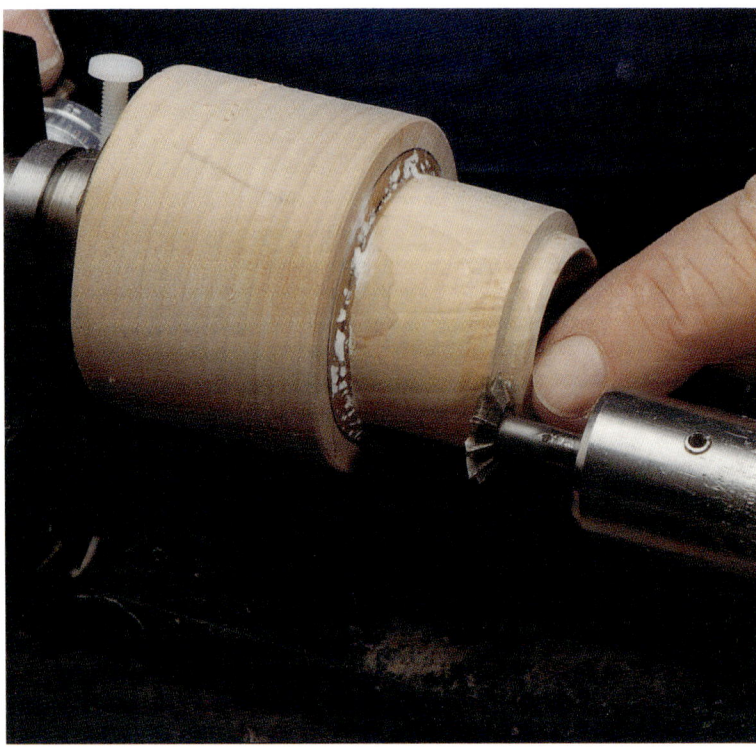

The cutter is again adjusted to just touch the tenon.

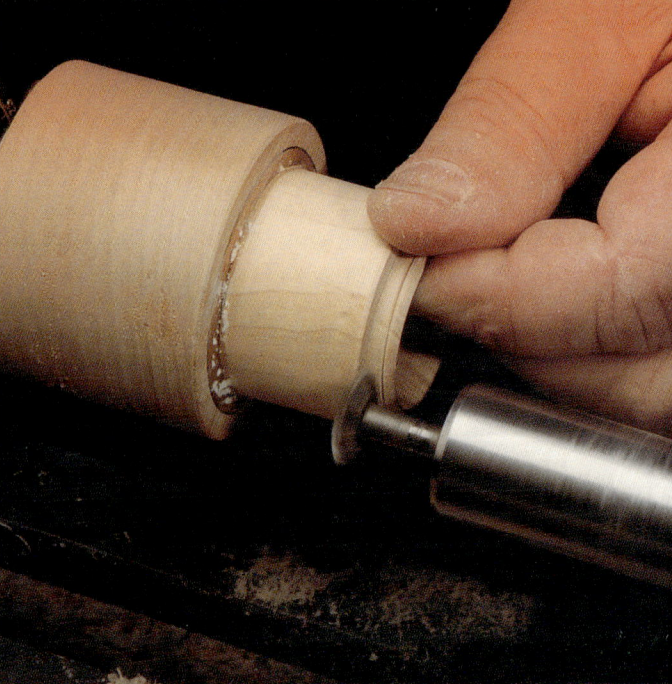

The cross vice is advanced one half turn and the cut is made.

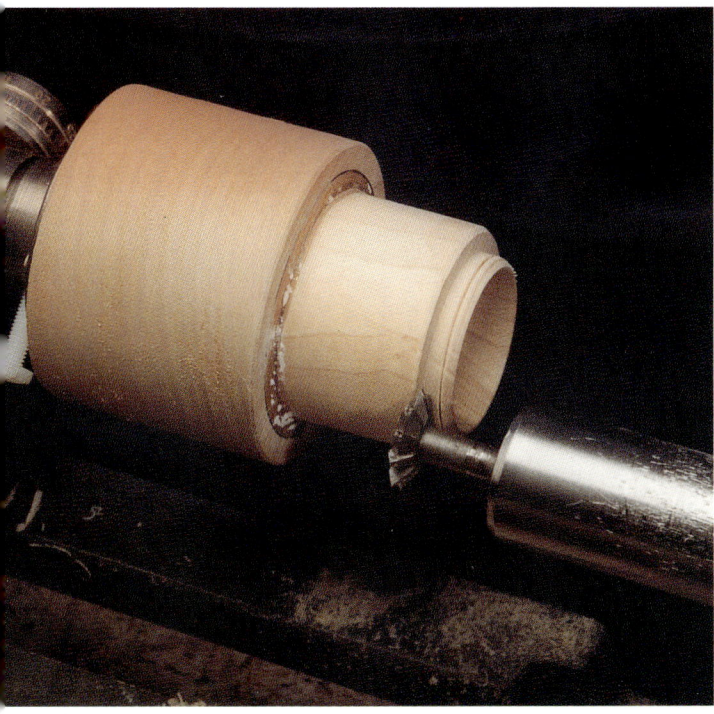

The threads are cut until the cutter just brushes the shoulder.

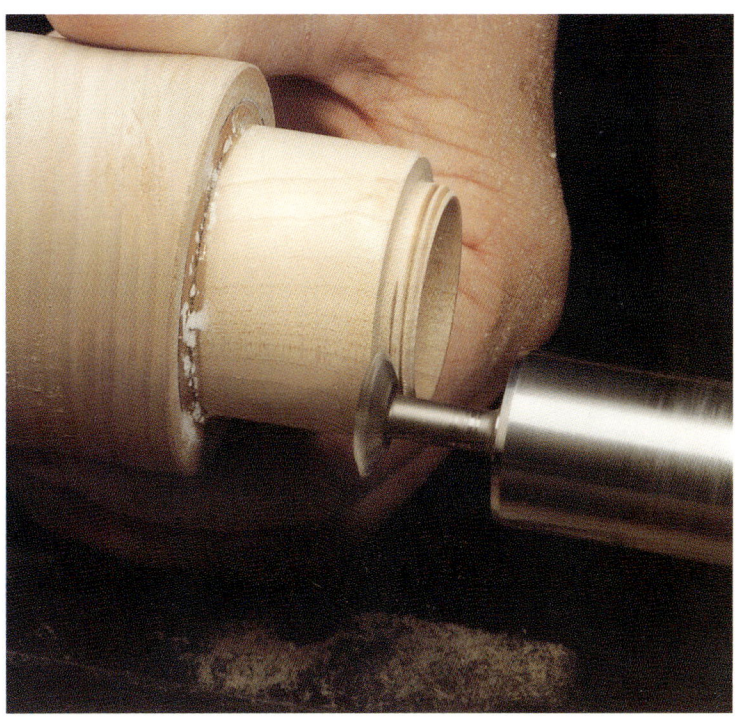

If the fit is too tight, advance the cross vice one quarter turn to cut the threads deeper.

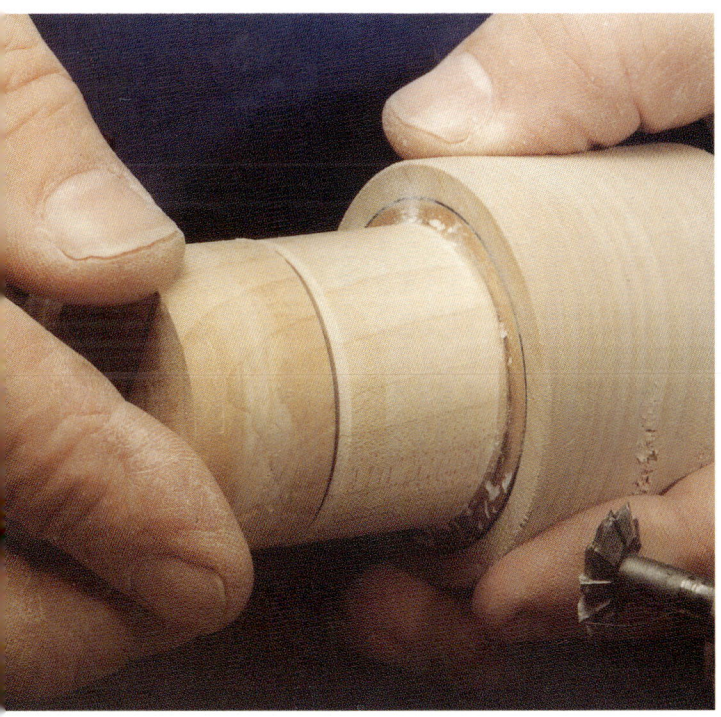

The lid is test fit to the bottom.

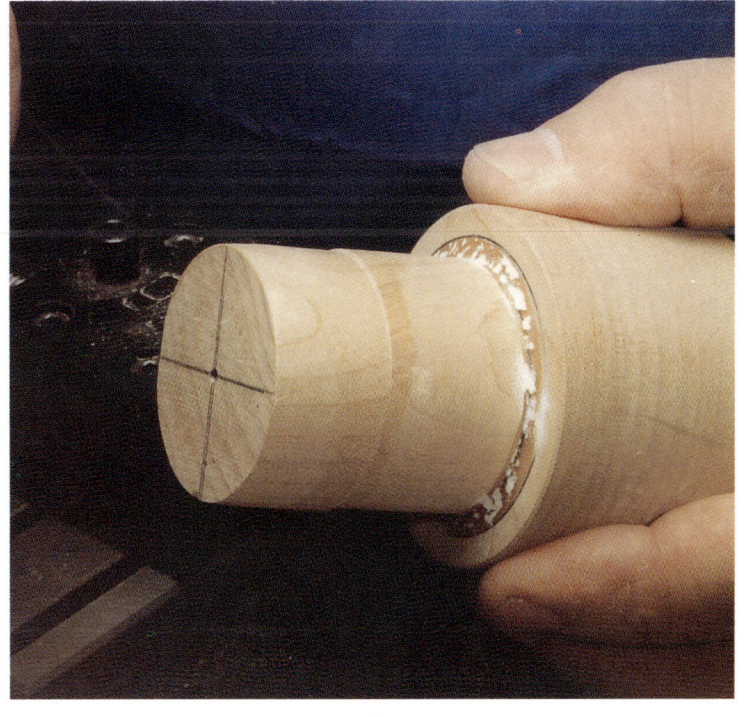

Success!

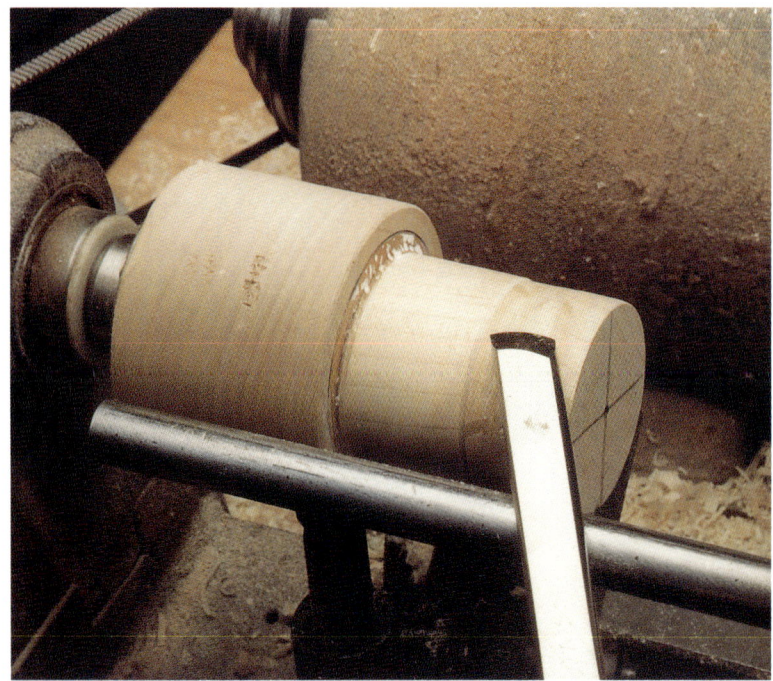

The exterior surface of the box is now smoothed with a 1/2" skew chisel.

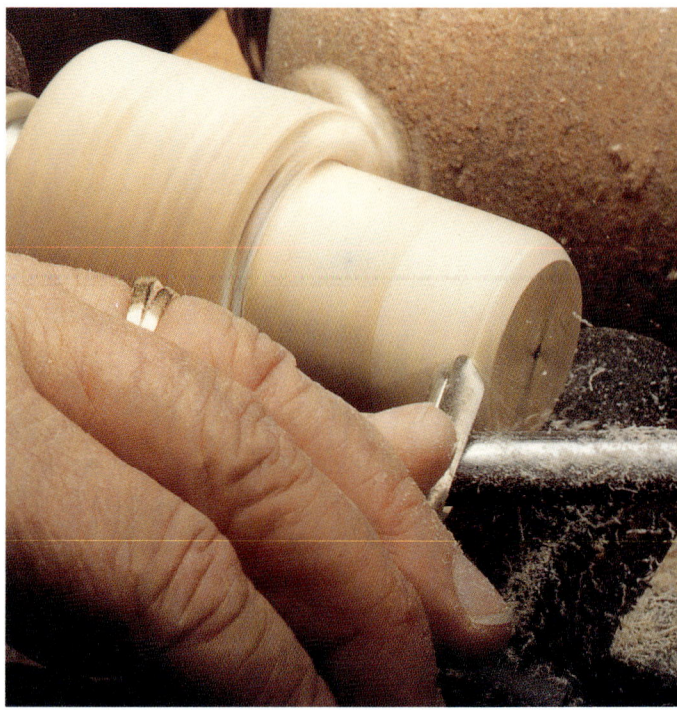

Using a 3/8" spindle gouge, shape the outside of the top.

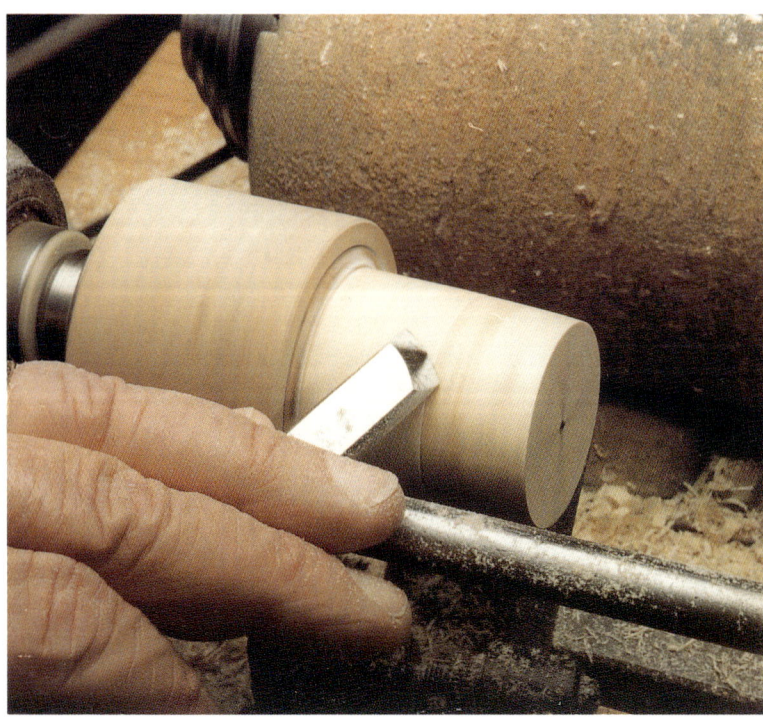

The outside is smoothed.

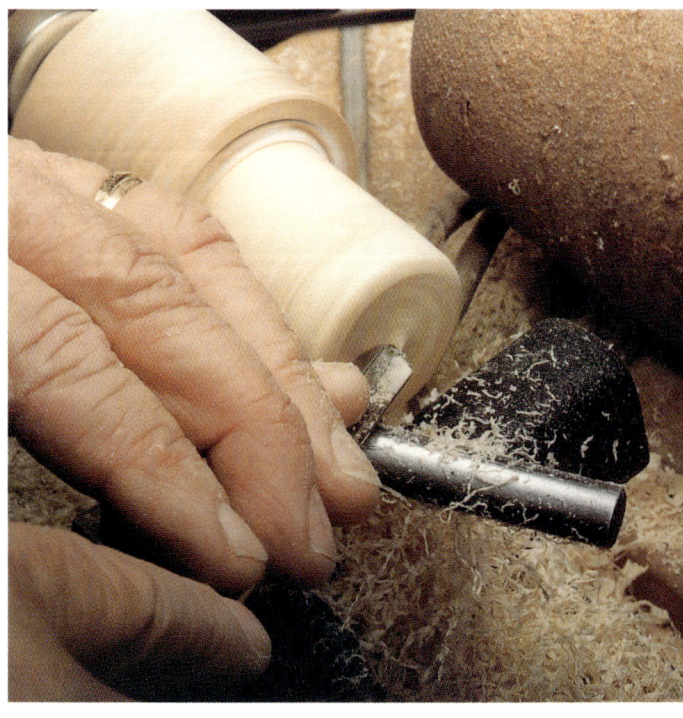

I like minimal decoration but will leave a rising tip at the center of the lid.

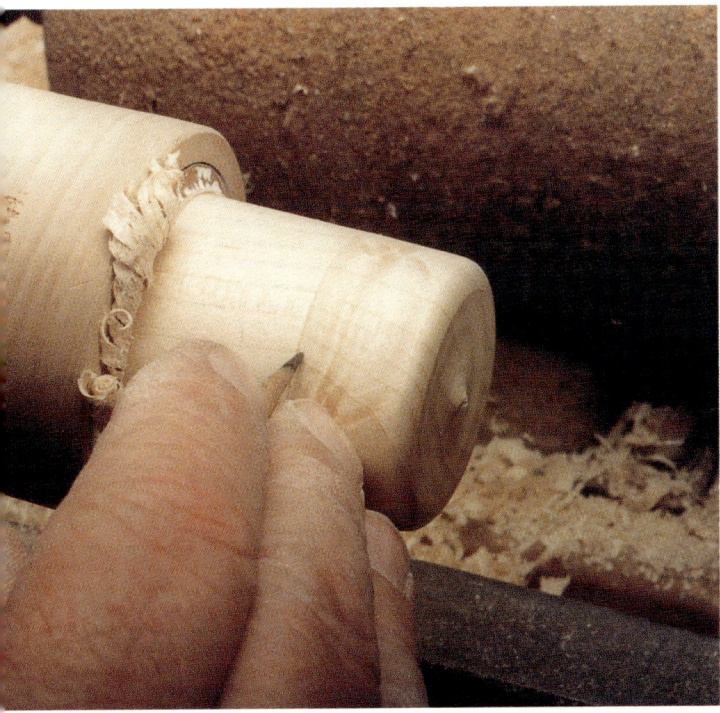

The grain does not match.

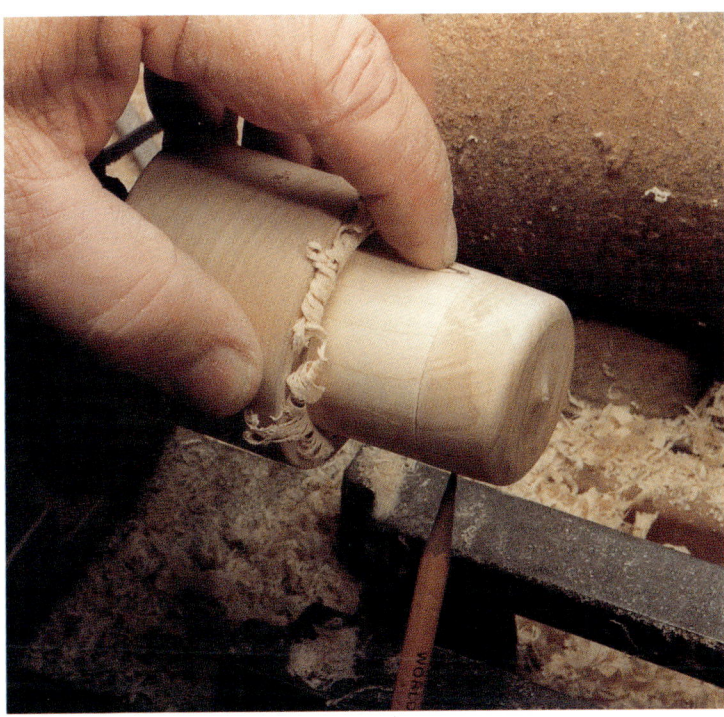

In our case, there is a 1/2 turn variation between the grain on the top and the bottom of the box.

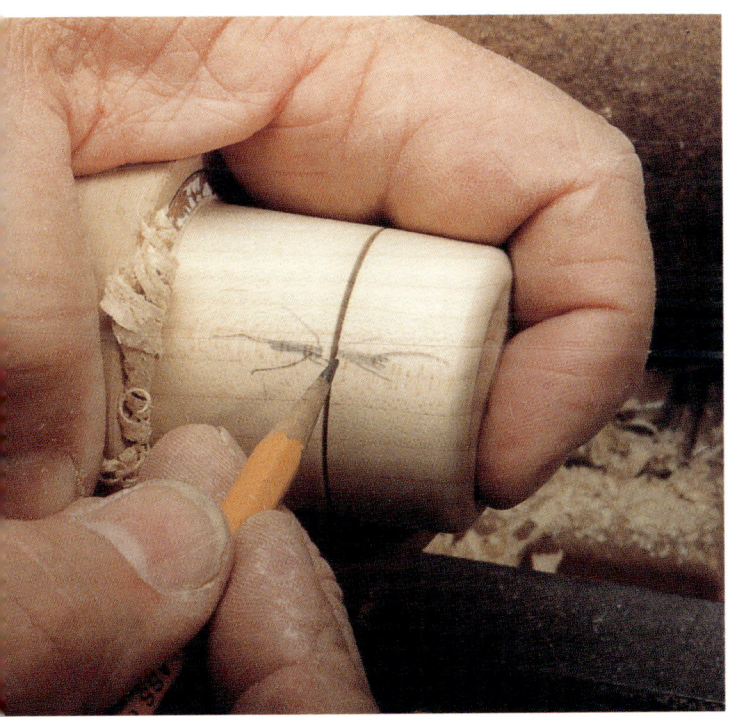

Lines are marked for grain matching.

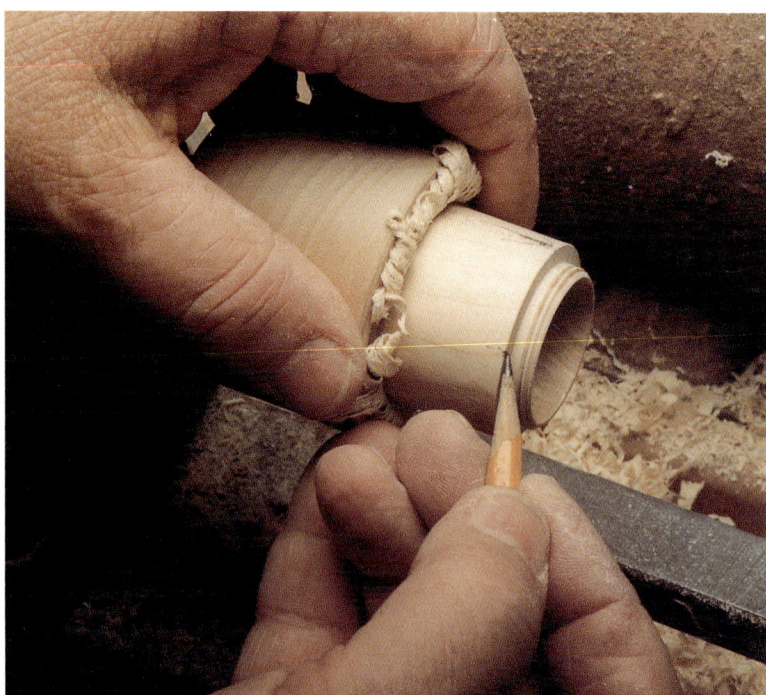

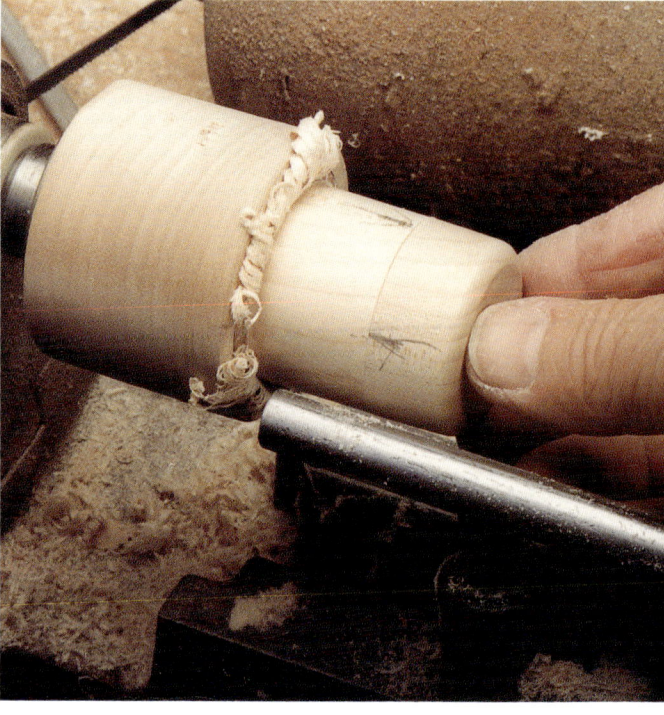

Getting closer.

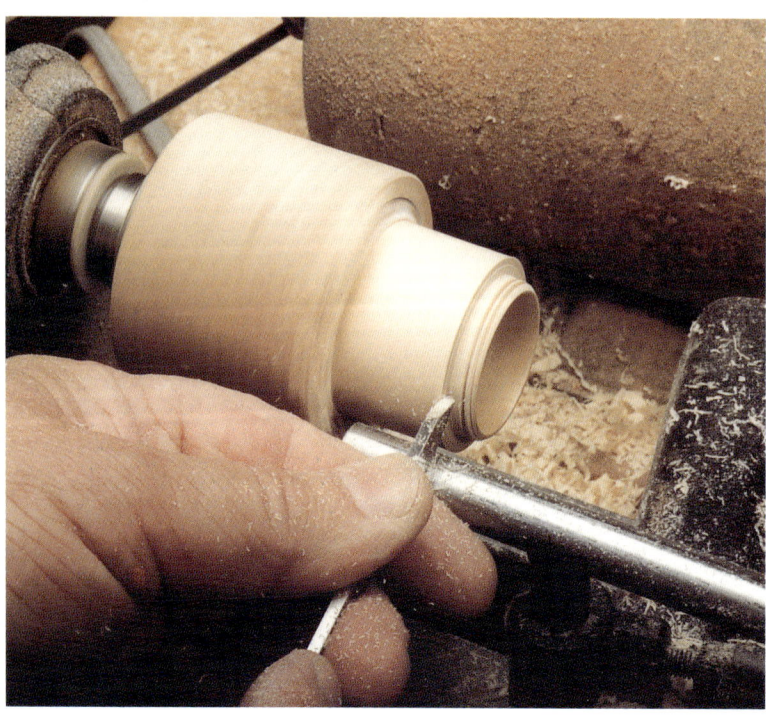

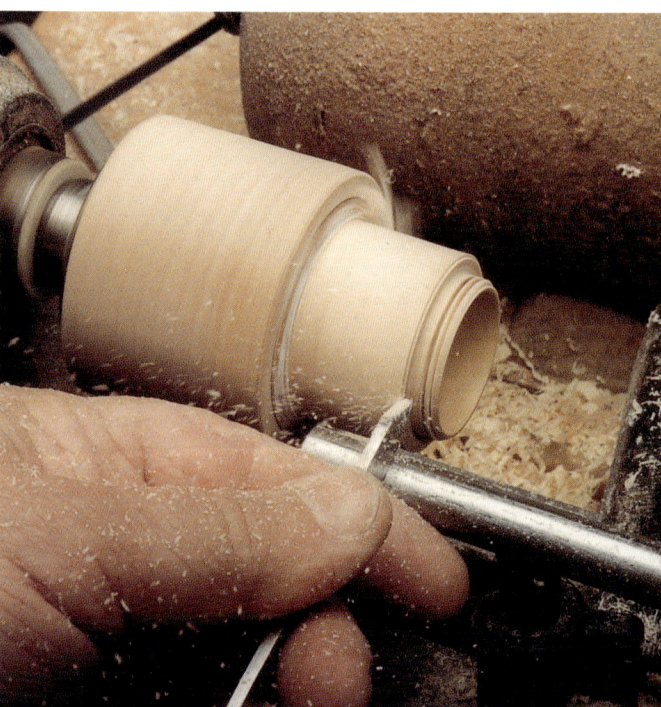

Making a small cut for the final adjustment.

With 16 threads per inch (tpi), one revolution is 1/16", one half revolution is 1/32". About 1/32" must be removed from the shoulder to match the grain.

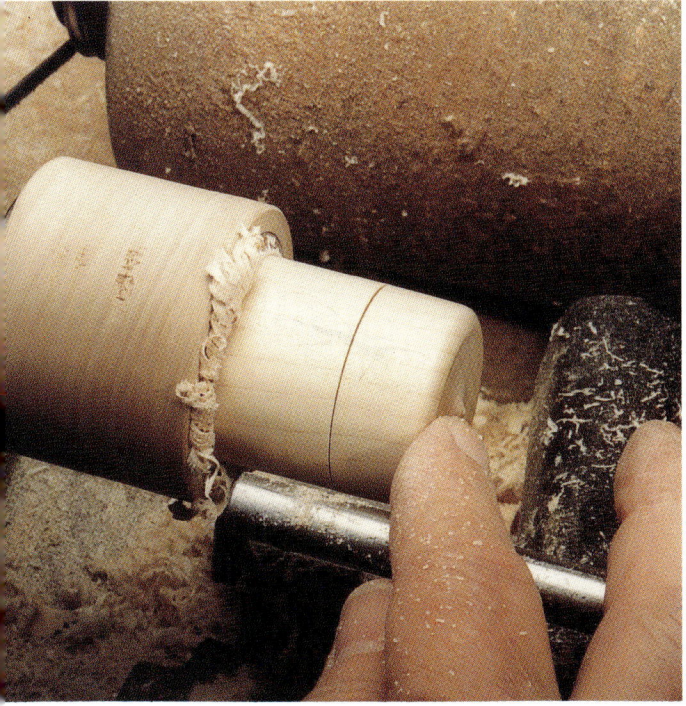

Success!

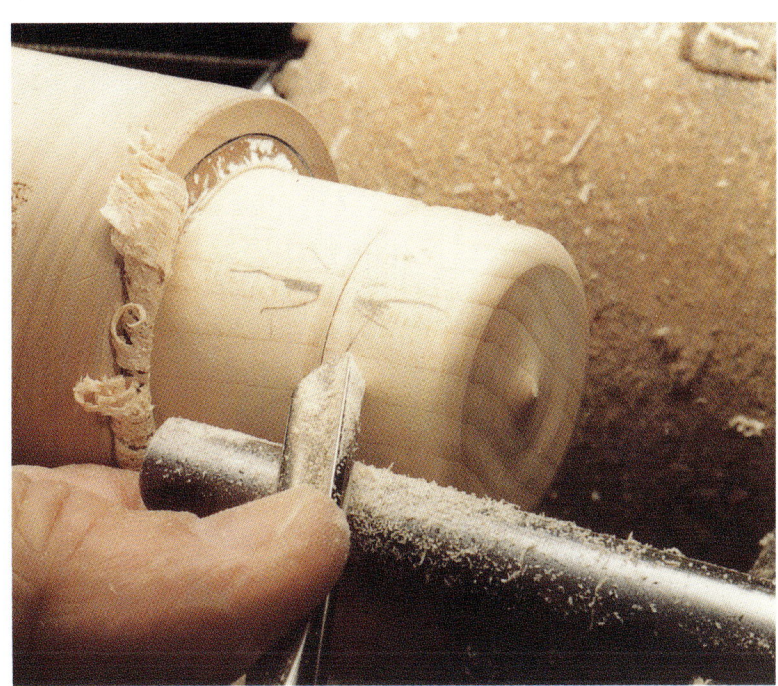

The cove is in place.

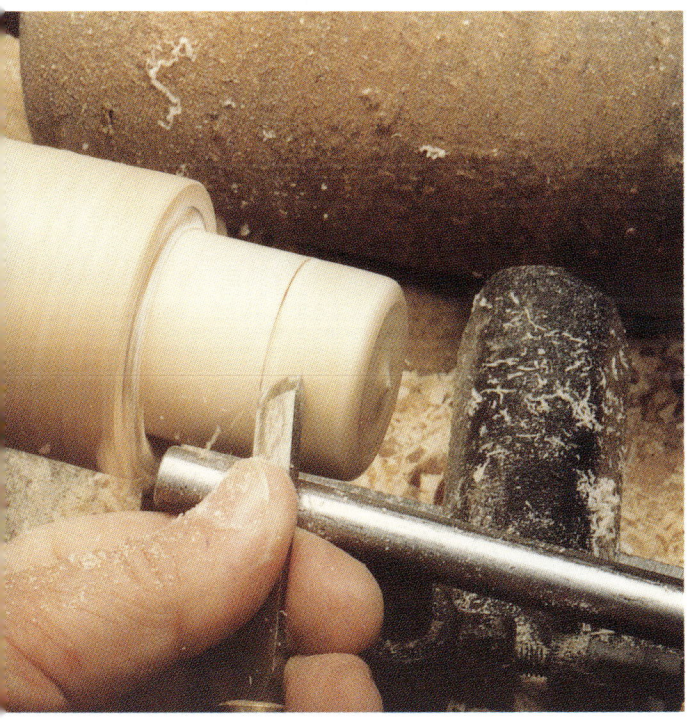

Since the joint itself cannot be completely hidden, a slight cove or chamfer is created on both sides of the joint using a 3/8" spindle gouge...or a small skew chisel for the brave of heart.

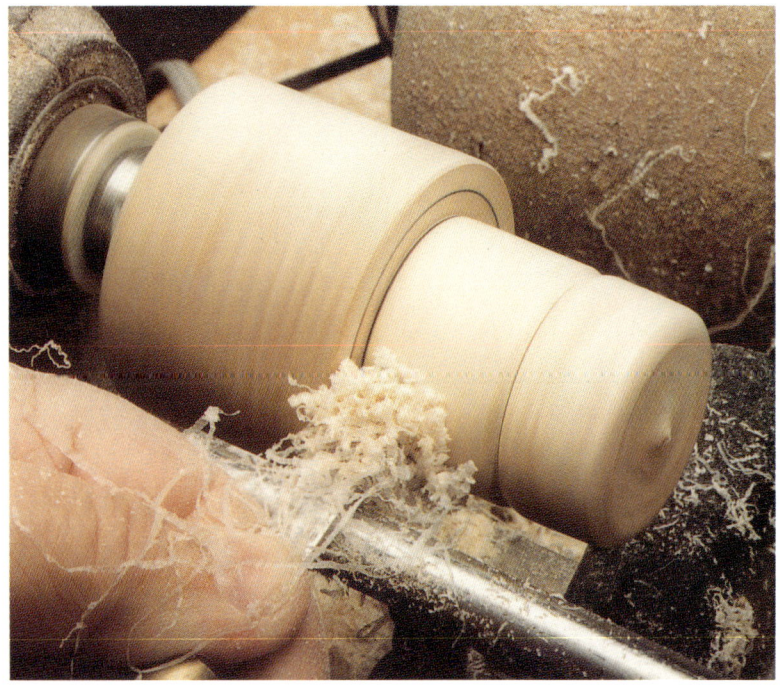

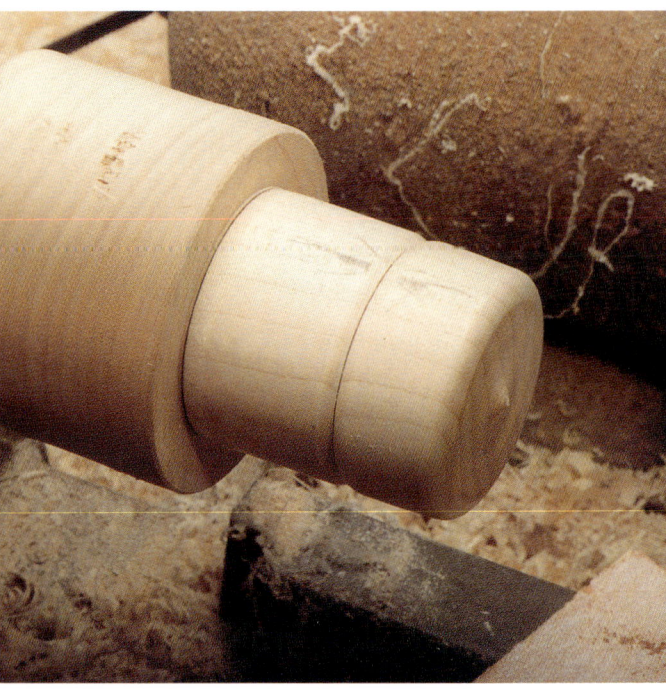

The exterior of the box is ready to be sanded.

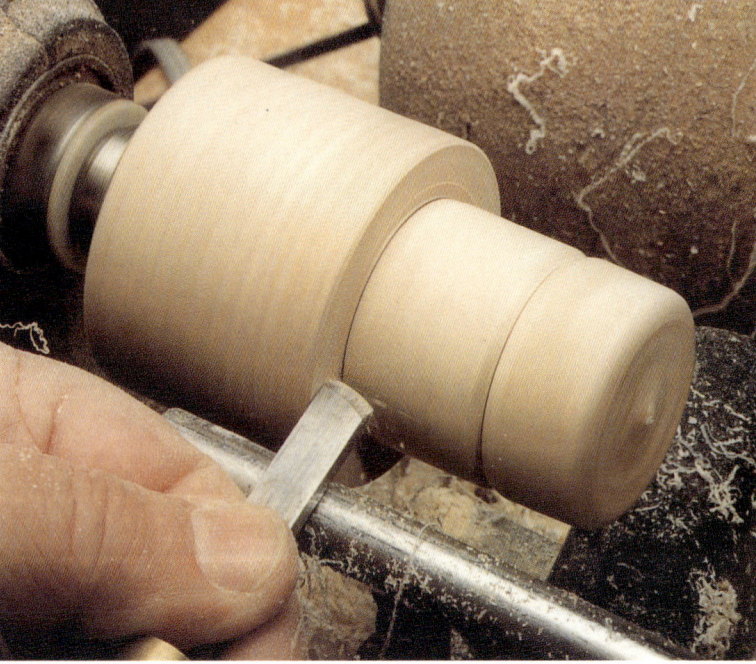

The base of the box can be trimmed using a small skew chisel in a scraping/peeling cut.

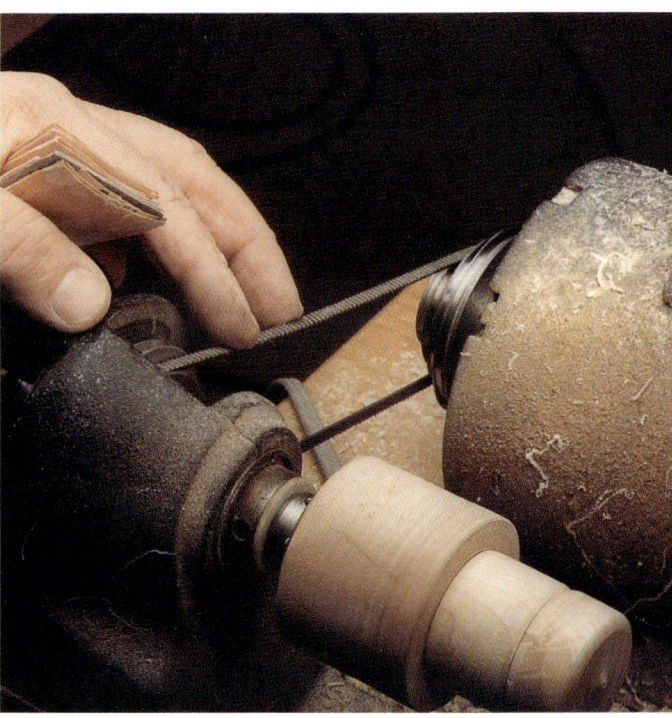

The lathe speed can be reduced. The faster the speed of the lathe, the faster you need to move the sandpaper to avoid scratches.

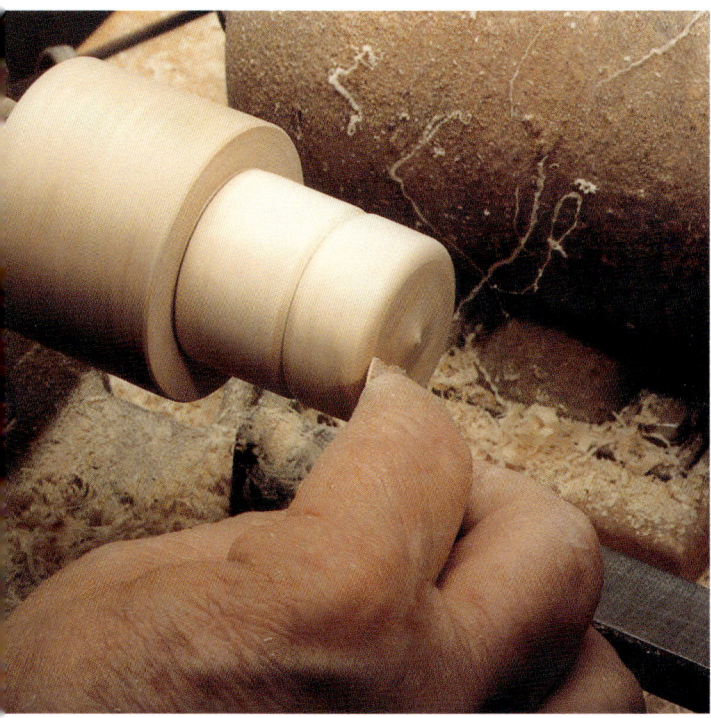

Stay away from the sharp lid tip with coarse sandpaper to maintain the profile.

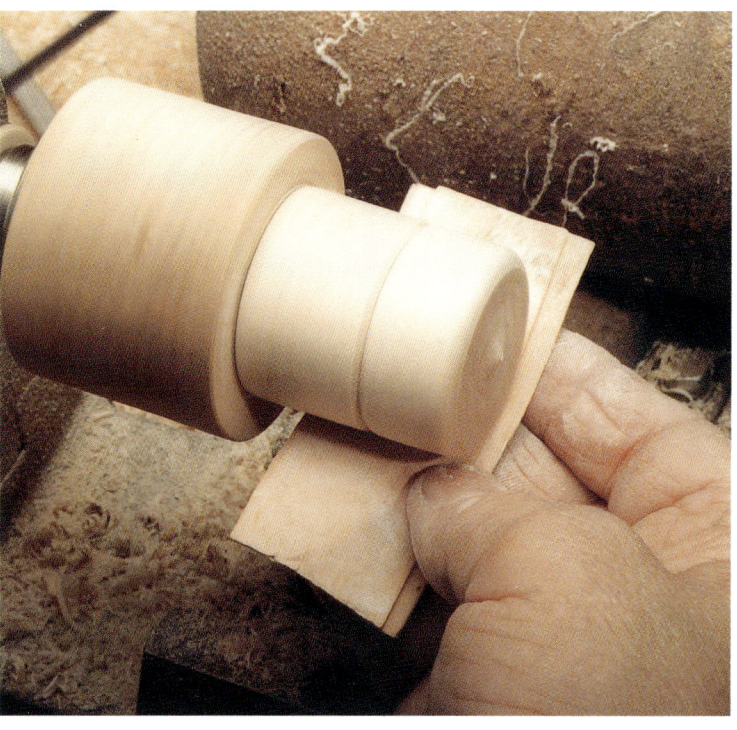

Sand the body of the box, moving up through your grits from 180 to 400.

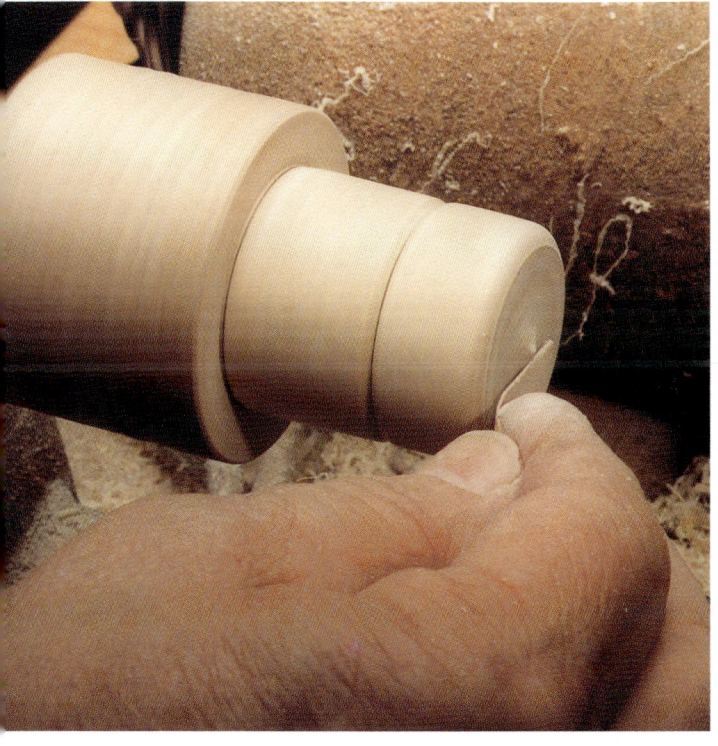

The tip can be sanded with 320 and 400 grit sandpaper.

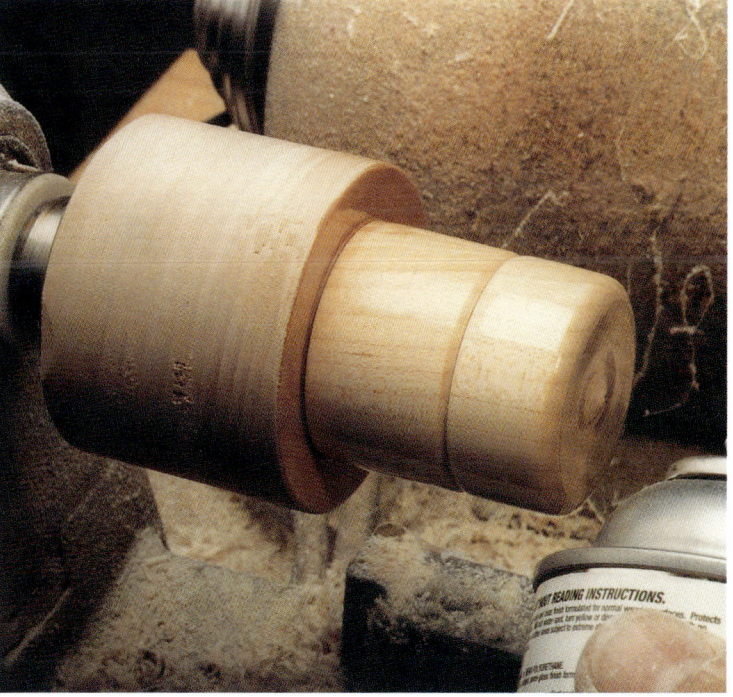

Sanding sealer is applied to the exterior.

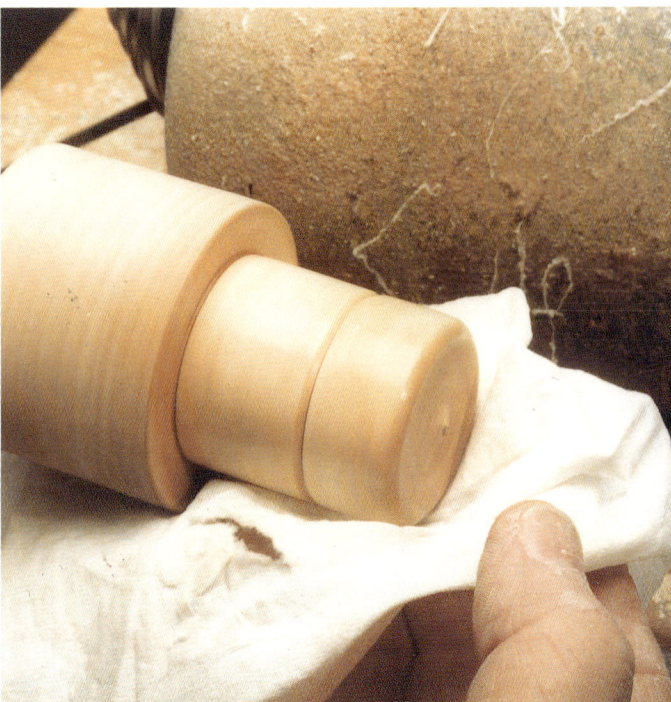

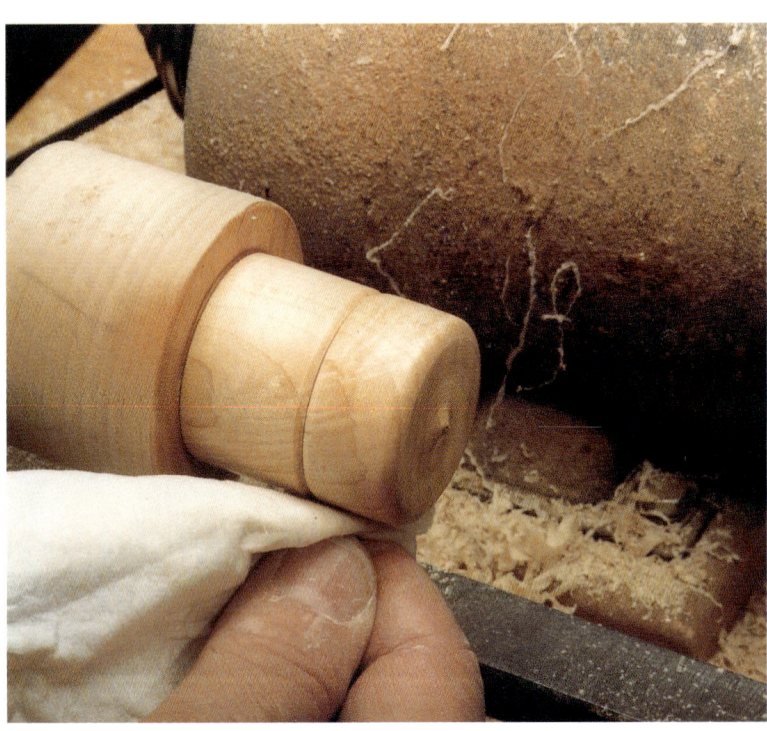

Final finish is your choice. Since boxes get handled a lot, a durable finish is needed. A lacquer based finish is recommended, such as Woodturner's Finish or French Polish.

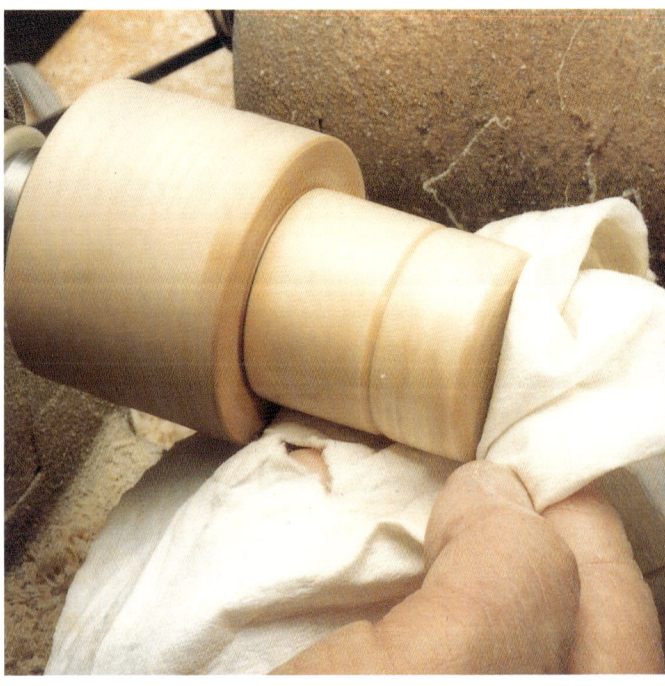

The finish should be friction dried.

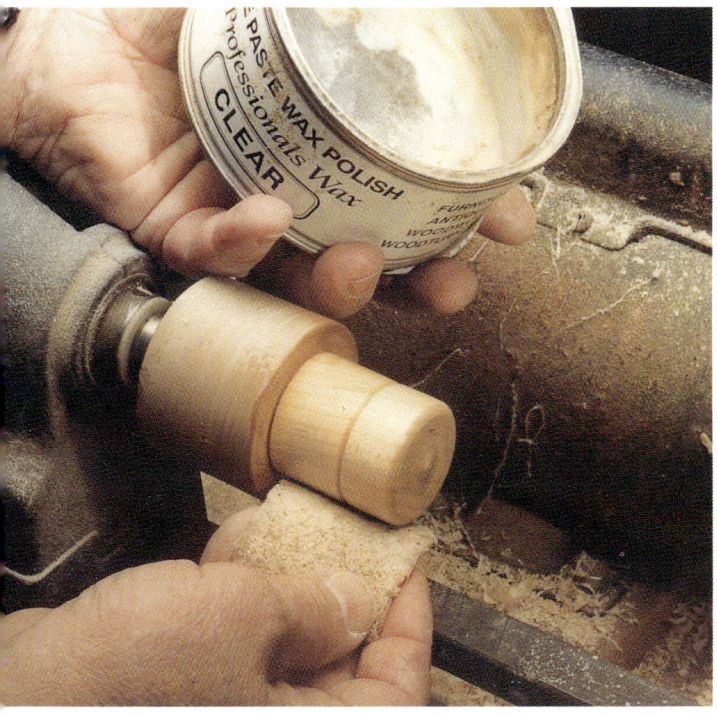

A wax can be applied to the exterior of the box to give a higher sheen.

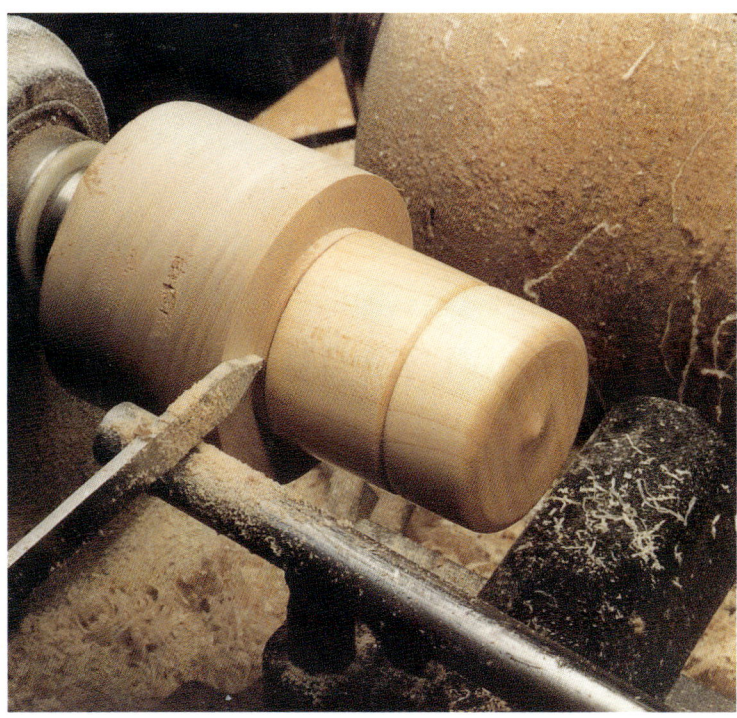

The box is parted off from the waste block with a thin parting tool. This cut is made in the waste block.

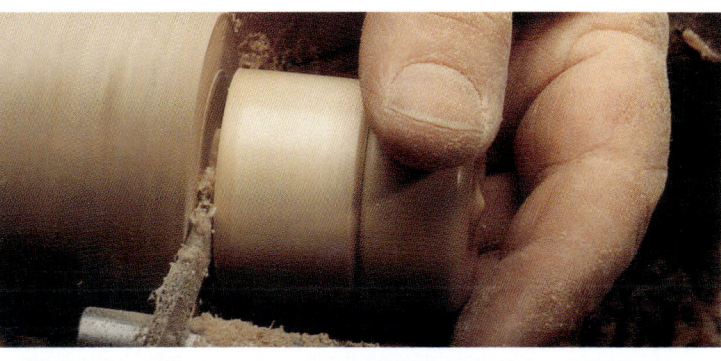

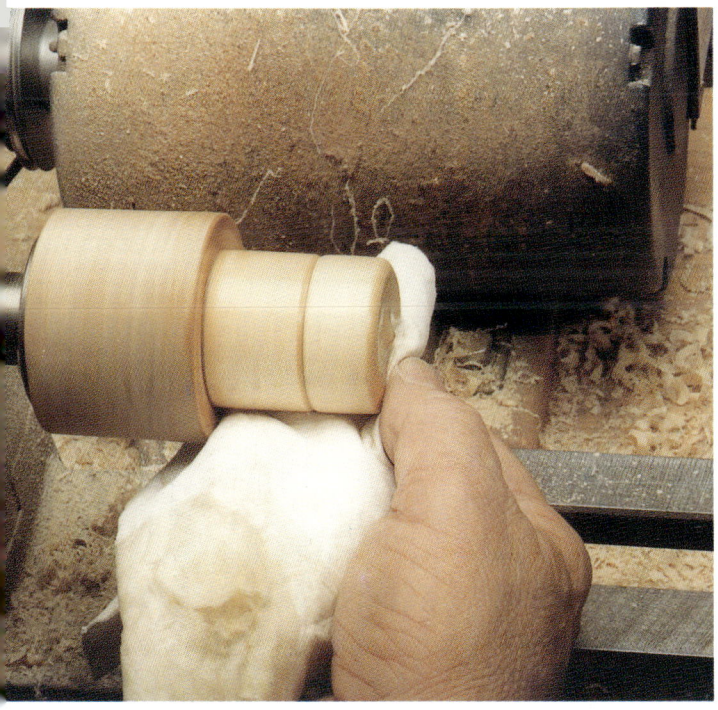

The box is friction dried with a paper towel.

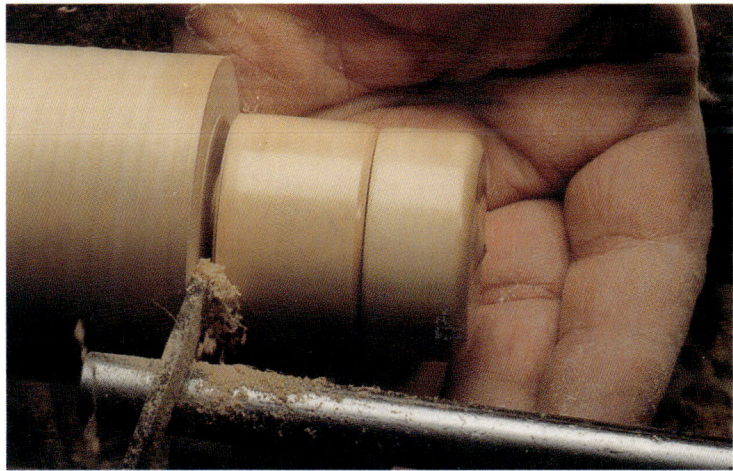

Be ready to catch the box when parting it off.

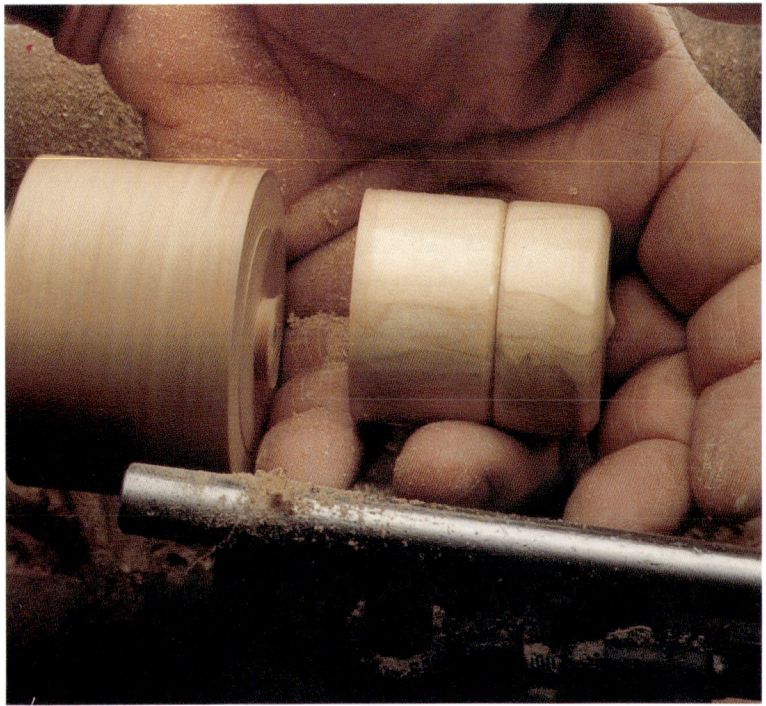

The box is parted off.

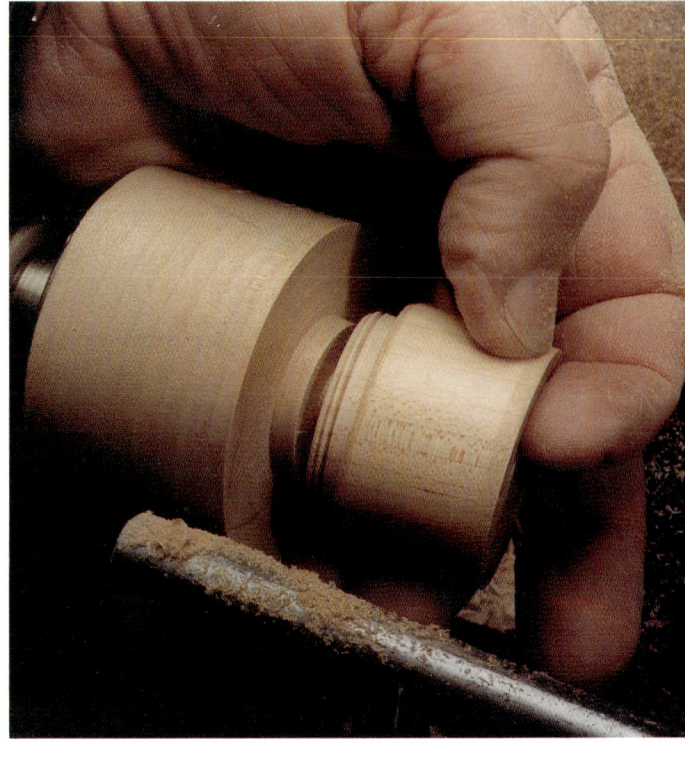

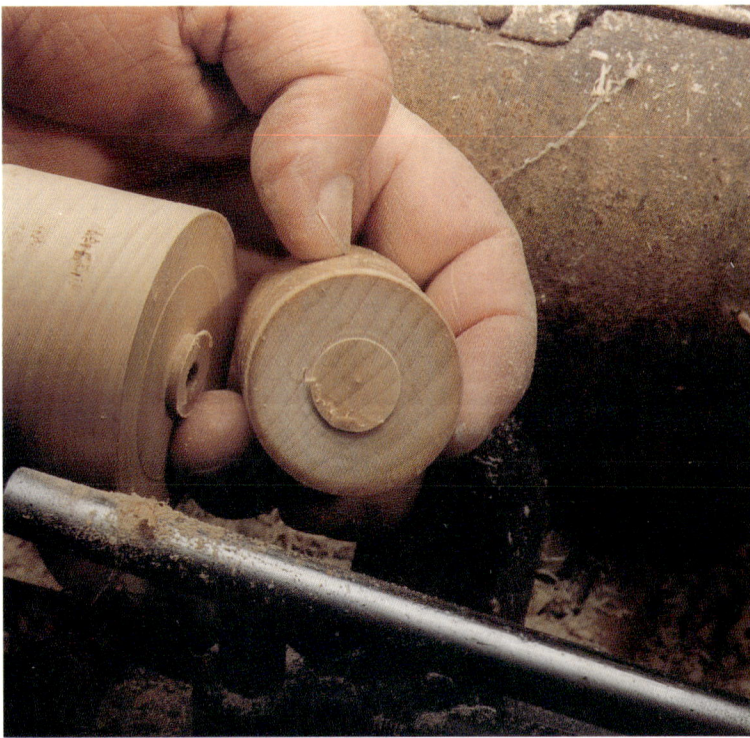

The bottom of the box needs to be shaped.

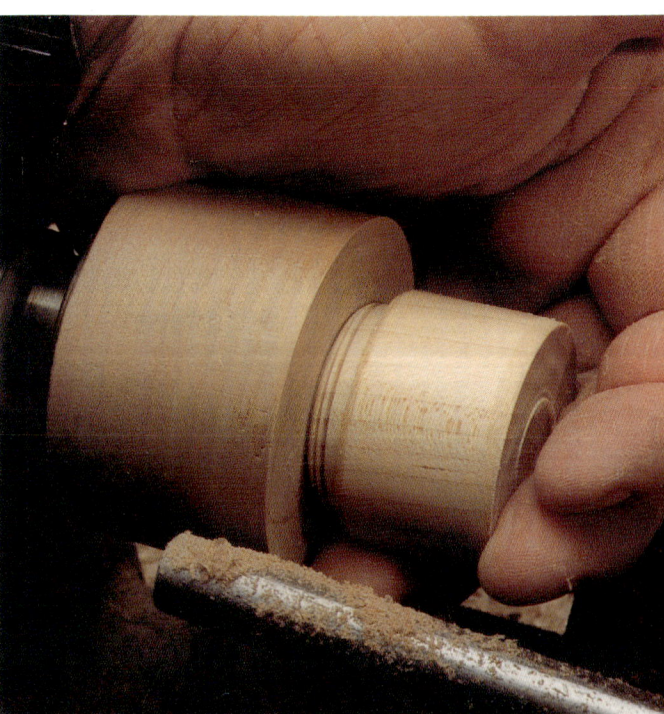

The box is fit on a jamb fit chuck that is made on the waste block.

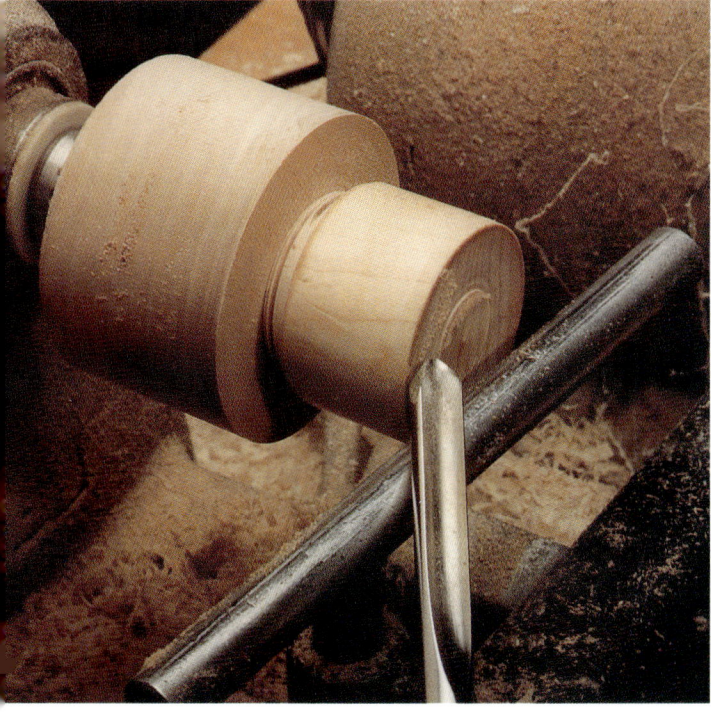

I'm using a 3/8" spindle gouge on the bottom.

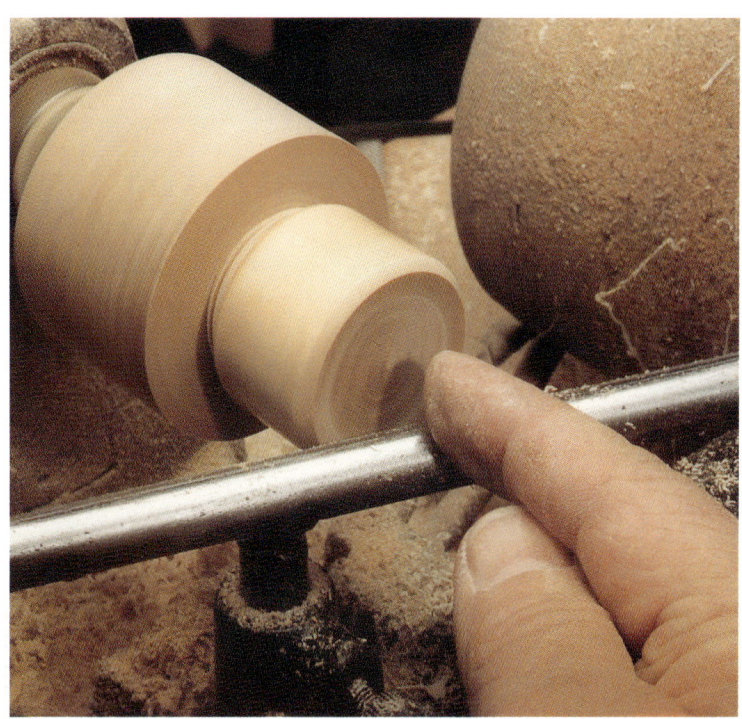

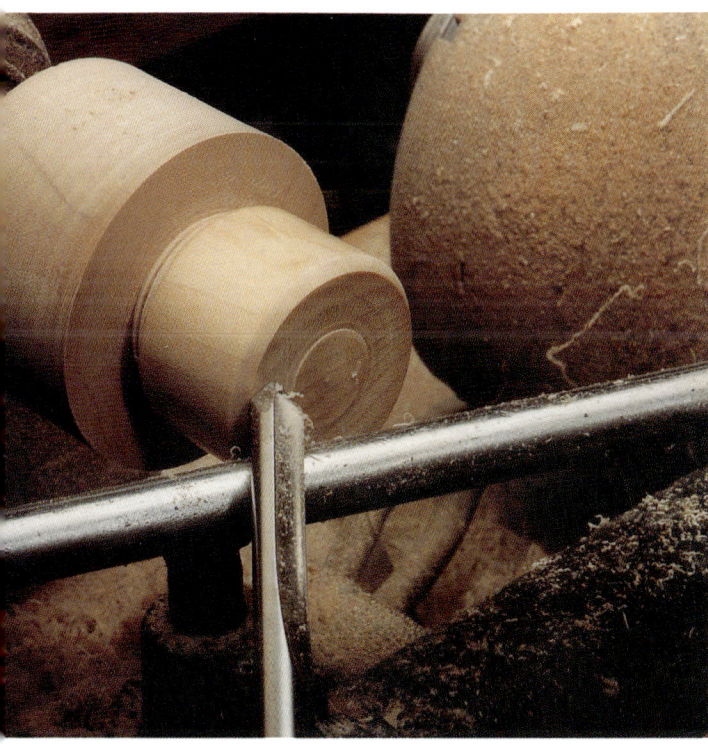

Be very gentle with your cuts, as the box is only held on the jamb fit chuck by friction.

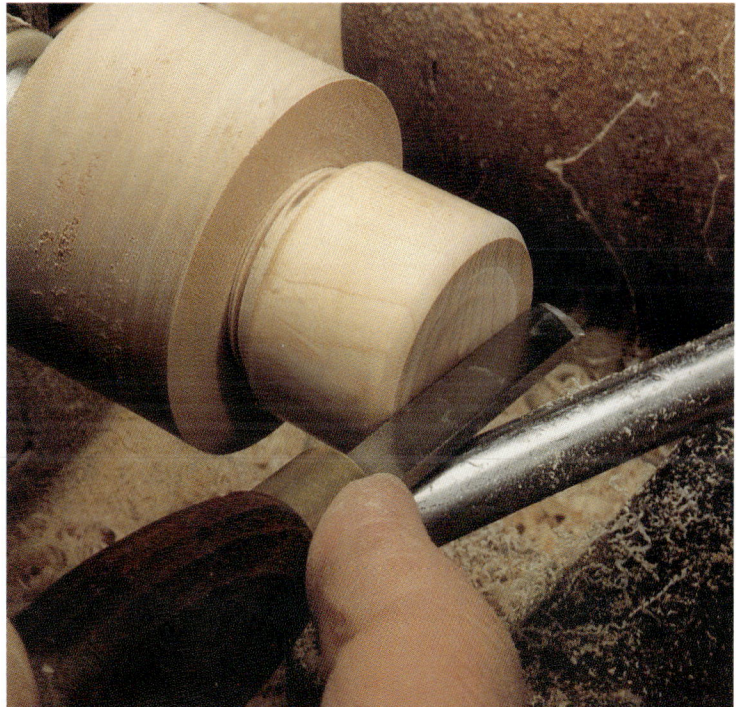

Make the bottom slightly concave.

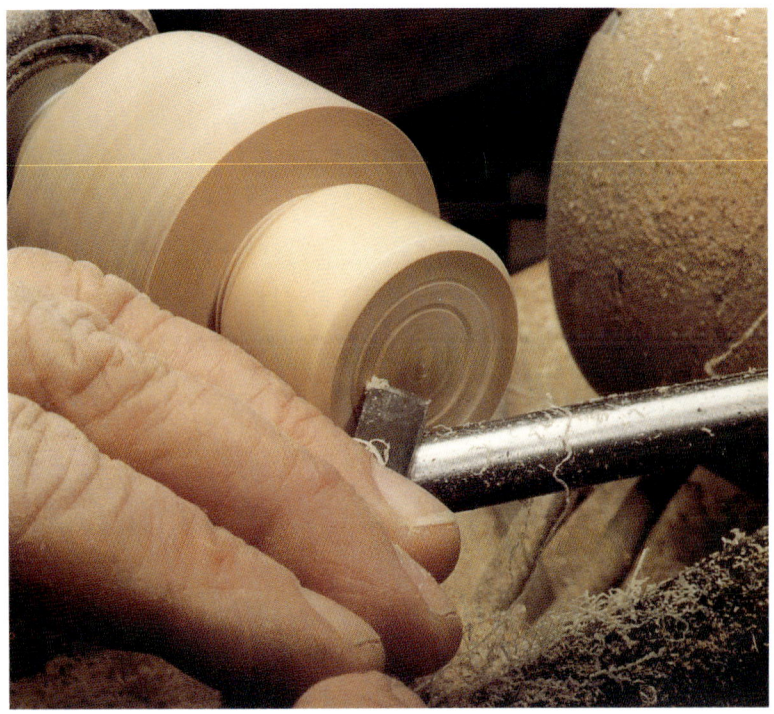

I add two circular lines to the base for my signature, the date, and the type of wood.

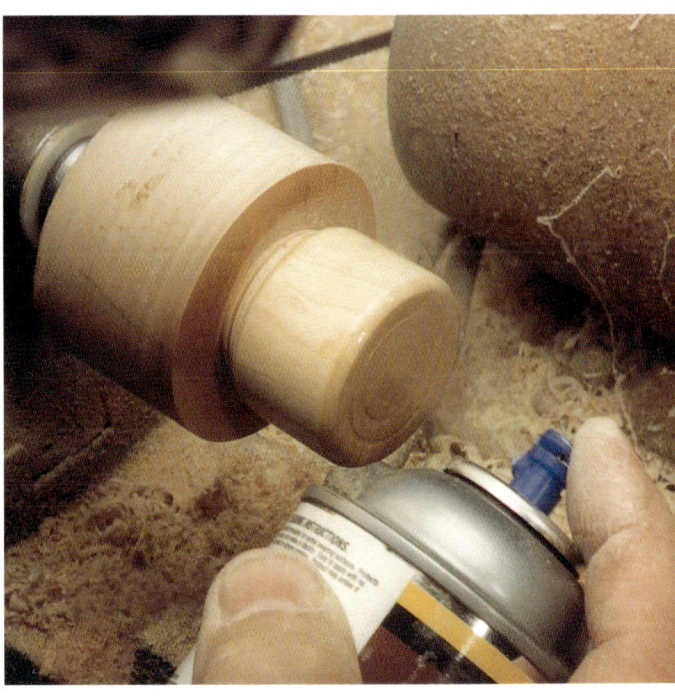

The same finishing process, sealing...

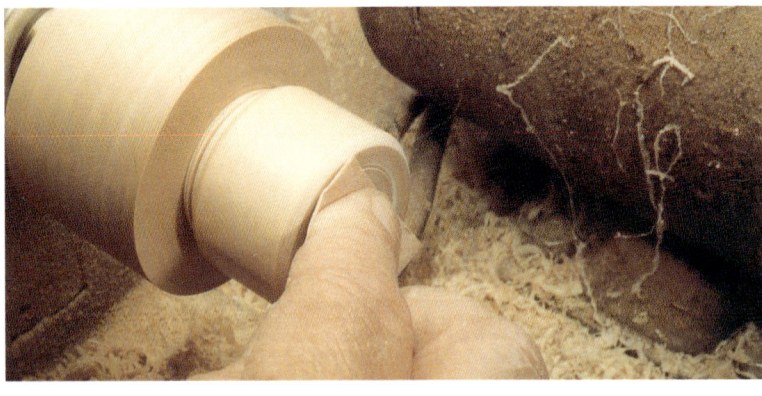

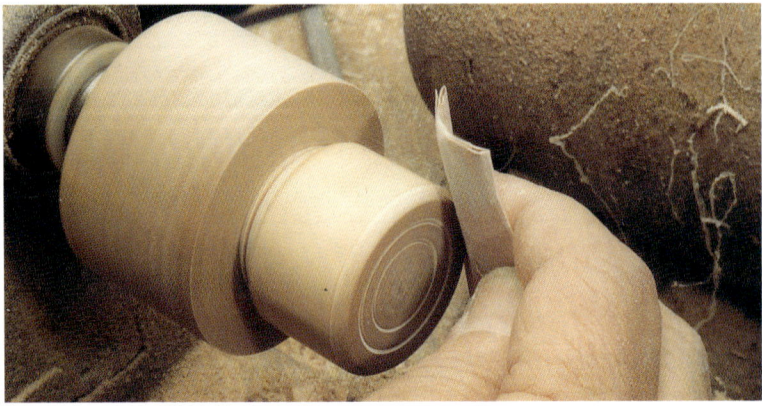

Again, the bottom is sanded from 180 through 400 grit sandpaper.

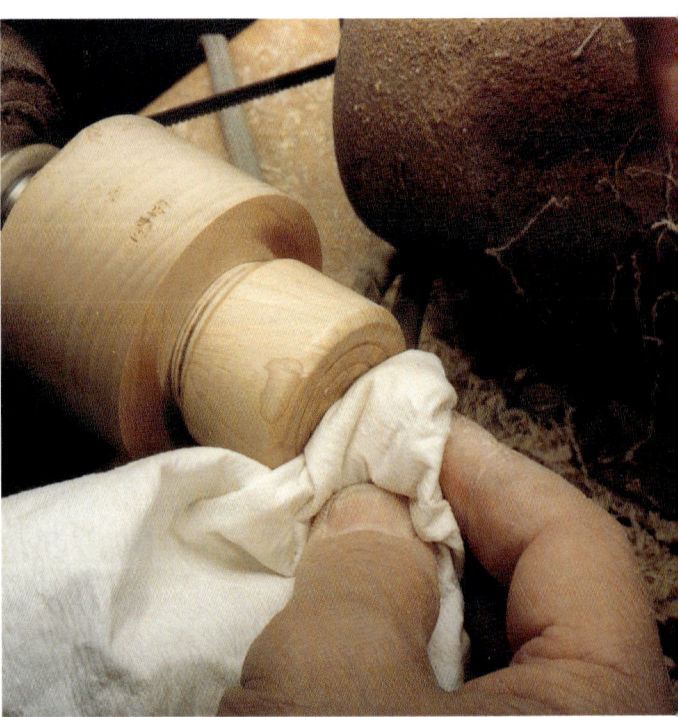

finishing...

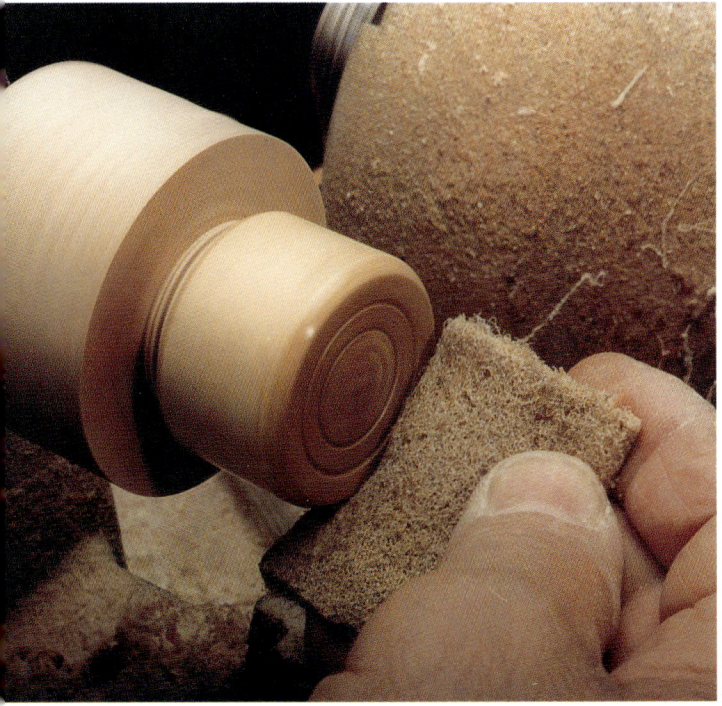

and waxing is used on the base.

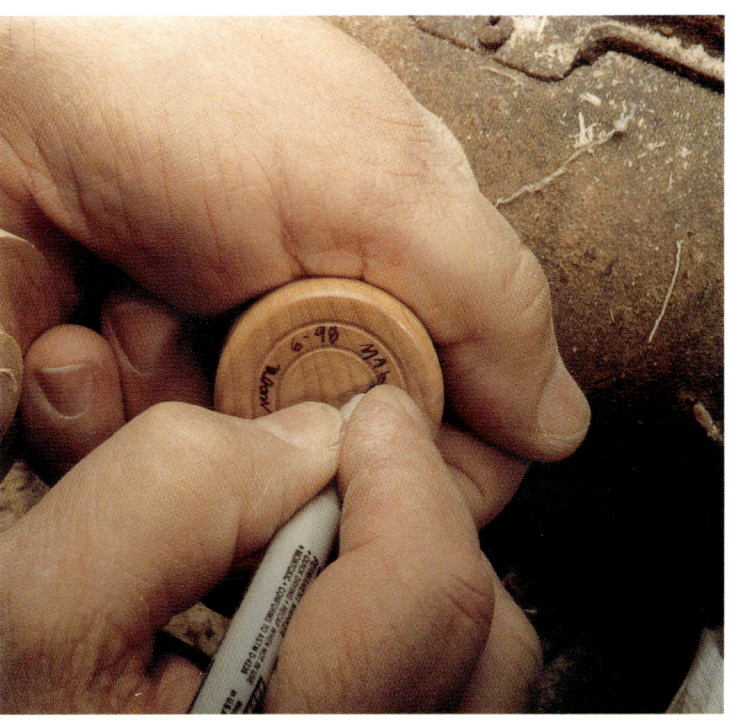

and dating the box.

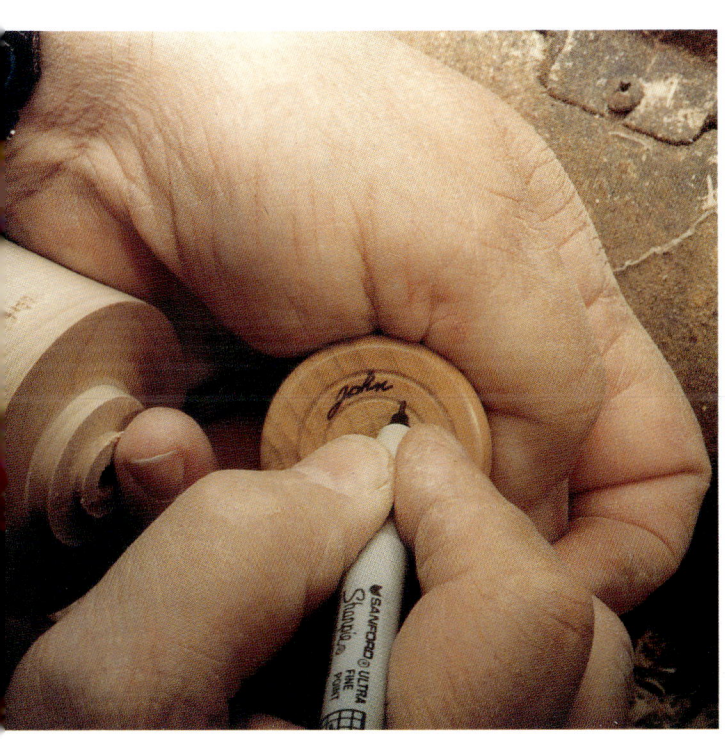

A last step is signing...

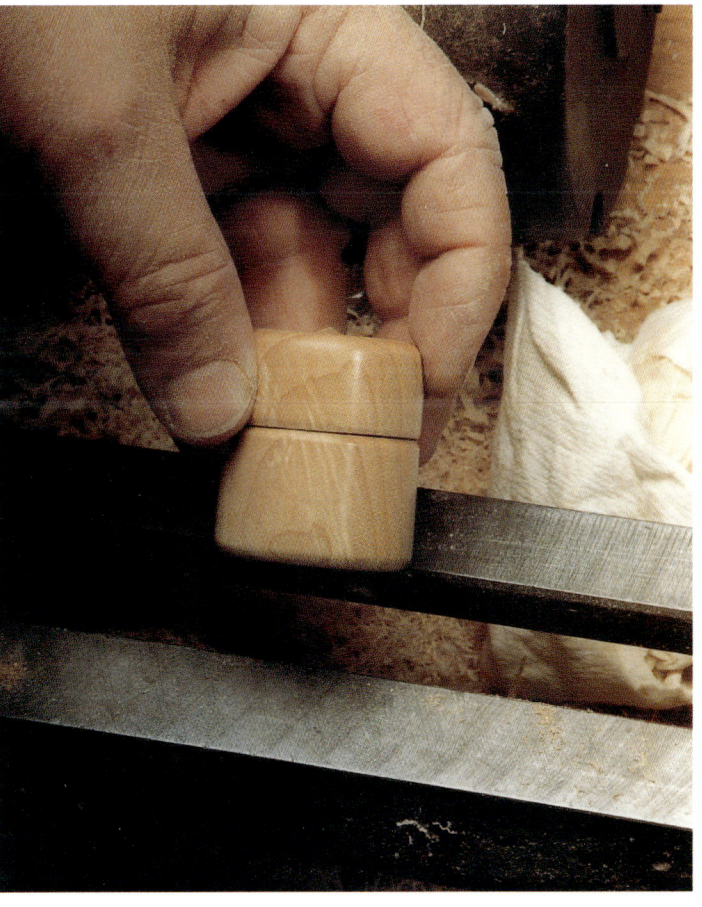

The finished box.

Project 2: A Threaded Box from a Maple Burl Block

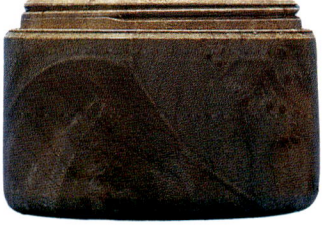
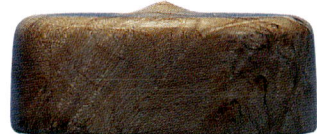

The second project.

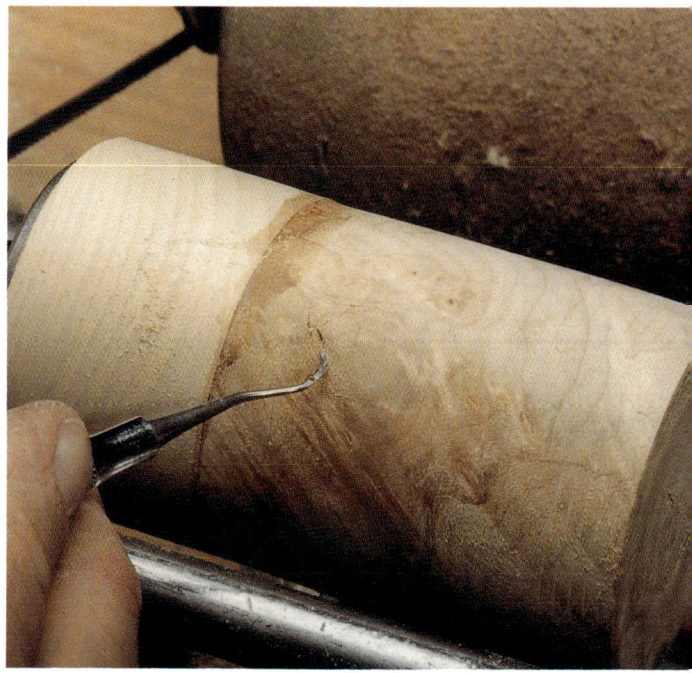

Sometimes there are defects in the wood that need to be cleaned out and filled in. Dental tools are excellent for this job.

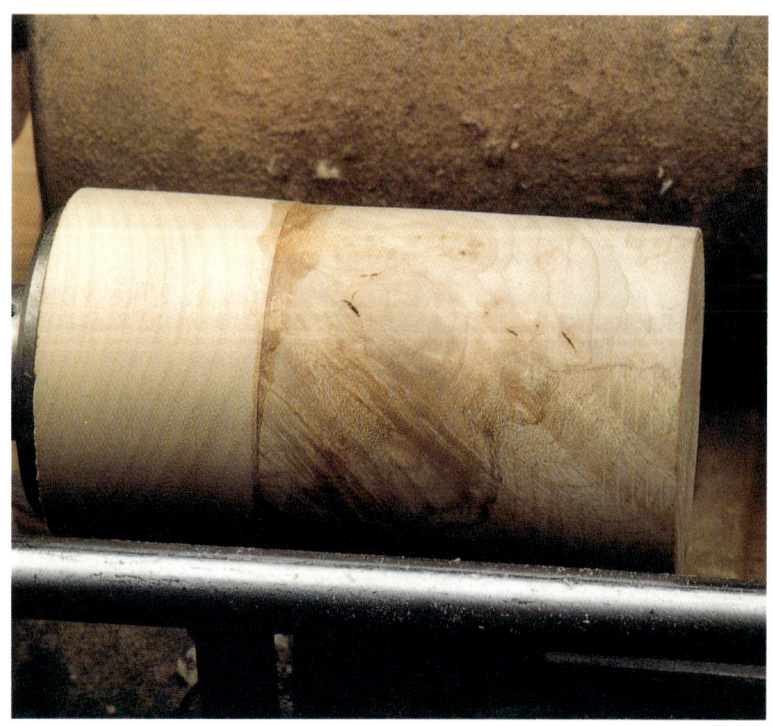

We have a maple burl blank that has been glued to a waste block for our next project.

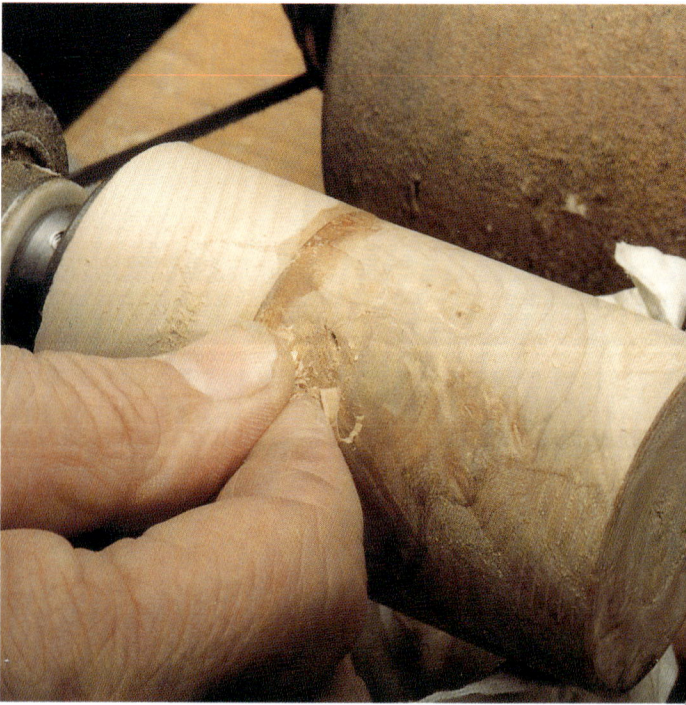

Shavings are rubbed into the hole.

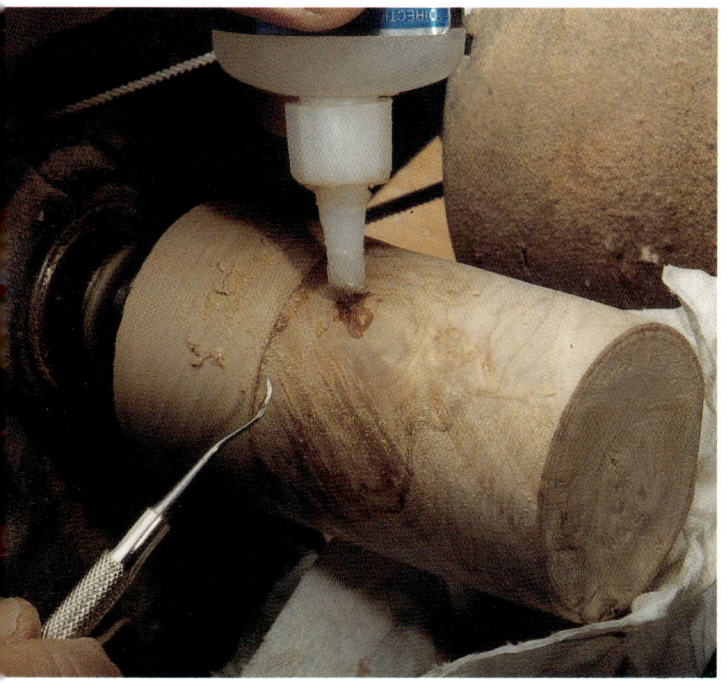

Coat the area with thin cyanoacrylate (CA) glue.

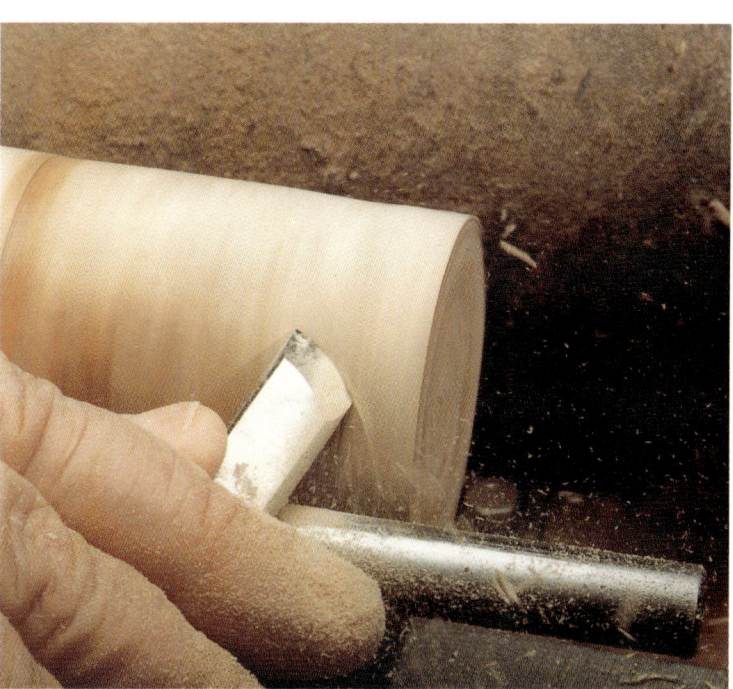

The blank is now shaped into a smooth cylinder using a 1/2" skew chisel.

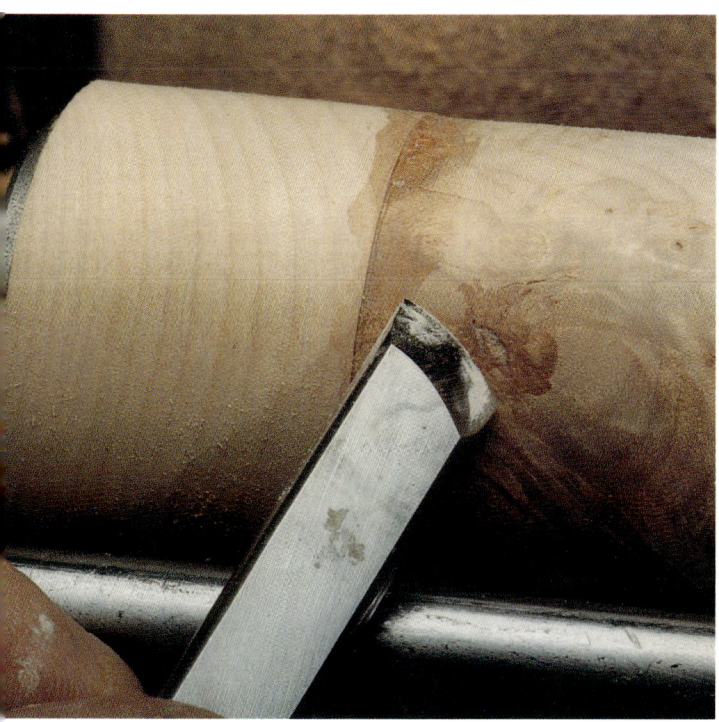

The defect is filled and the blank is now ready to turn.

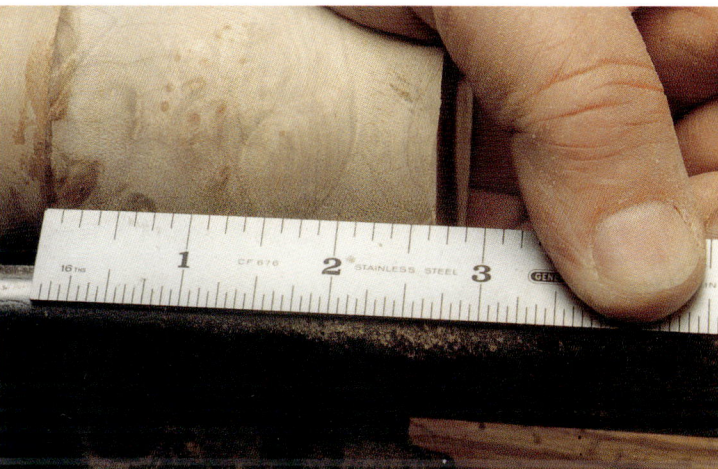

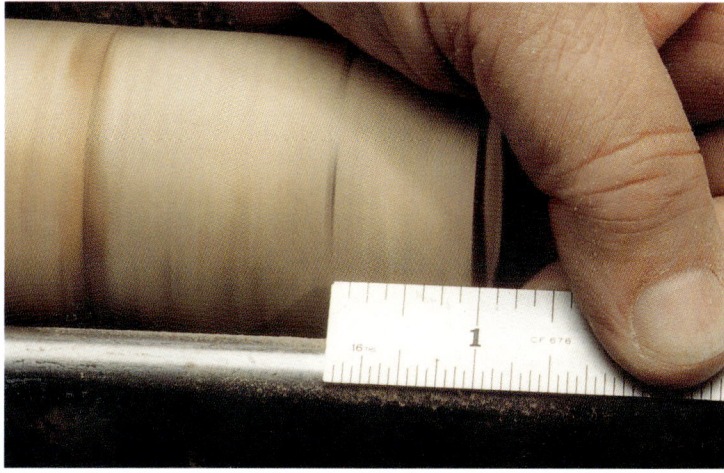

For this 2 1/2" blank, the properly proportioned block should have a lid of 7/8"—which is marked on the blank.

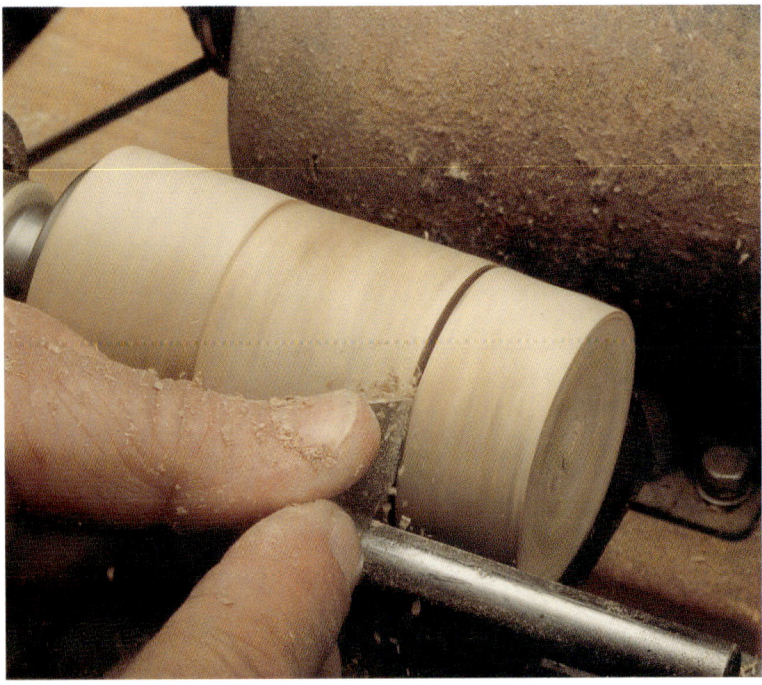

The lid is parted off just below the line with an ultra-thin parting tool.

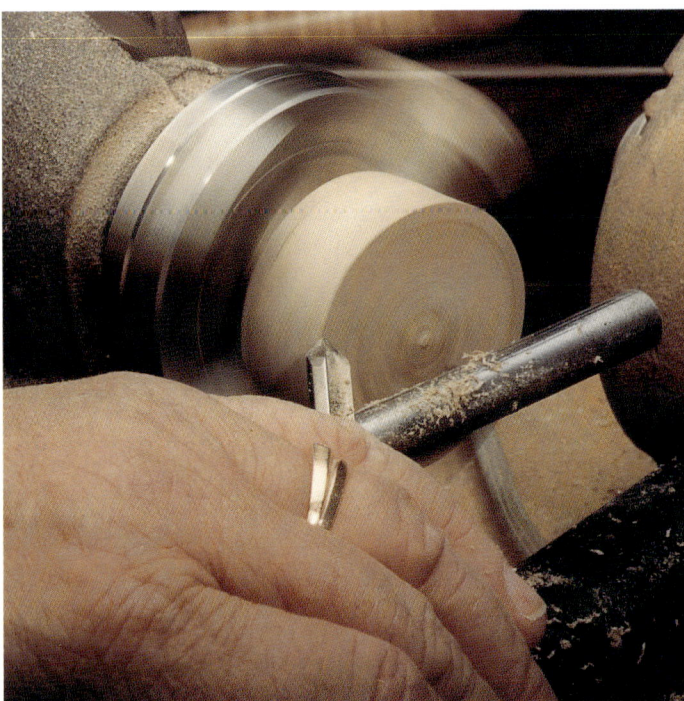

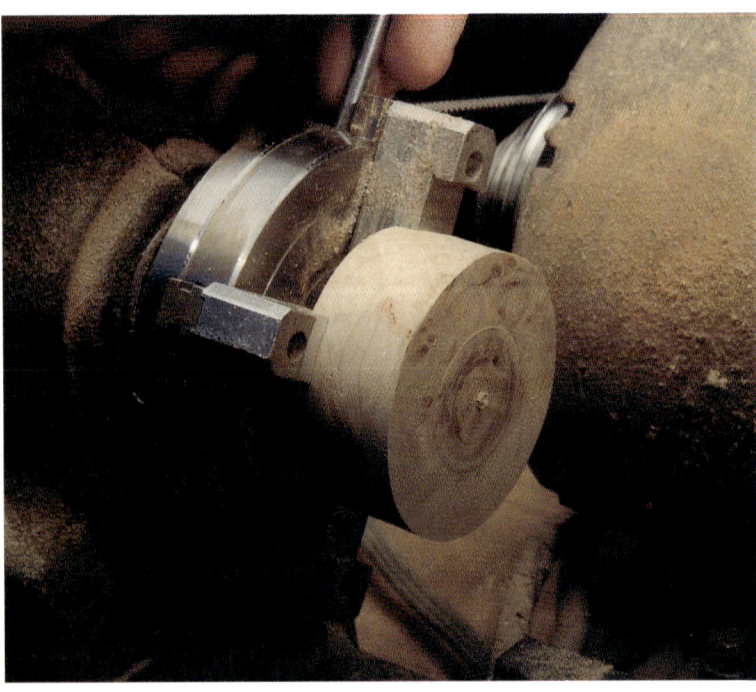

The lid is mounted into the four jaw chuck.

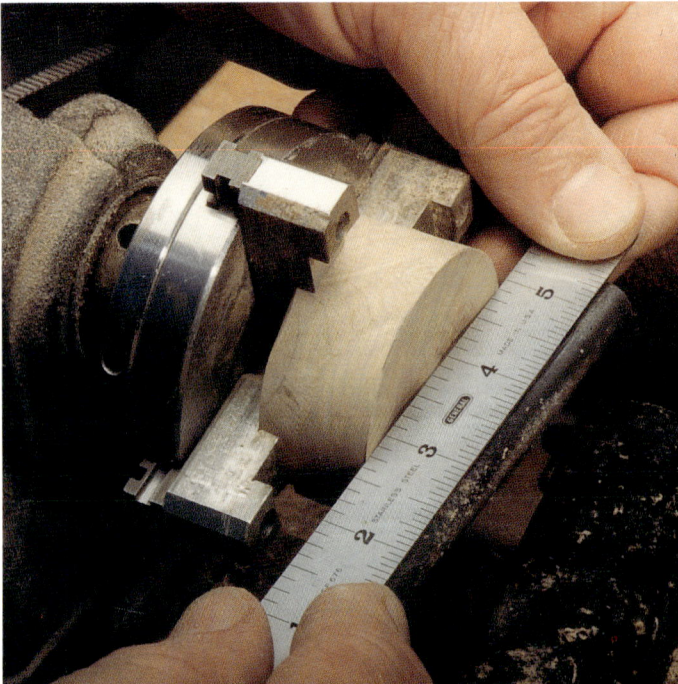

The base of the lid is made slightly concave with the 3/8" spindle gouge. This will ensure the lid contacts the base on the outside edge.

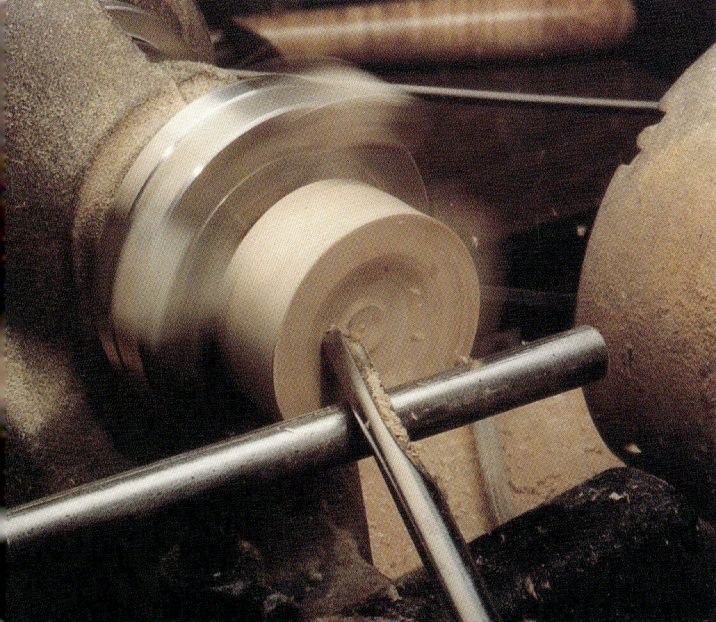

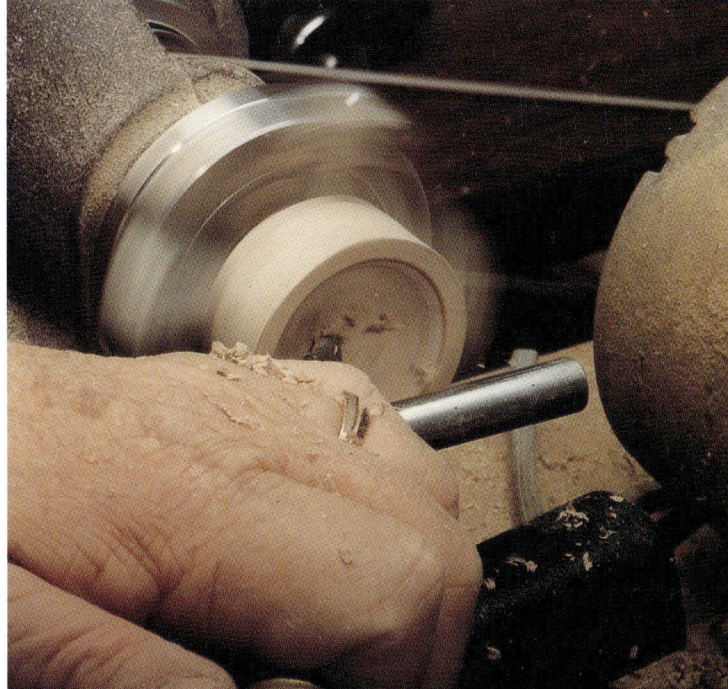

To make a domed top, use a small round nosed scraper.

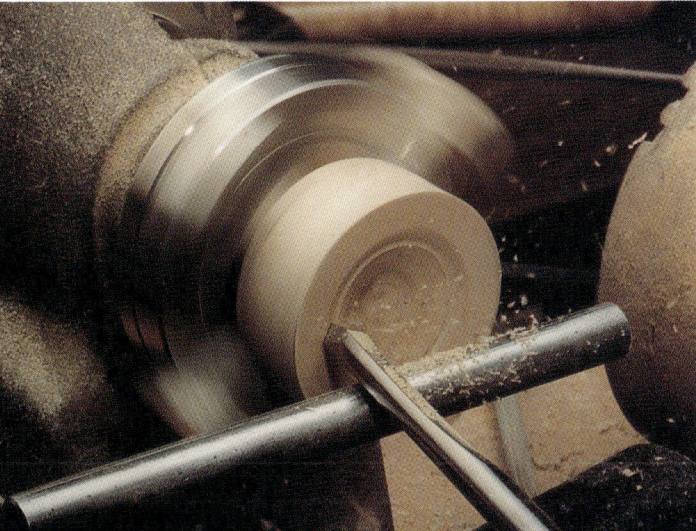

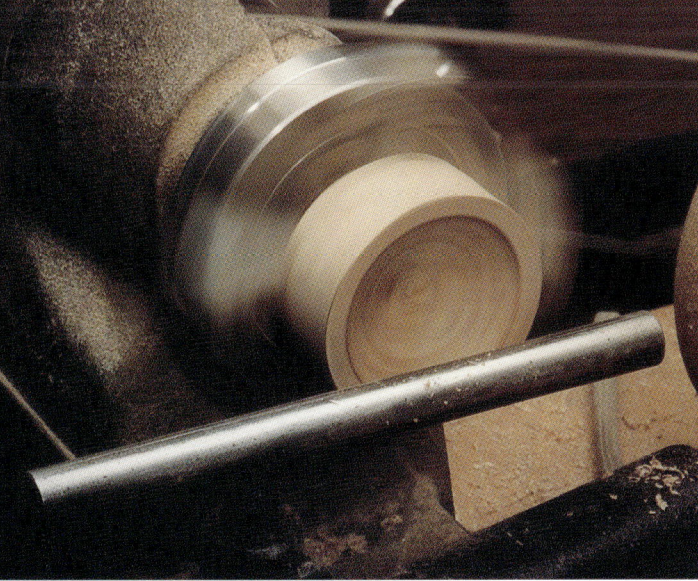

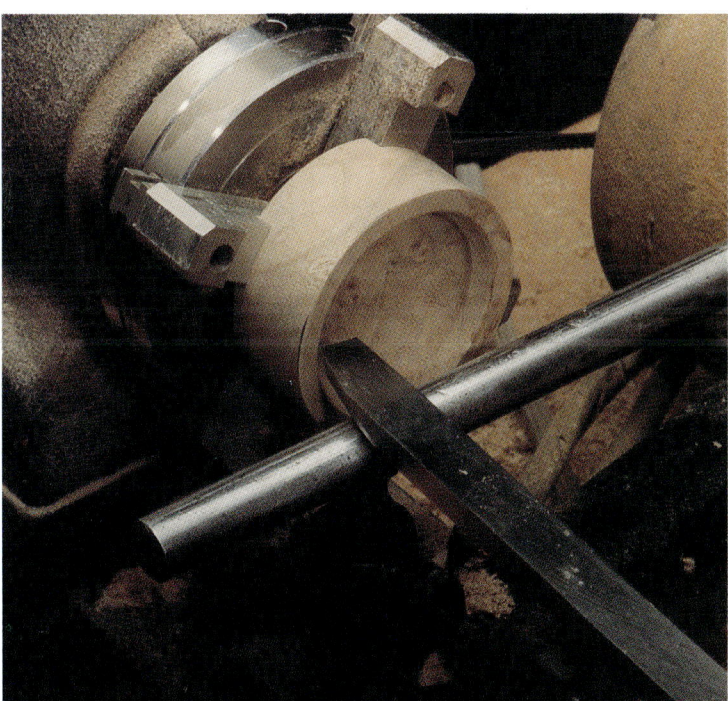

I want to leave a sidewall thickness of 1/8" to 1/4" when turning burled wood. I use a square nosed scraper for this cut.

Beginning to hollow out the lid with the 3/8" spindle gouge.

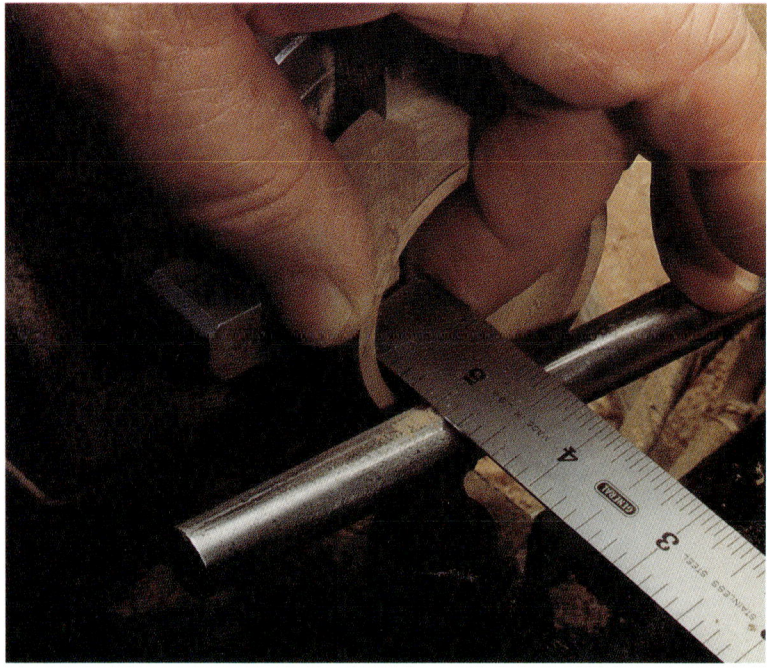

Make sure that the area for the threads is parallel to the ways of the lathe.

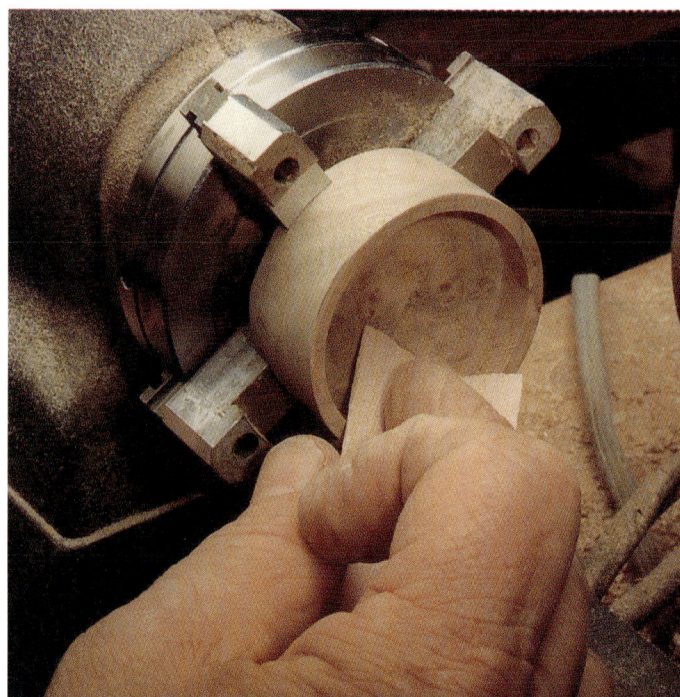

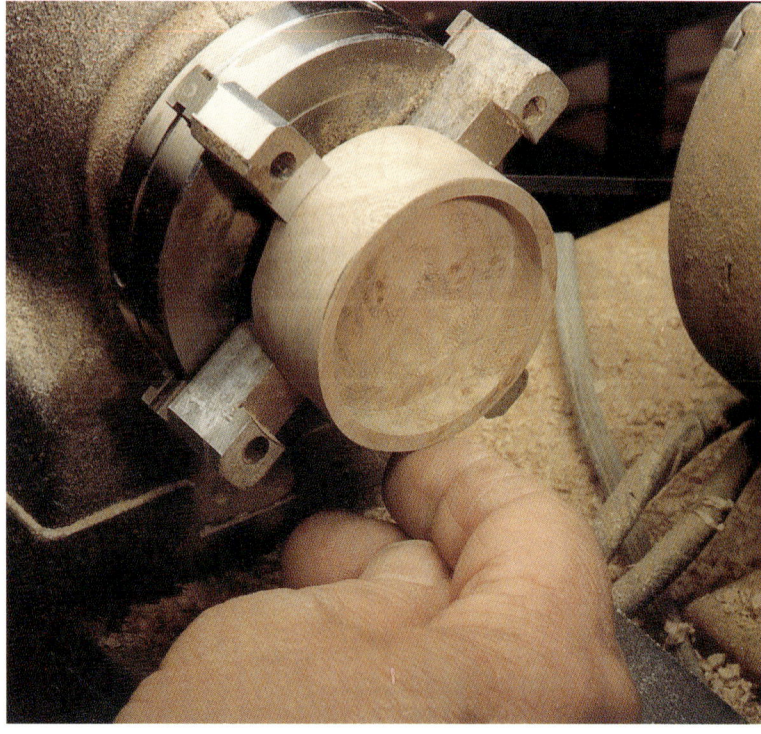

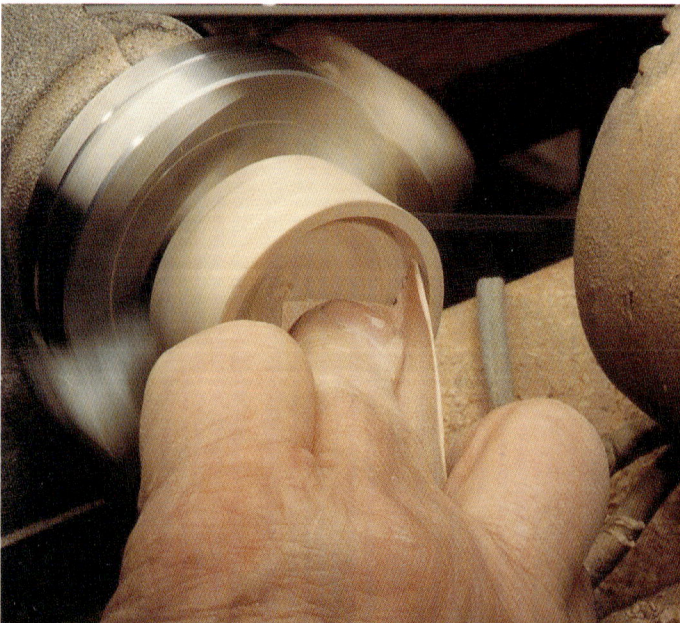

starting with 180 grit sandpaper and working up to 400 grit.

With sharp tools, the interior of the box should be ready for sanding ...

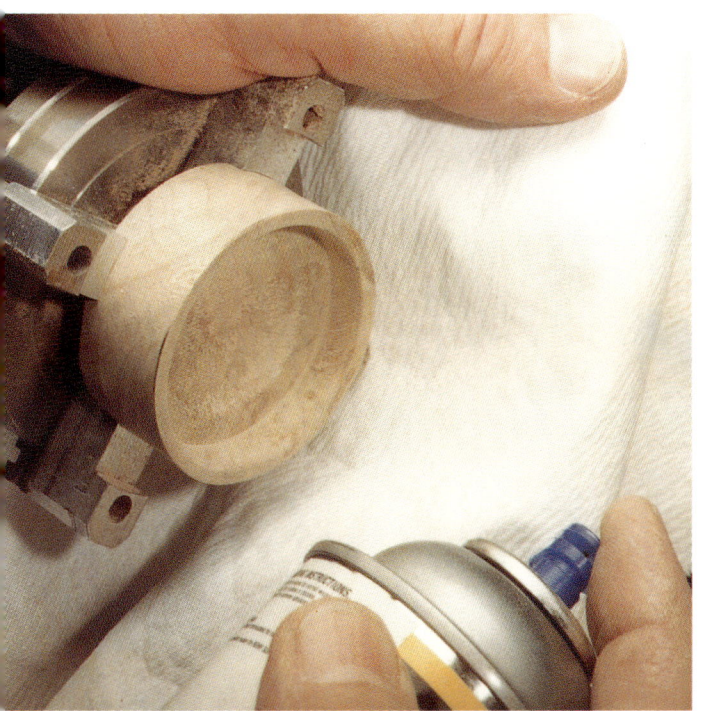

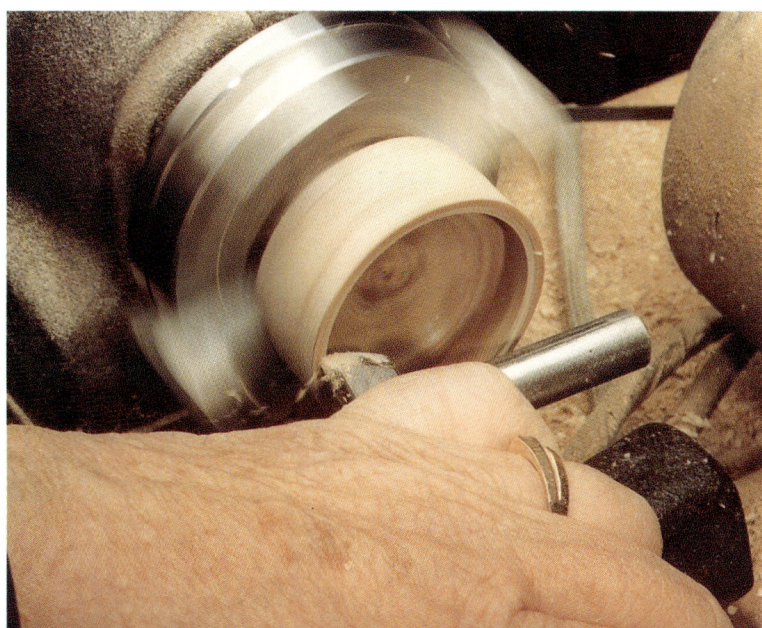

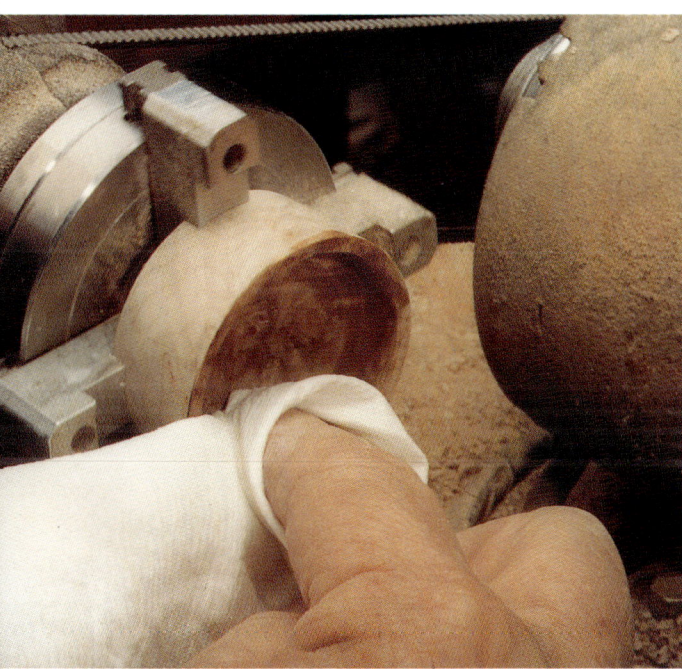

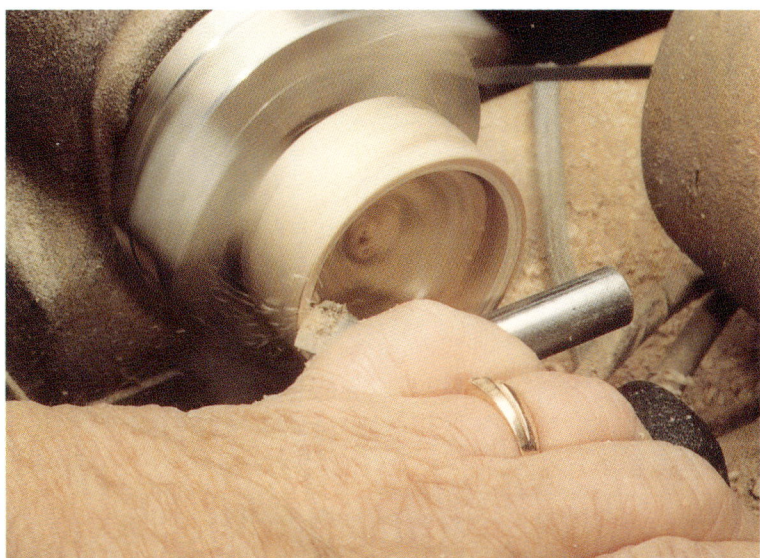

Apply sanding sealer to the inside of the box lid and buff dry with a paper towel.

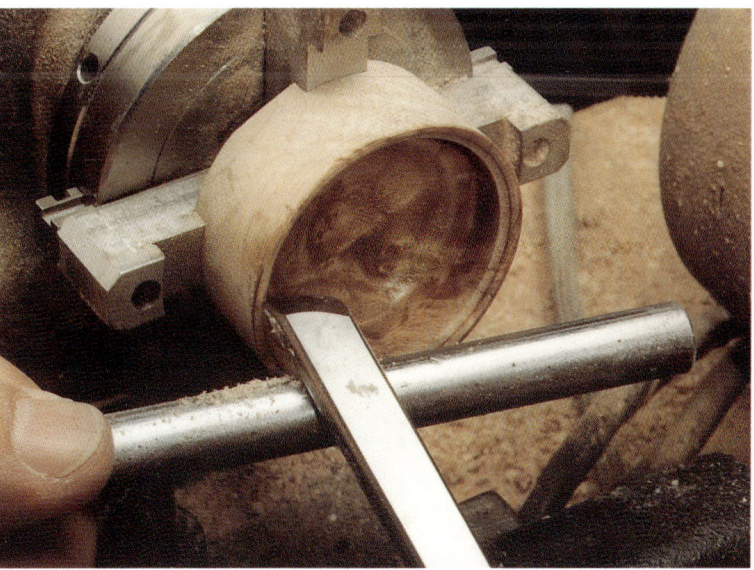

Cut a 1/16" rabbet to allow for adjustment at final fitting.

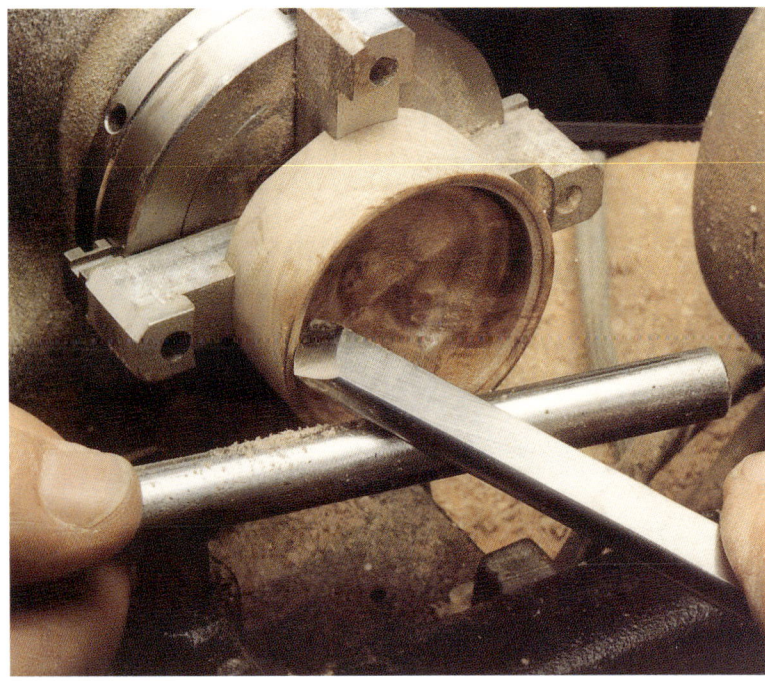

The inside edges are chamfered to remove sharp corners.

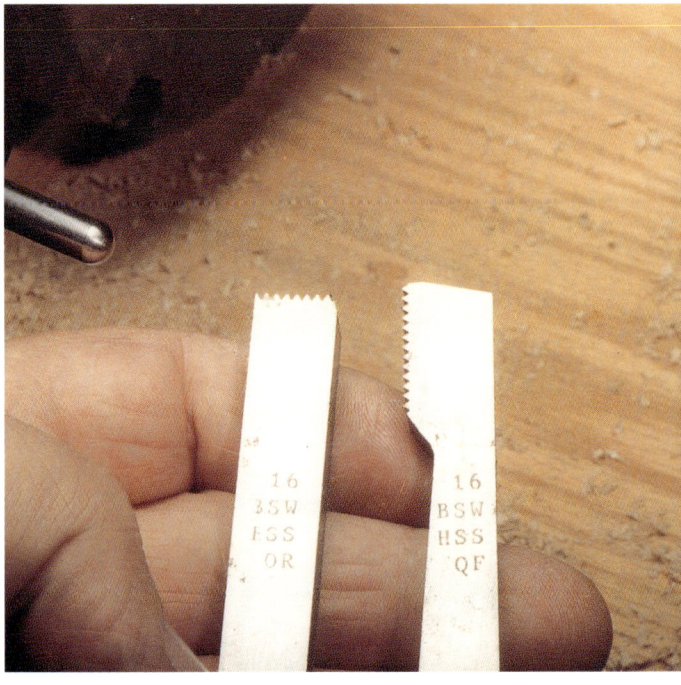

Threads can be hand chased using old fashioned methods. There are two world renouned turners, Bill Jones and Allan Batty, from England who have a marvelous touch and years of experience chasing threads. It takes much time and experience to learn to use these tools satisfactorily.

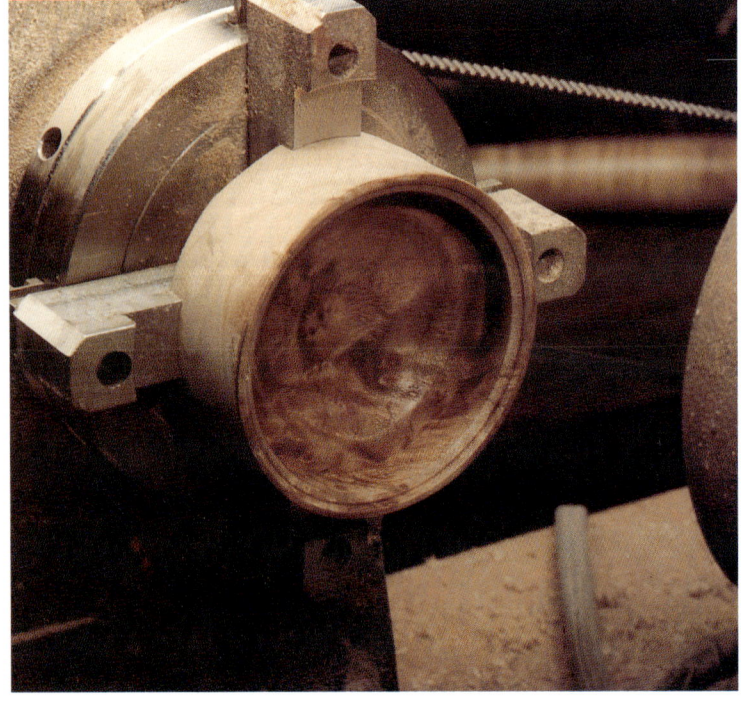

The lid is ready for threads.

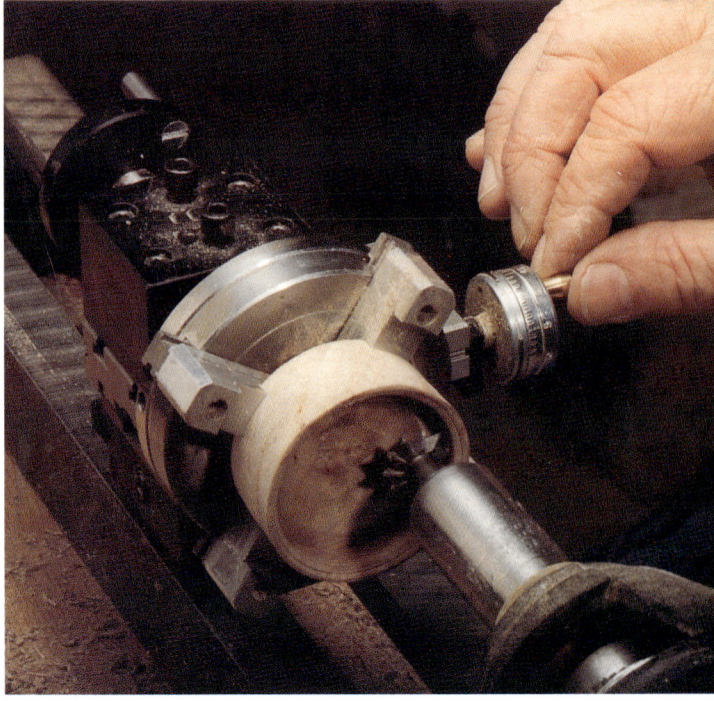

Adjust the cross vise until the cutter just contacts the surface of the lid.

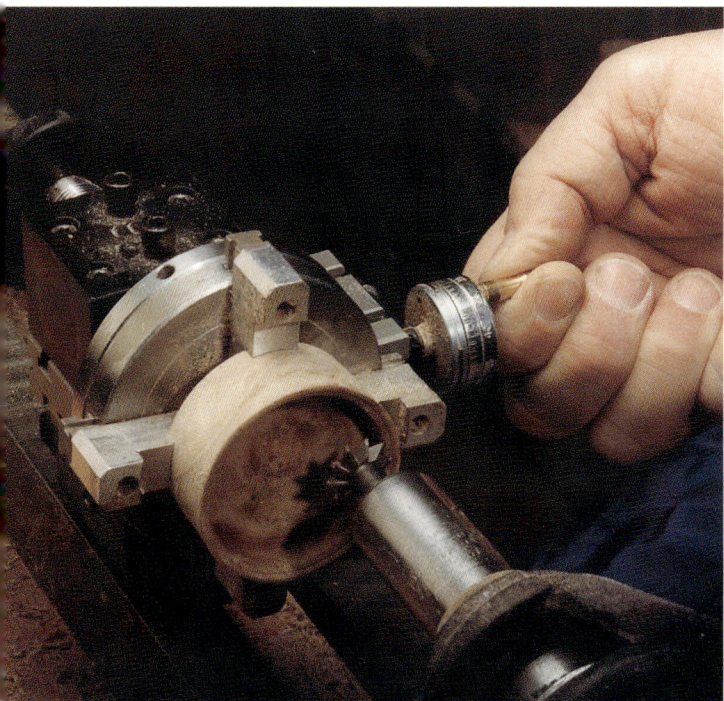

After the box has been moved away from the cutter, advance the cross vise 3/4 of a turn. This will produce threads that are approximately 40 thousandths of an inch deep.

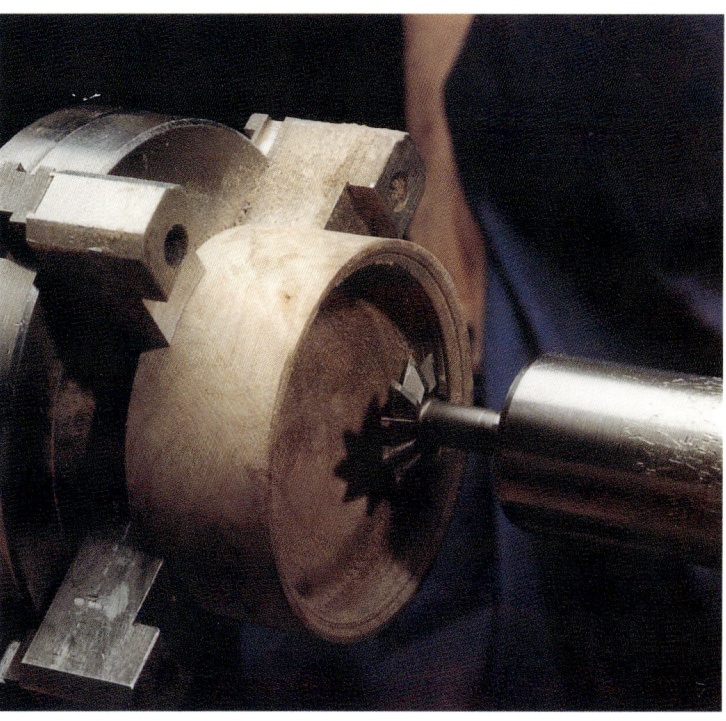

The threads are in place.

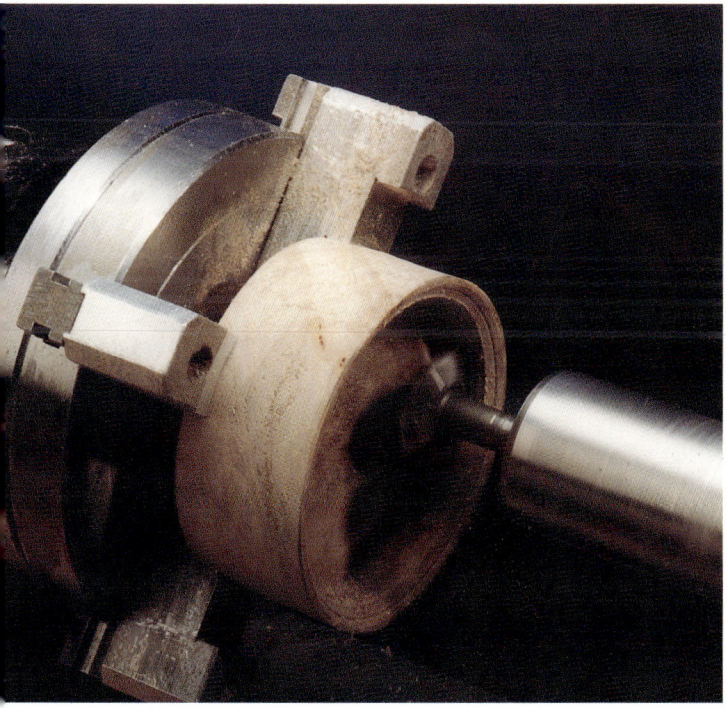

Cutting the threads. Three to four threads are sufficient for closure.

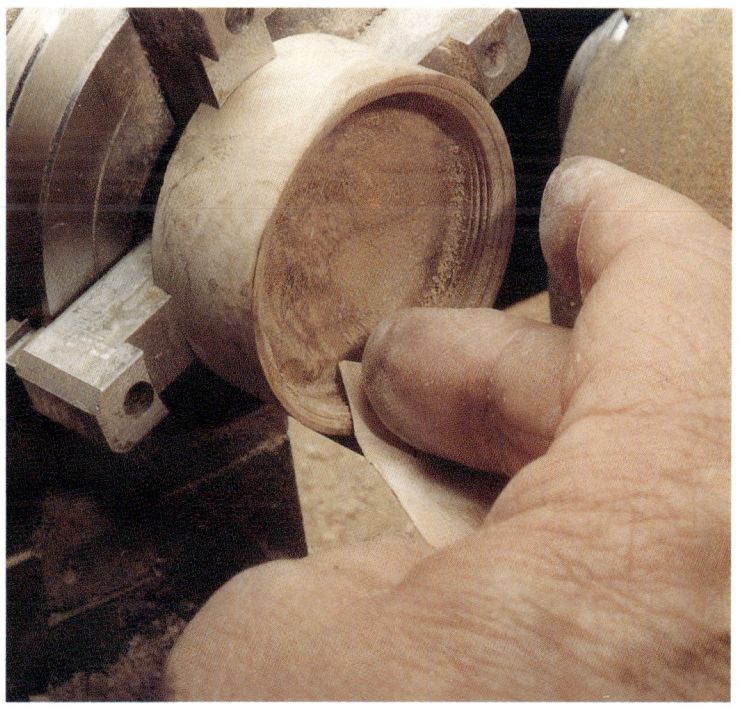

The threads are lightly sanded with 400 grit to remove burrs left during cutting.

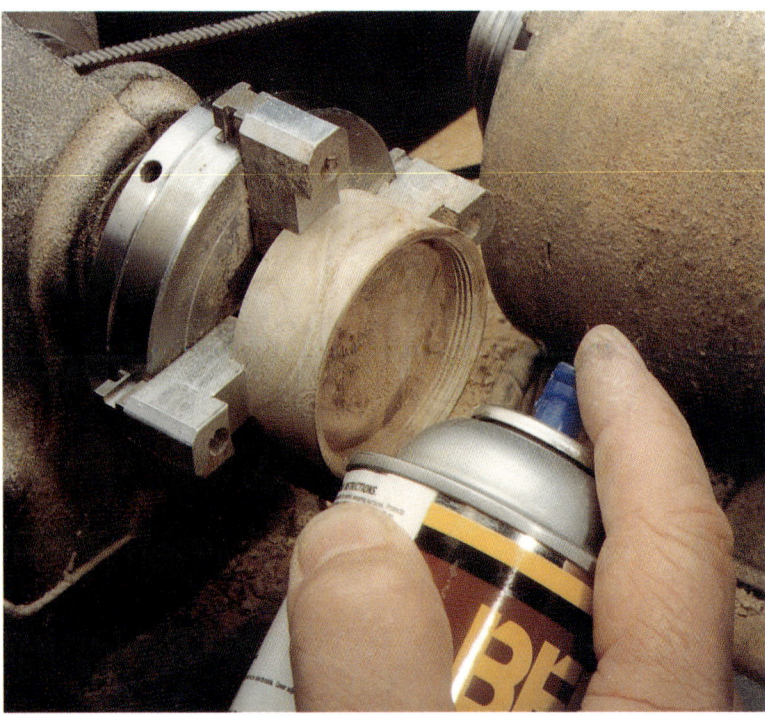

Apply sanding sealer to the inside of the lid.

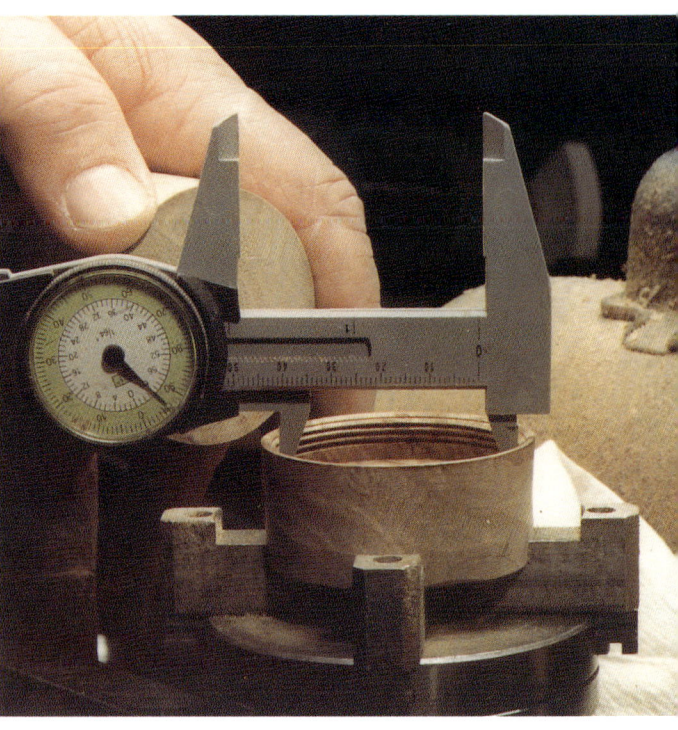

The diameter across the box at the threads is 1.91".

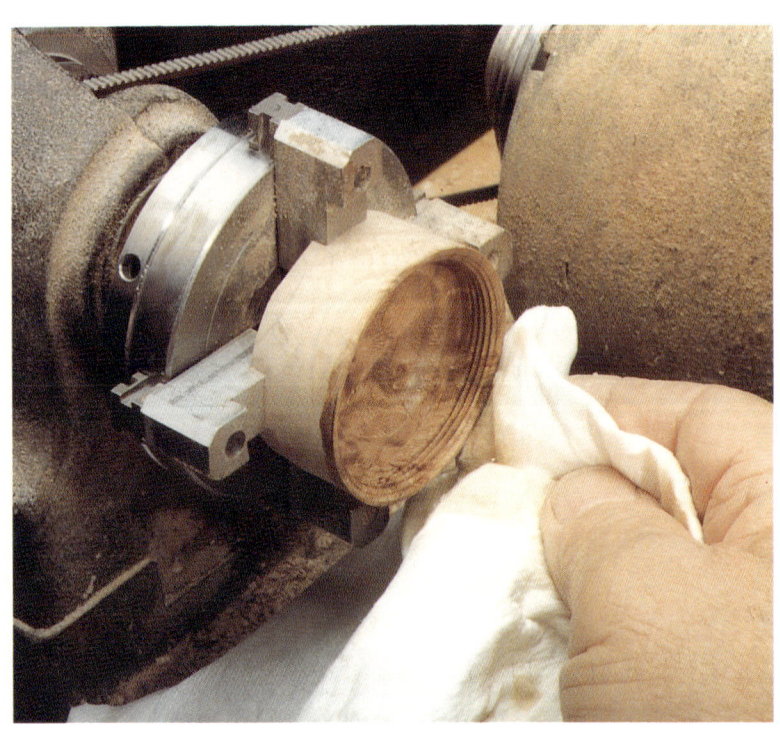

Buff and dry the sanding sealer with a paper towel.

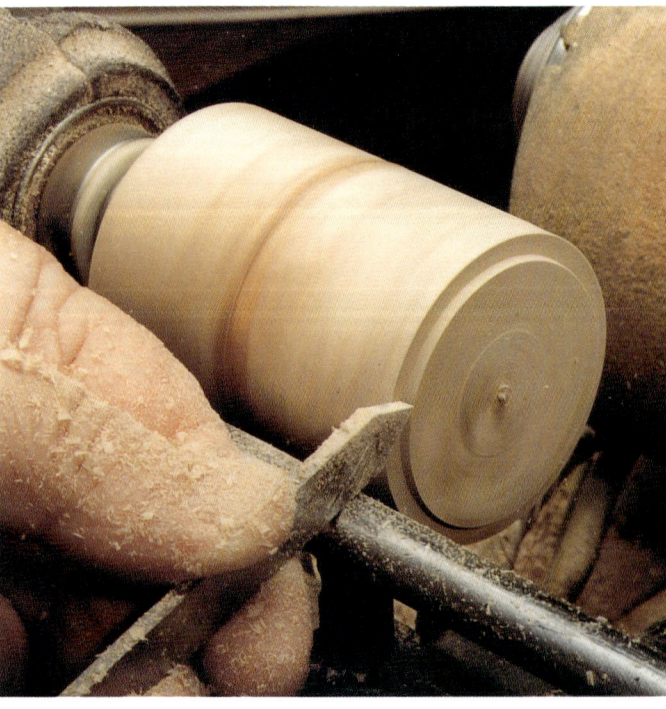

Moving on to work on the bottom of the box. Cutting a short tenon (about 60 thousandths greater than the lid diameter at the threads—or 1.97") is required for sizing the interior of the box.

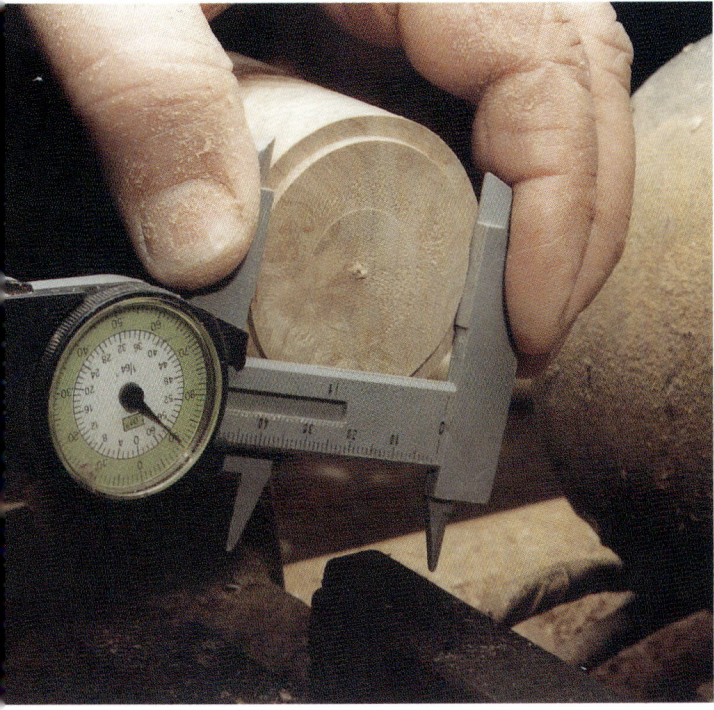

This tenon is too small, therefore a new one must be cut. That is why a short tenon is initally cut.

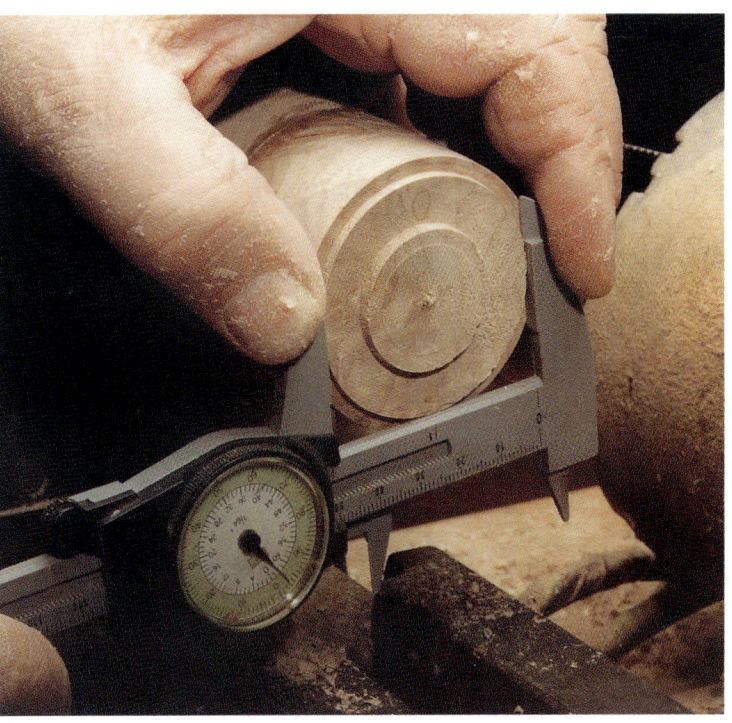

Success! The second tenon is 1.97". The reason for leaving this tenon oversized is that the box may change shape when the interior is removed.

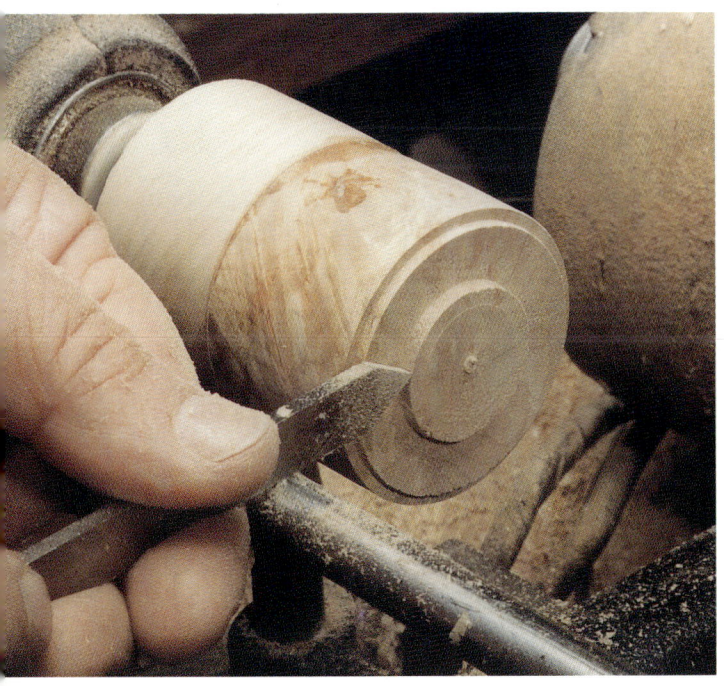

Cut away the mistake and try again.

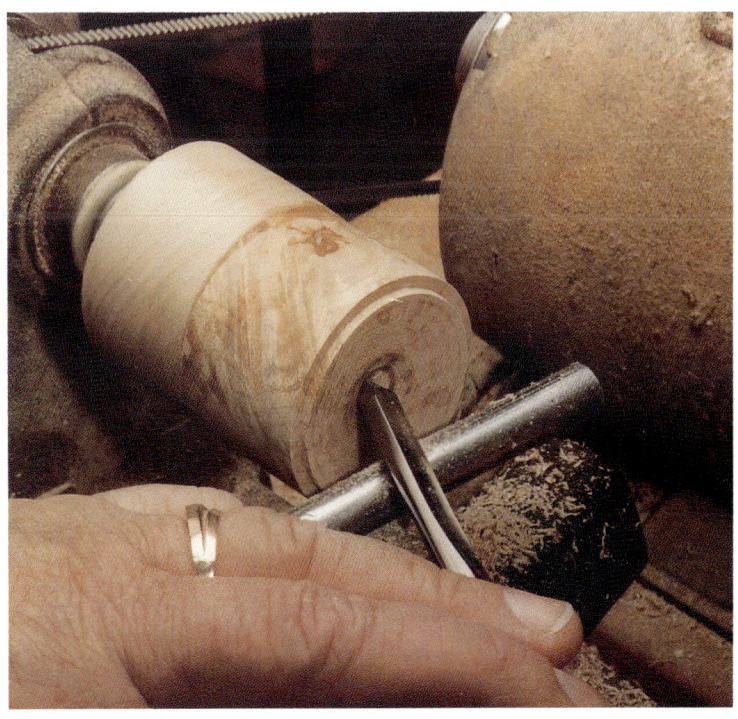

Cut a recess in the center of the box bottom with a 3/8" spindle gouge.

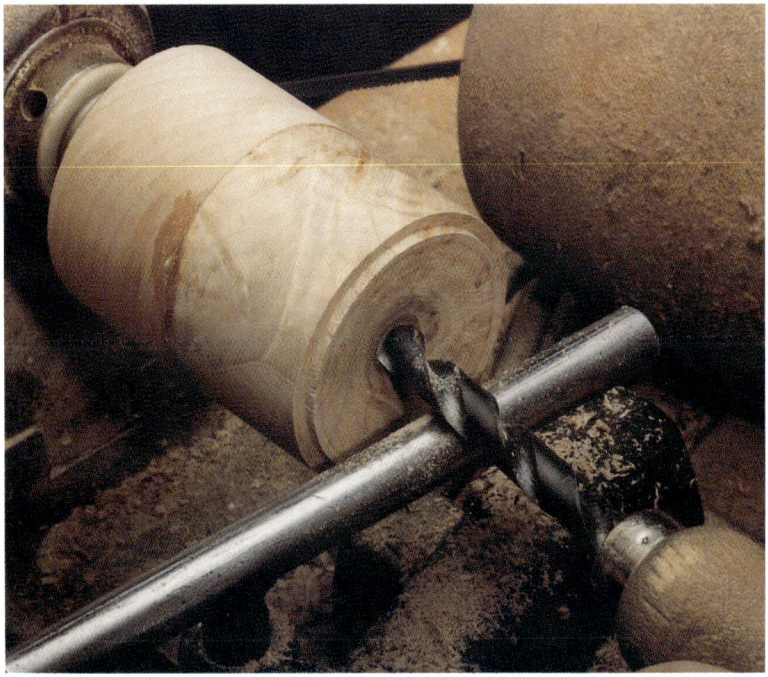

With the recess in place, I bore a 3/8" hole to make hollowing easier.

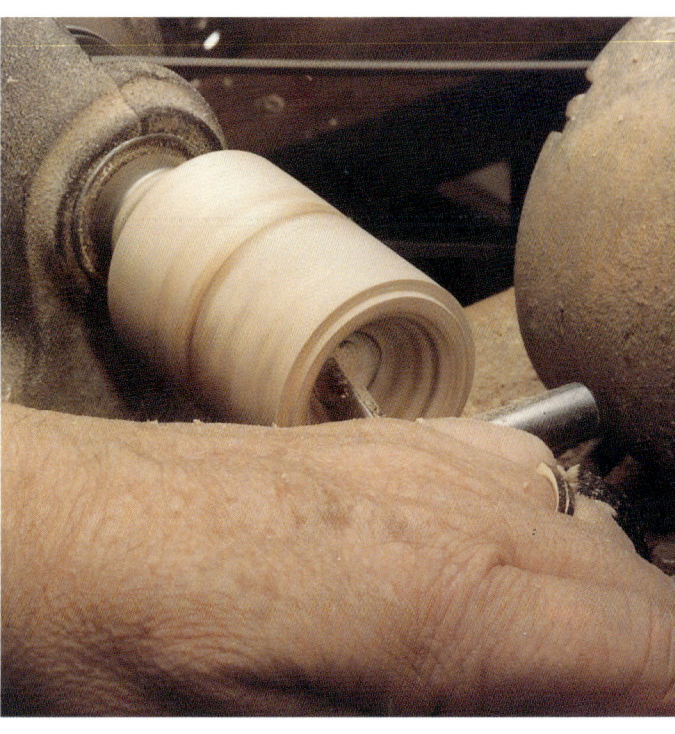

Hollow out the interior with a 3/8" spindle gouge.

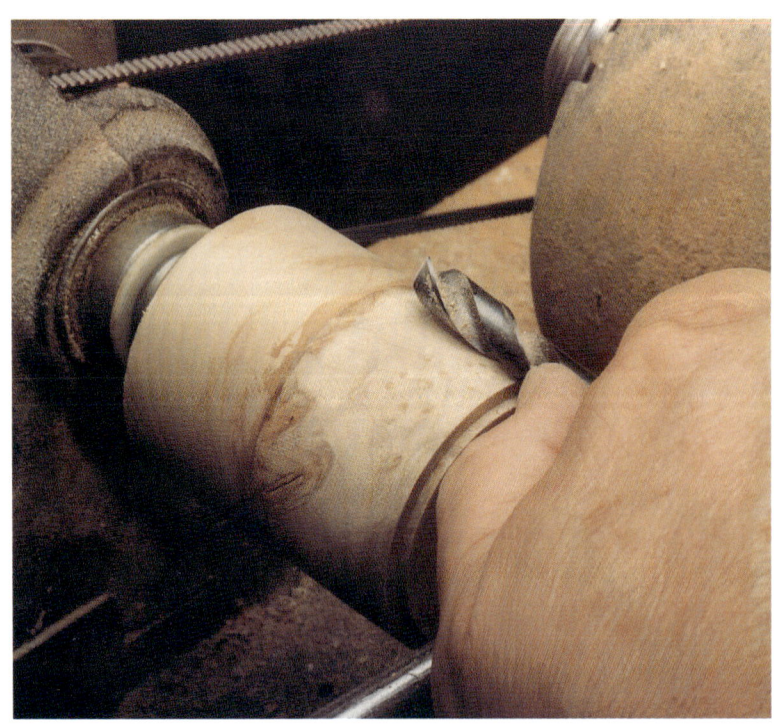

Check the depth to ensure that you do not bore too deep. The intent is to make a box, not threaded napkin rings.

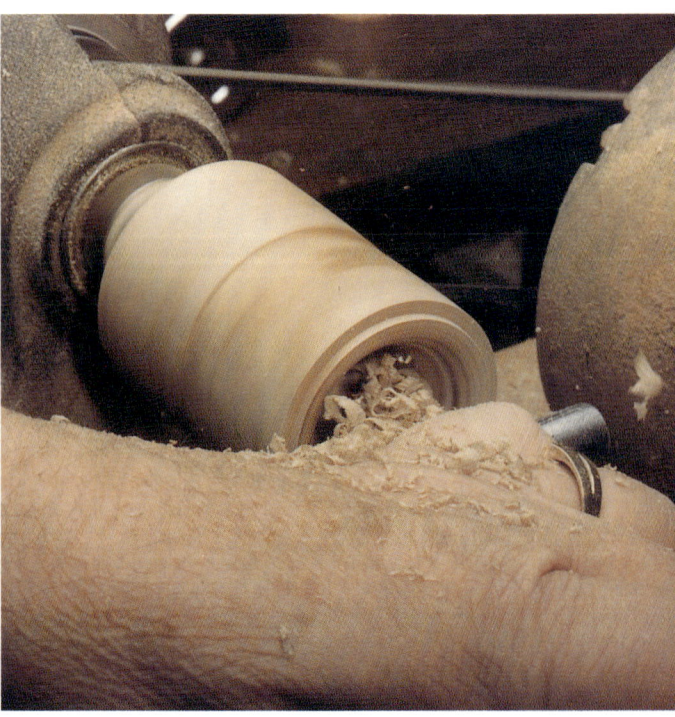

Hollowing out the interior

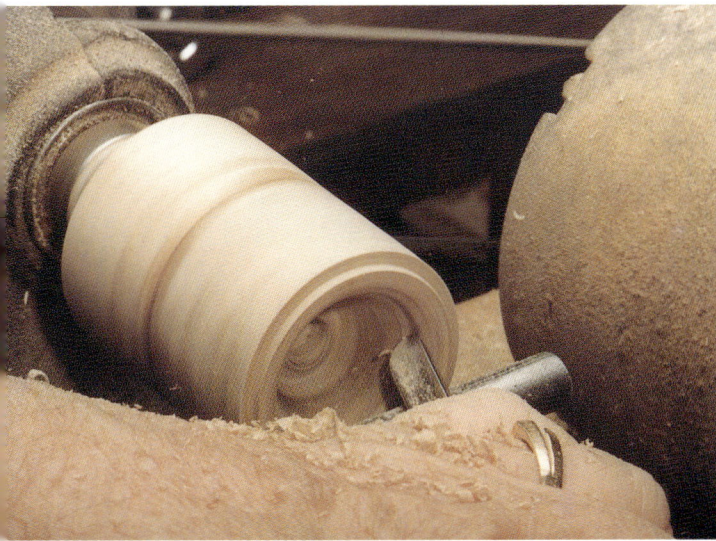

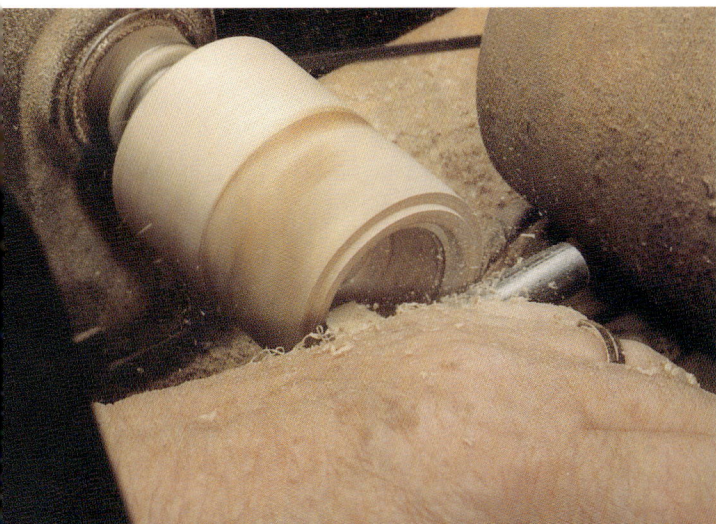

If your lathe has a reverse switch, you can cut from the opposite side.

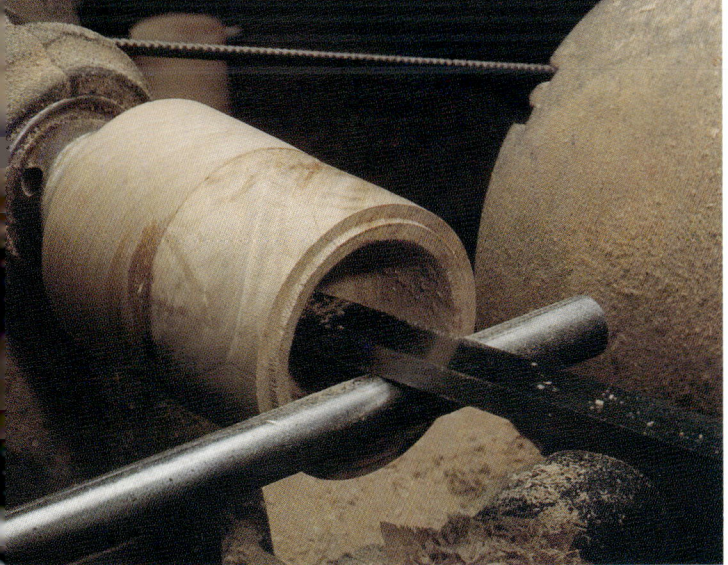

Use a square ended scraper to hollow out the box.

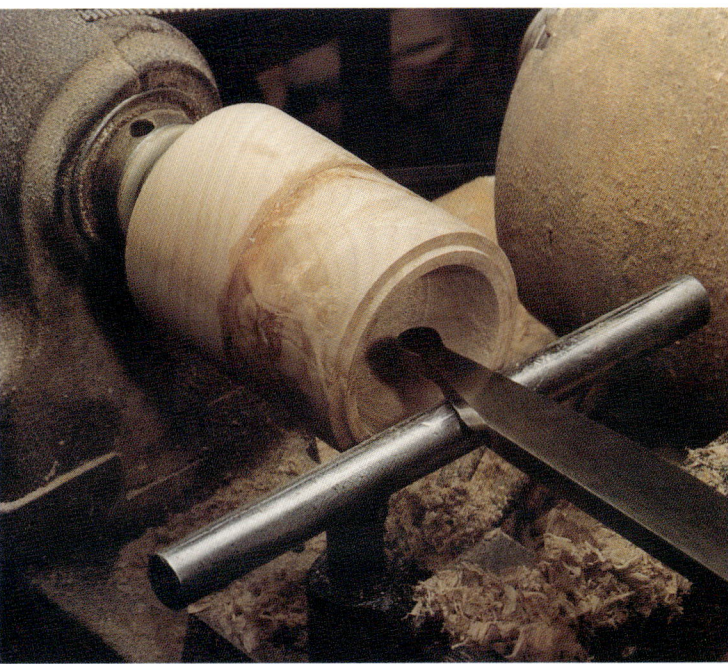

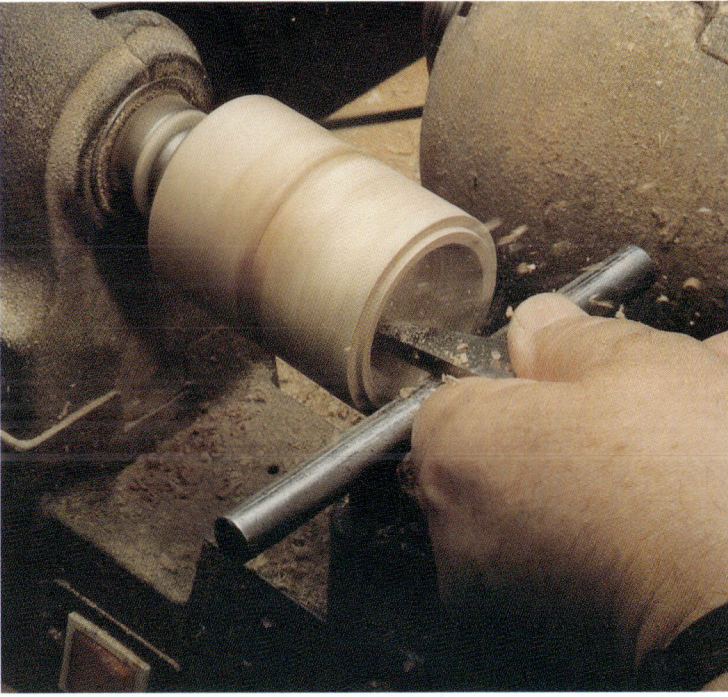

Since I have a rounded top, I want a rounded bottom. Use a round nosed scraper to achieve this.

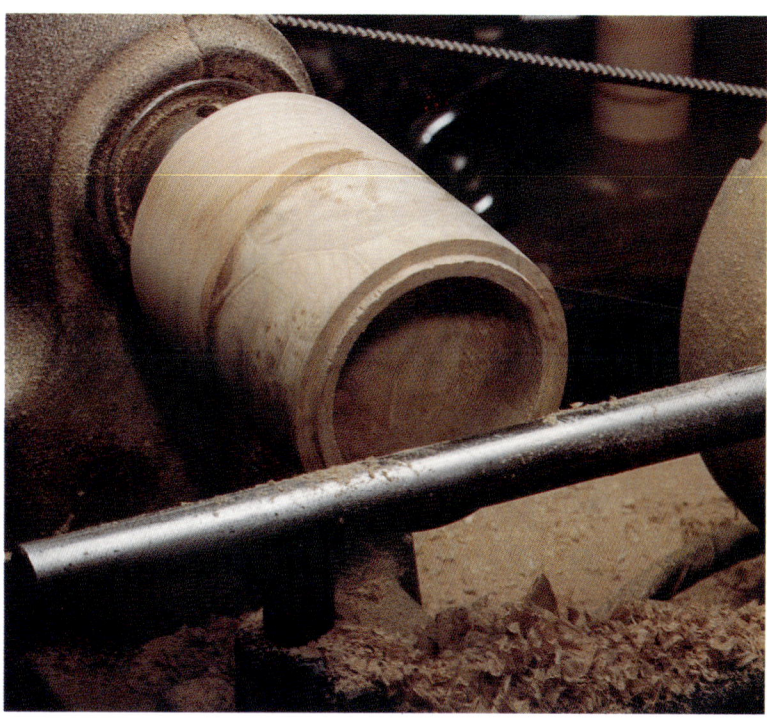

The rounded bottom. The hollowed interior is ready for sanding.

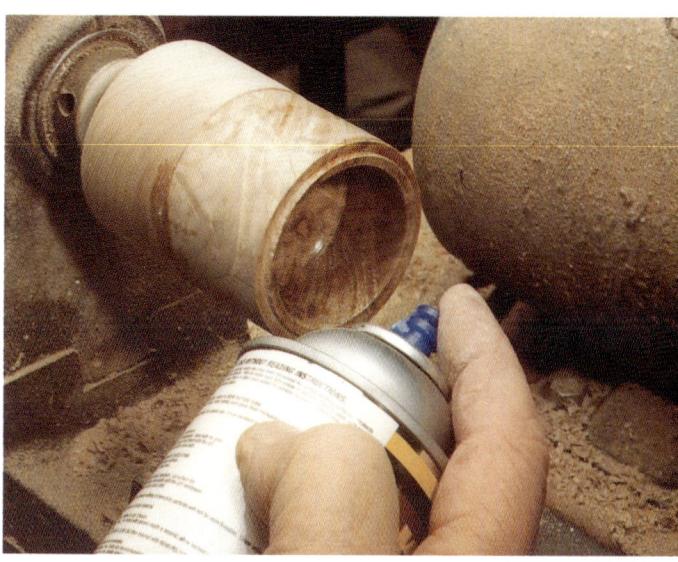

The interior of the base is sealed.

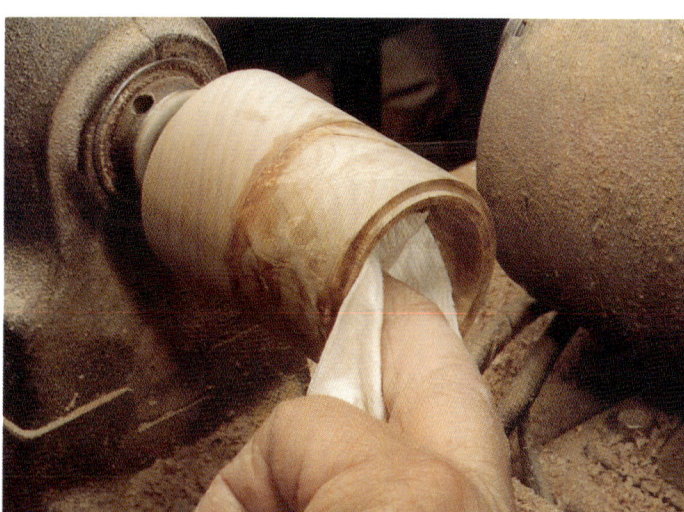

Friction dry the sealer with a paper towel.

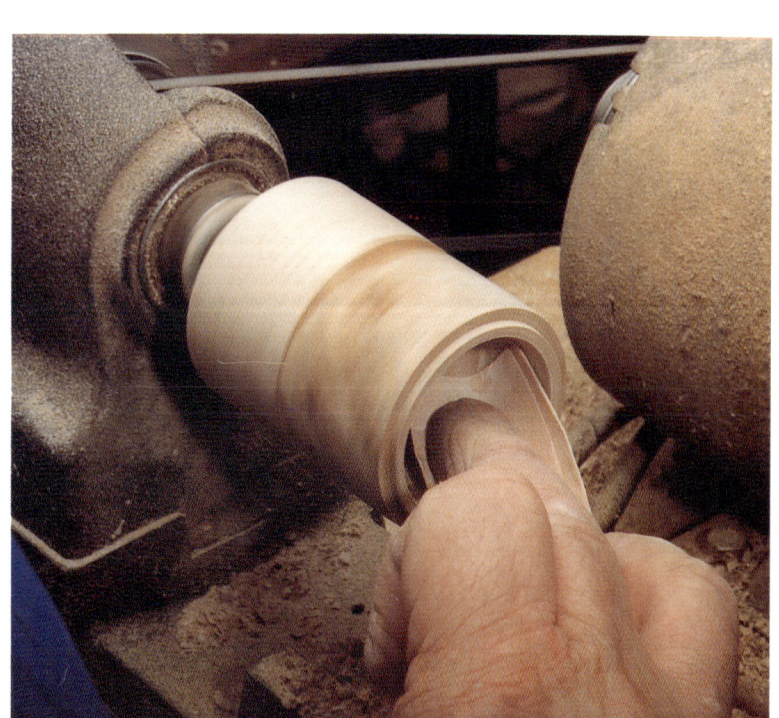

Sand the interior, using 180 grit through 400 grit sandpaper.

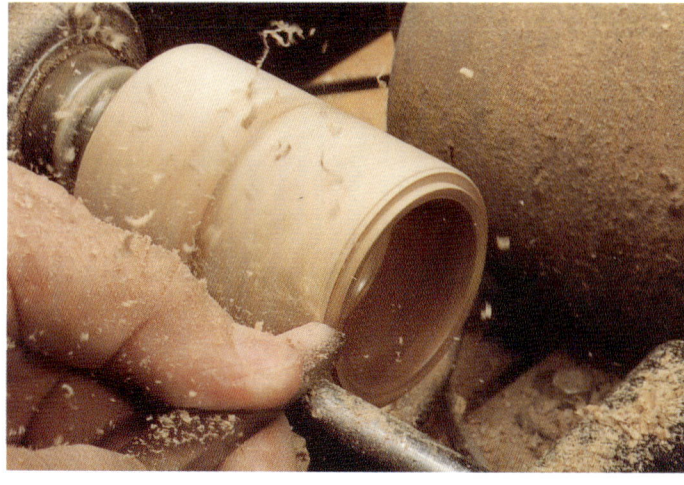

A 3/16" long tenon is cut with the square end scraper or a parting tool.

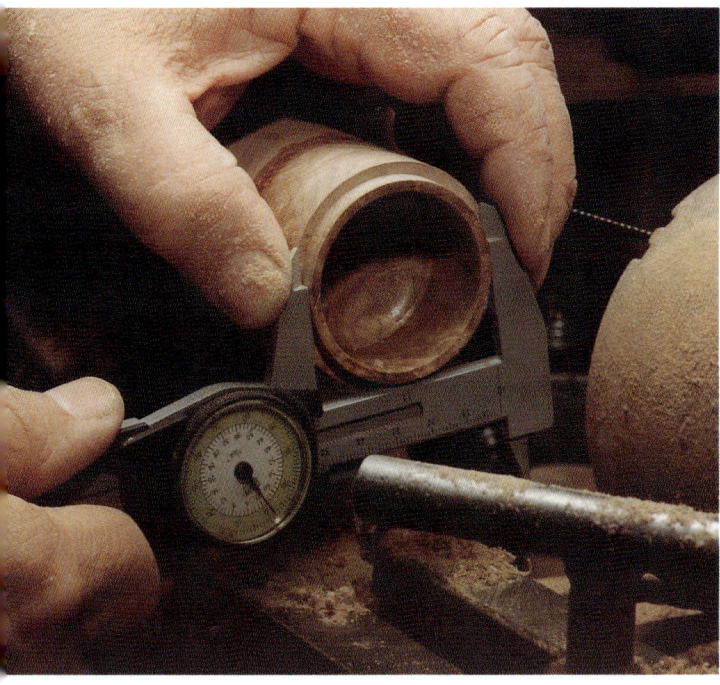

The tenon measures 1.97", as it should.

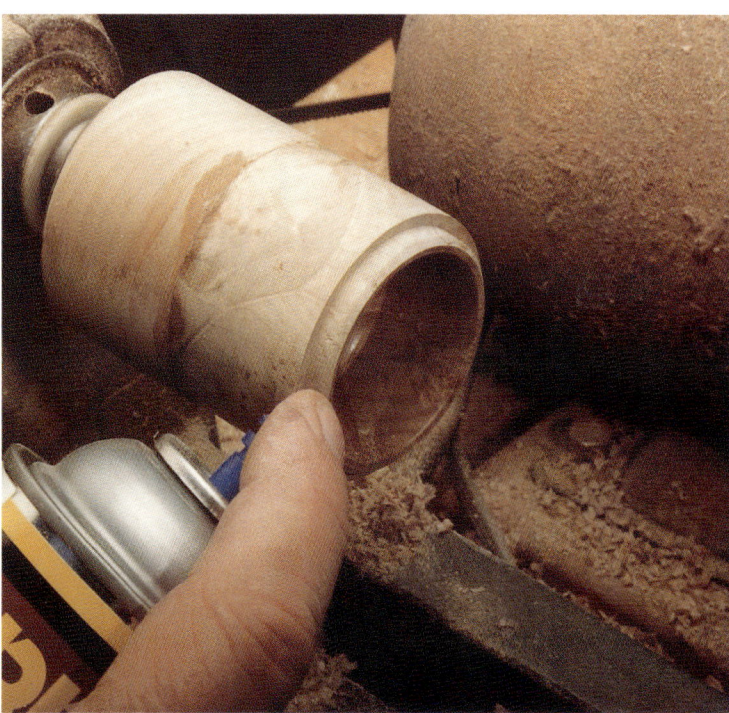

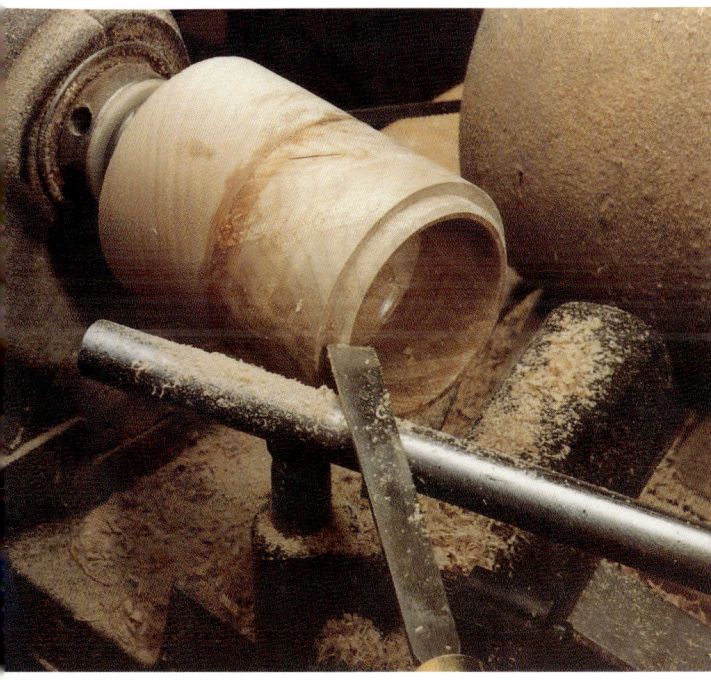

A chamfer is put on the exterior lip.

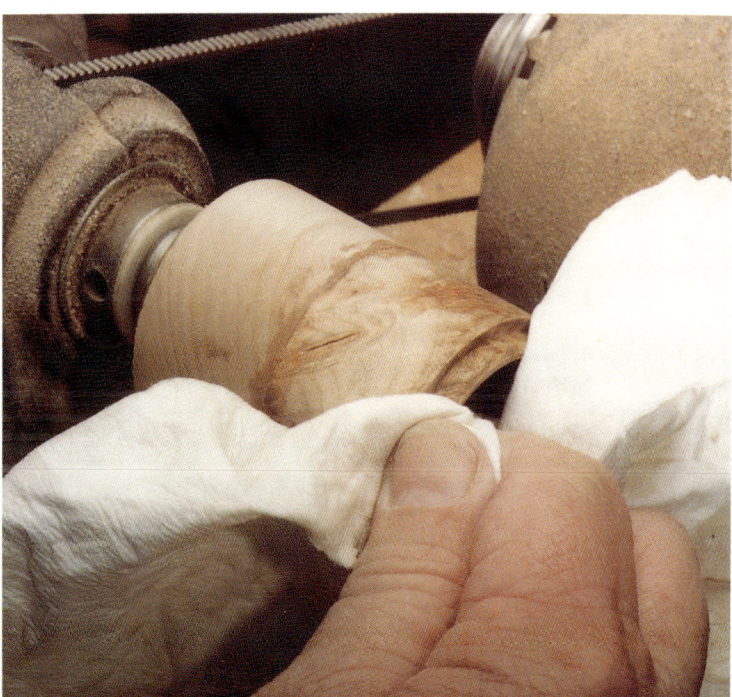

The exterior is sealed and buffed.

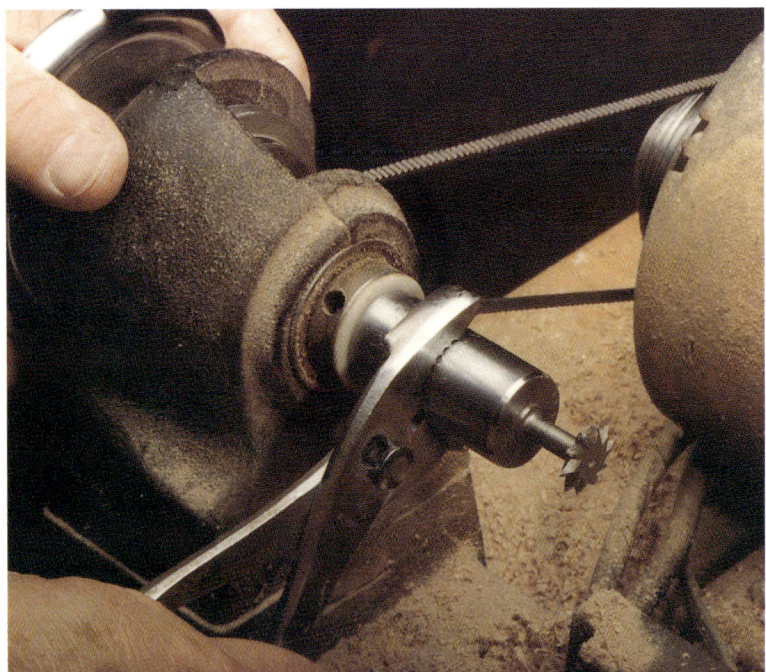

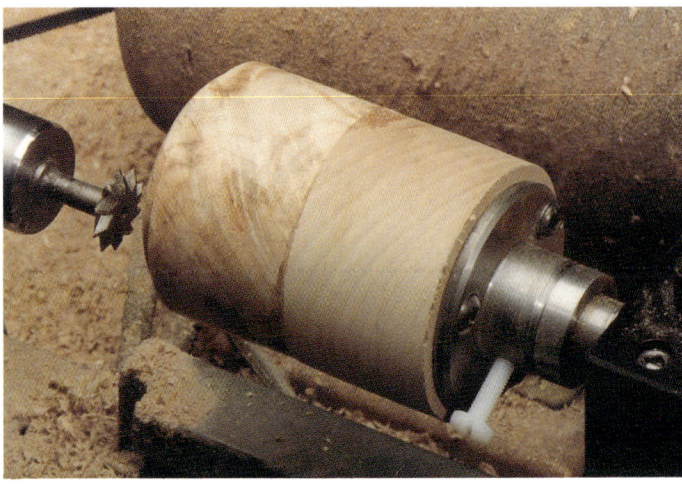

A nylon screw is inserted into the thread on the face plate.

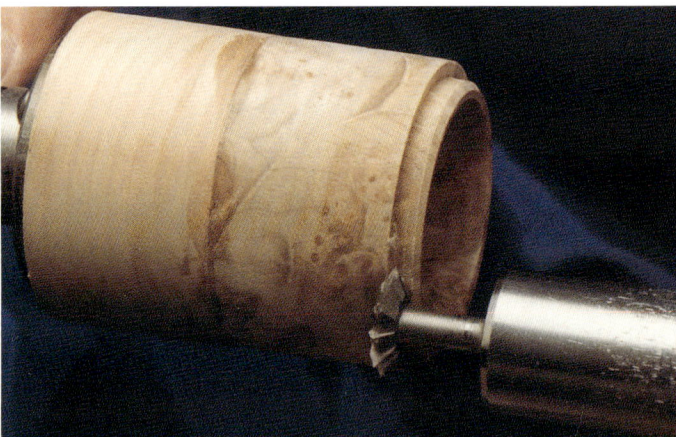

The cross vise is adjusted until the box just touches the cutter.

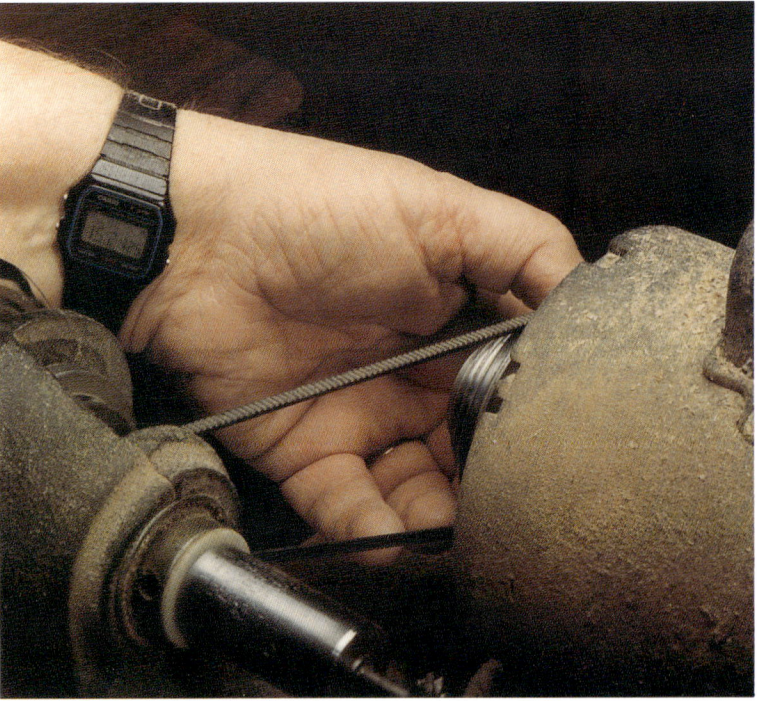

The cutter is tightened and the lathe speed is set to maximum.

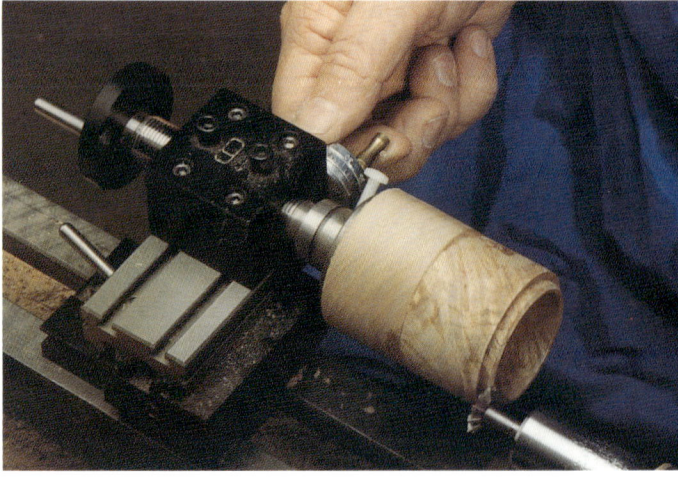

The cross vise is advanced one half turn. The threads are now ready to be cut.

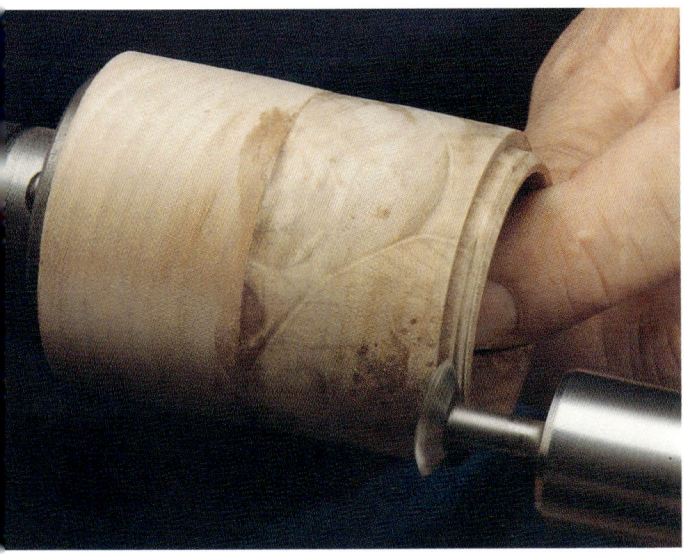

Cutting the threads.

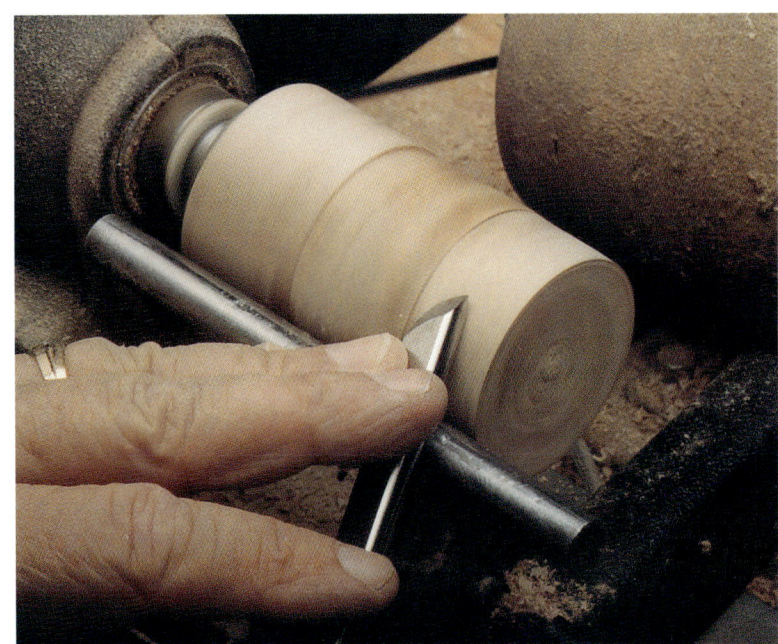

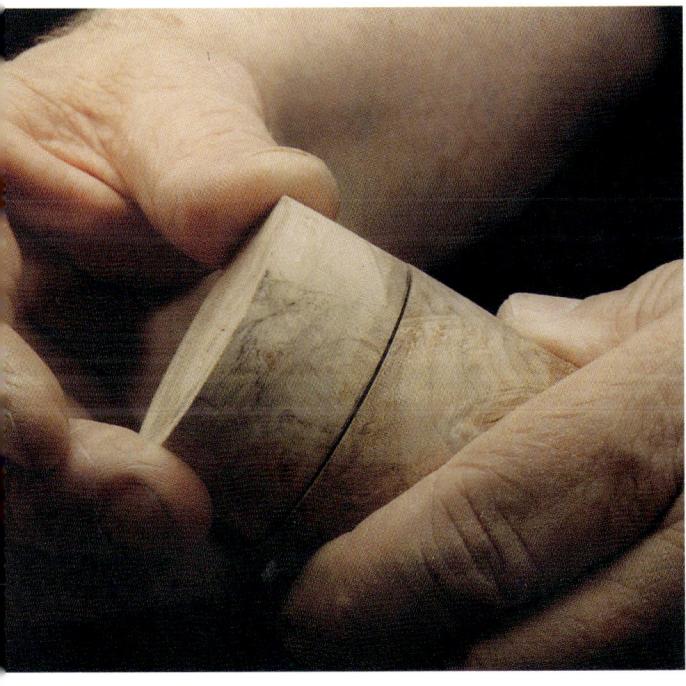

Testing the fit.

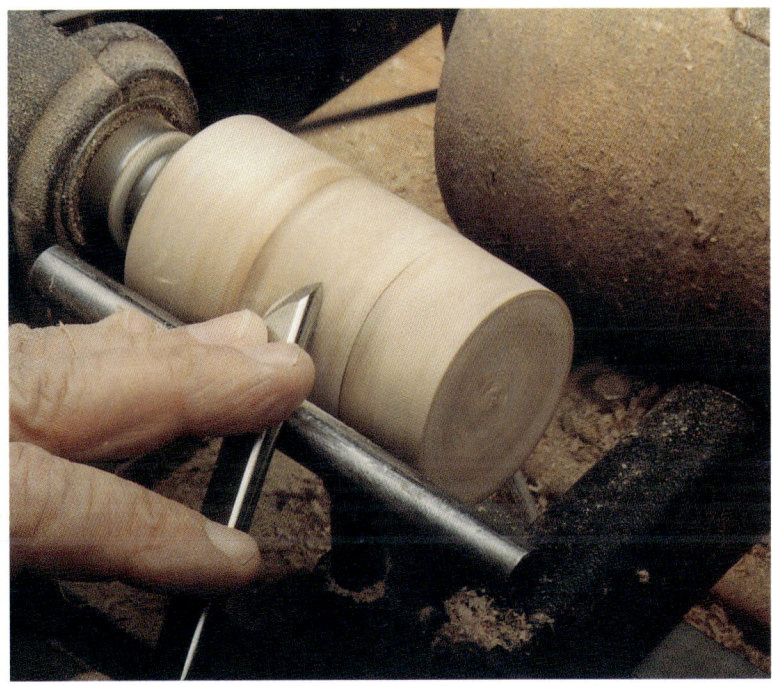

The exterior of the box is ready for final shaping and smoothing with a 1/2" skew chisel.

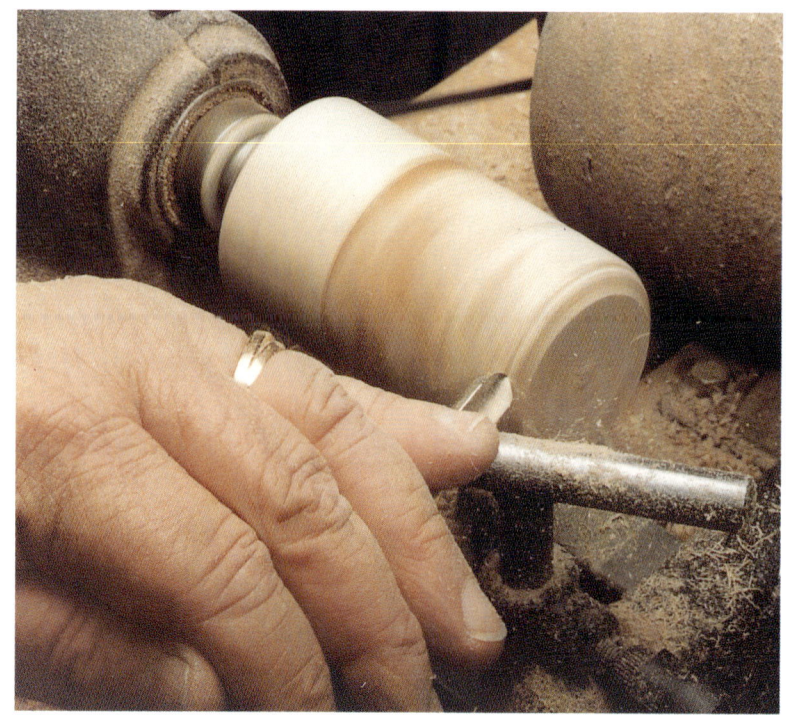

Since the interior is rounded, a rounded profile on the exterior would be appropriate. A 3/8" spindle gouge is an excellent tool for this purpose.

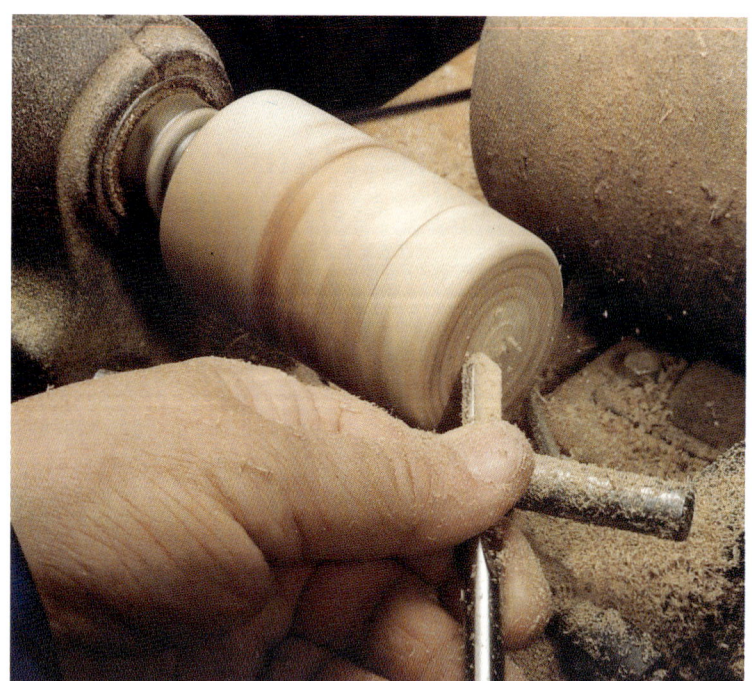

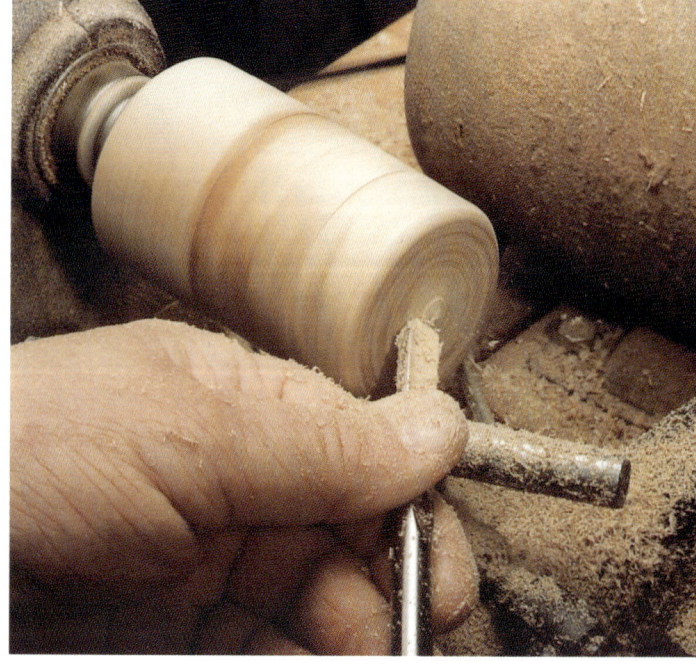

When cutting a curve on the top, pivot from your ankles to get a smooth flowing curve.

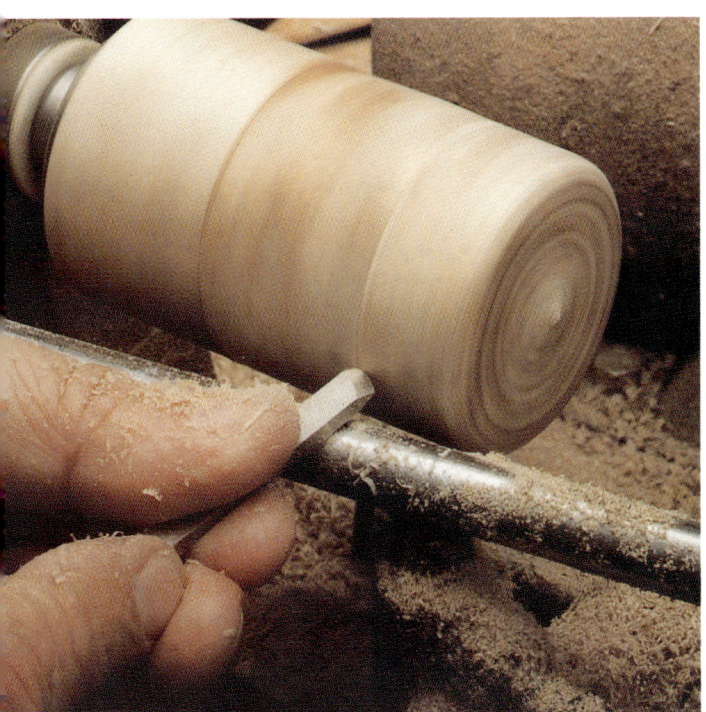 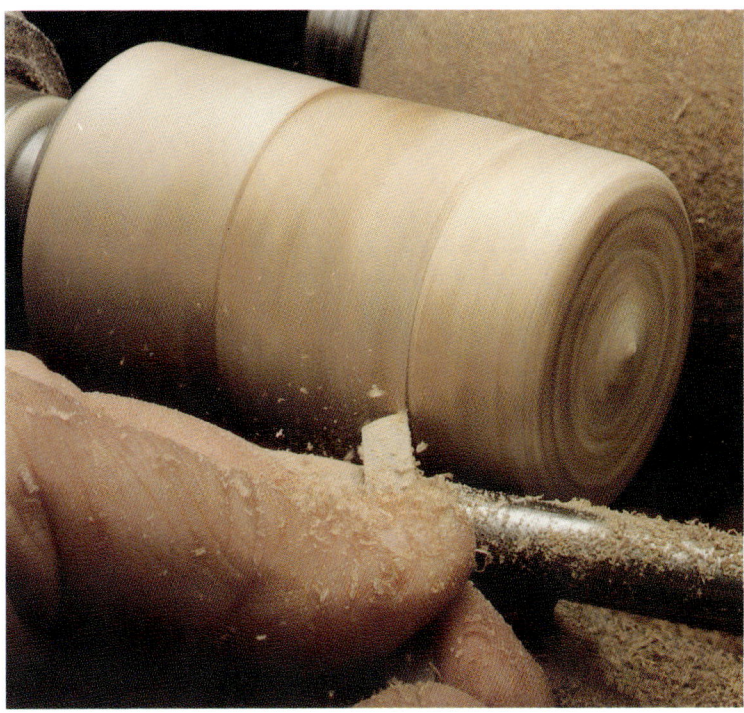

Place a small V groove along the separation line between the lid and the base of the box. A 1/4" skew chisel makes a very sharp V groove.

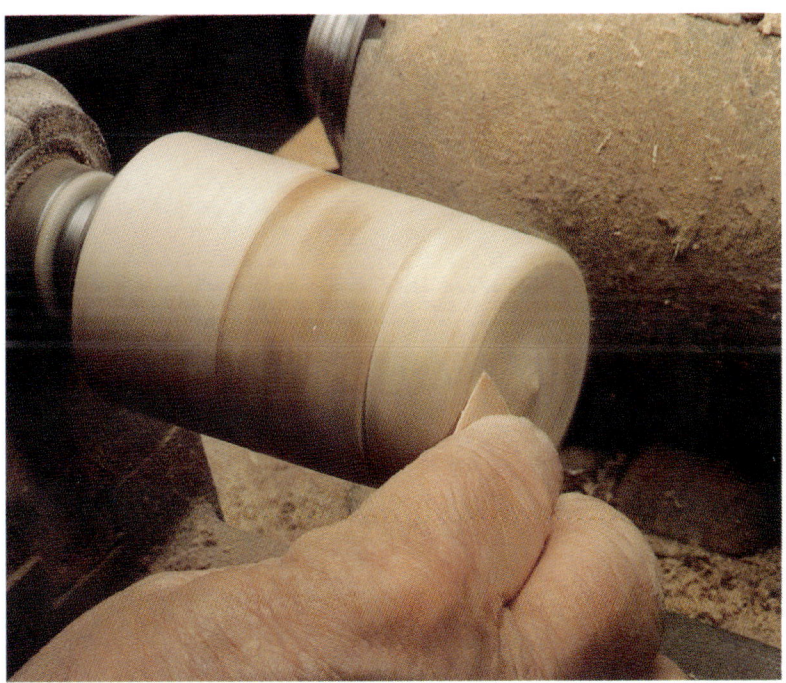

Sand the exterior of the box as before, remembering to stay away from the pointed tip with the coarser paper.

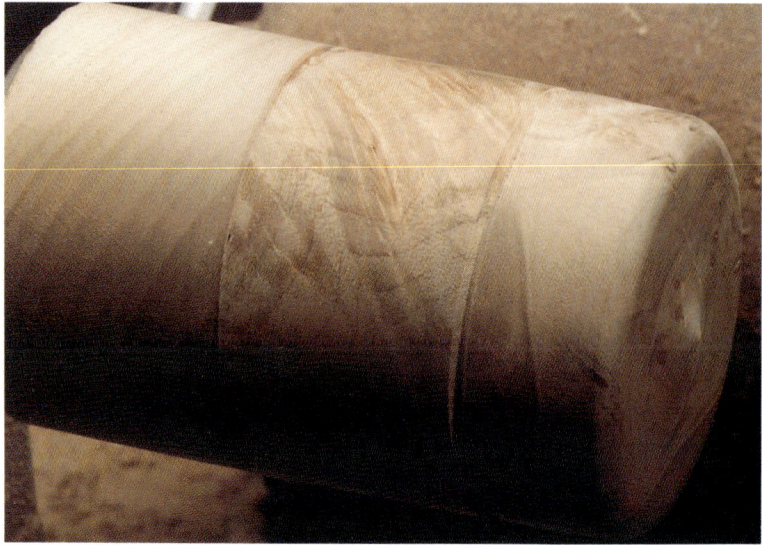

The sanding is complete. On some woods, grain match can not be accomplished, so it is better to leave the joint as it was originally cut.

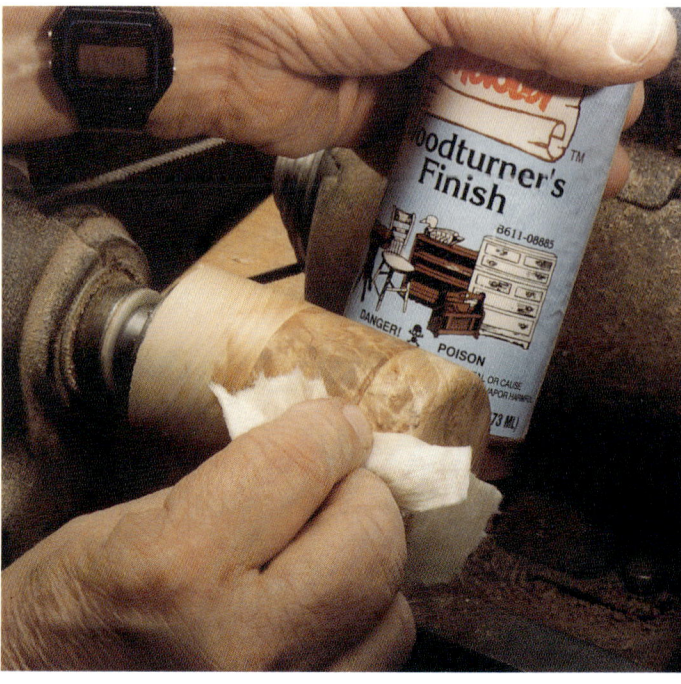

Apply a coat of Woodturner's finish. It gives a very hard surface that is good for boxes as they receive a lot of handling.

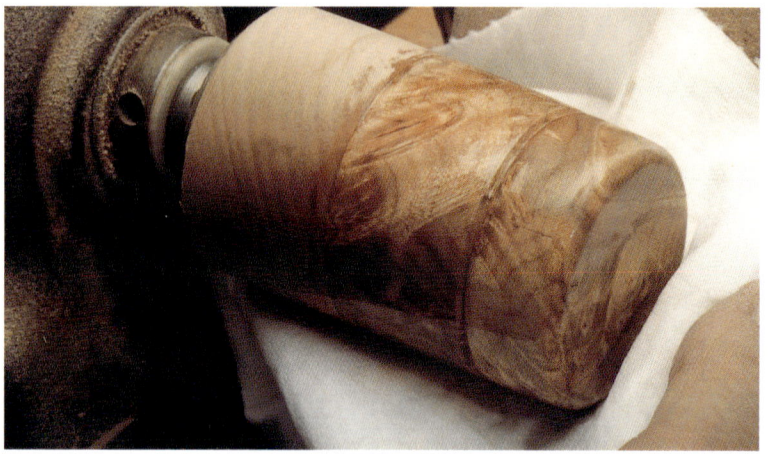

The exterior of the box is sealed with spray lacquer. Buff the lacquer with a paper towel.

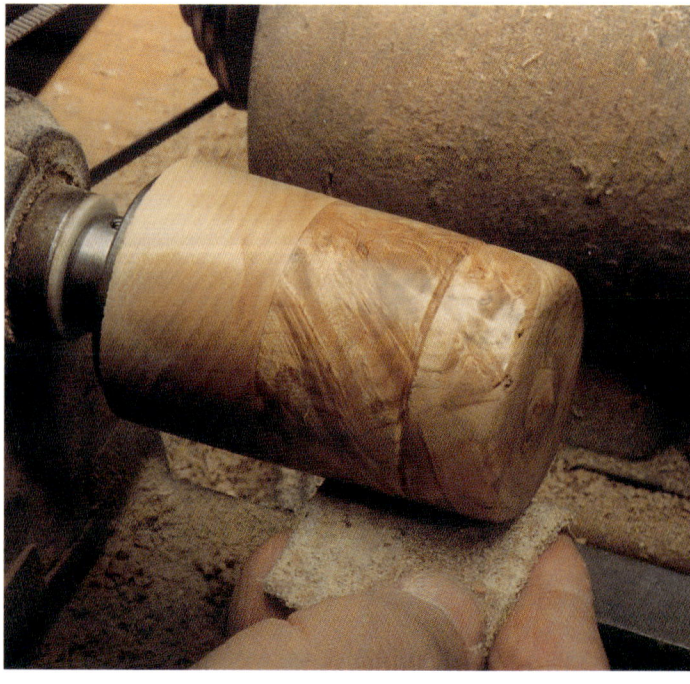

A good quality wax will produce a slightly higher sheen.

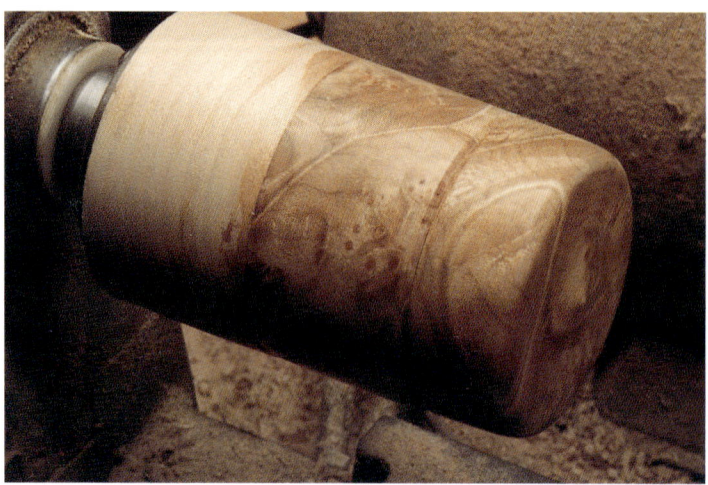

The buffed box.

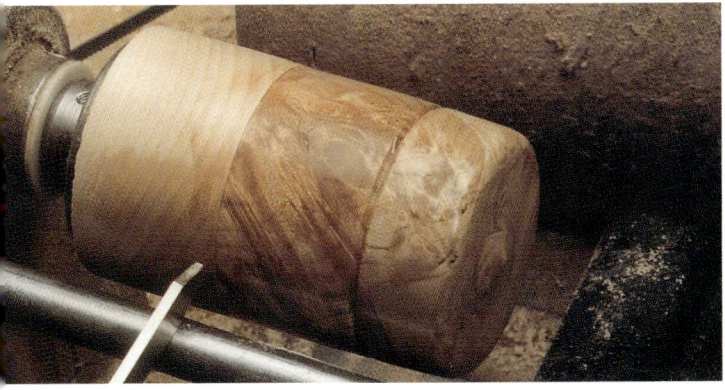

The box is ready to be parted off from the waste block.

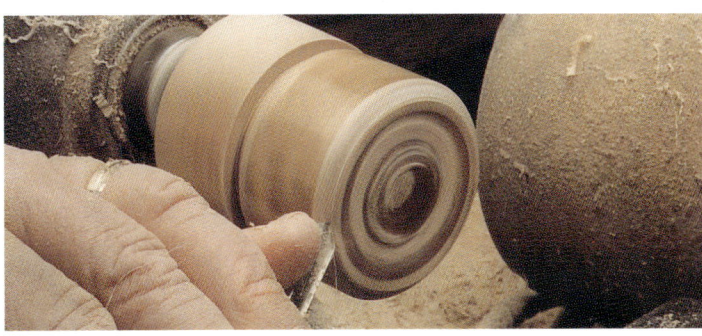

Fitted to the waste block, the bottom can now be finished with a 3/8"spindle gouge.

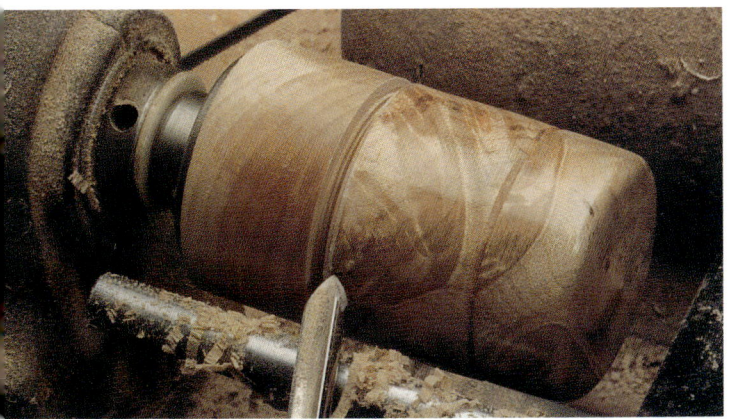

Since the base is going to be slightly rounded, you can use a 3/8" spindle gouge to create the curve before completely separating the box from the waste block.

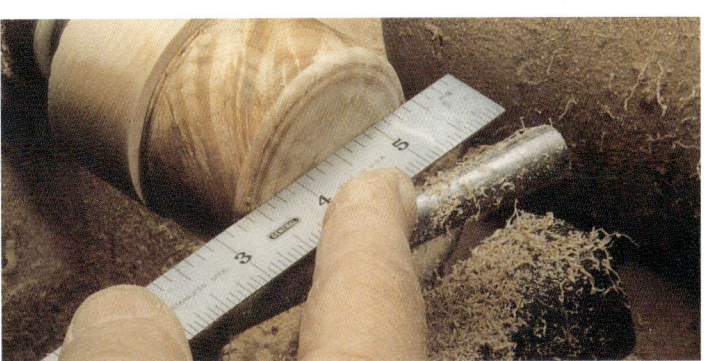

The bottom is slightly concave. The box will rest on its outer edges.

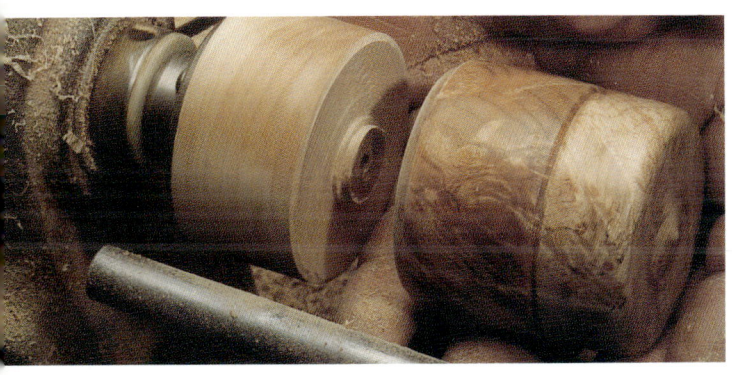

The box is separated.

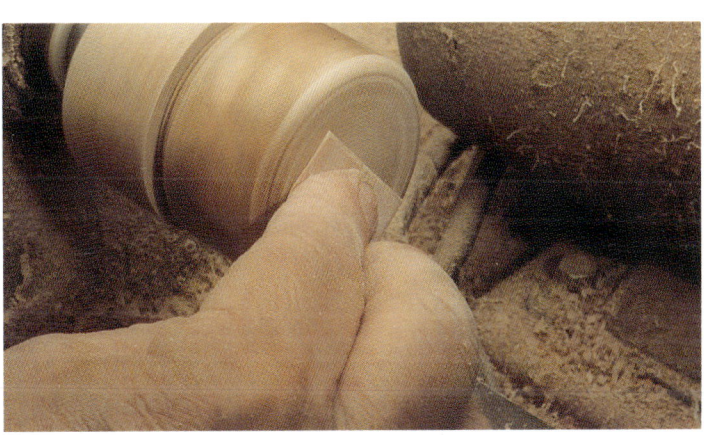

The bottom needs to be sanded and finished, just like the rest of the box.

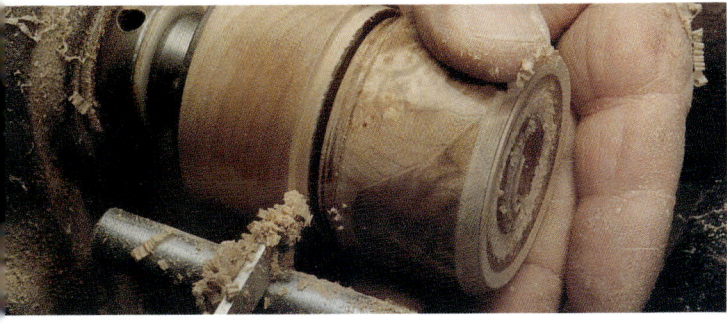

A spigot is cut into the waste block to make a jamb fit chuck.

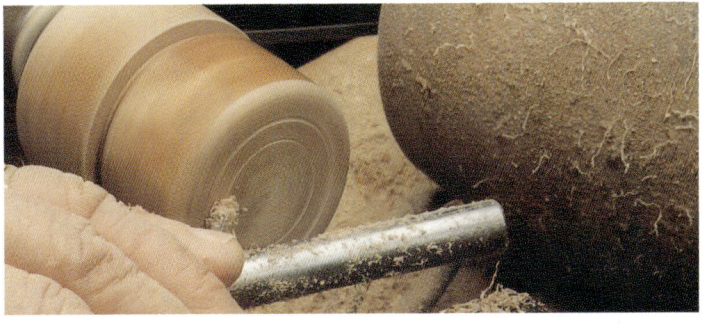

Two small grooves are cut as before.

59

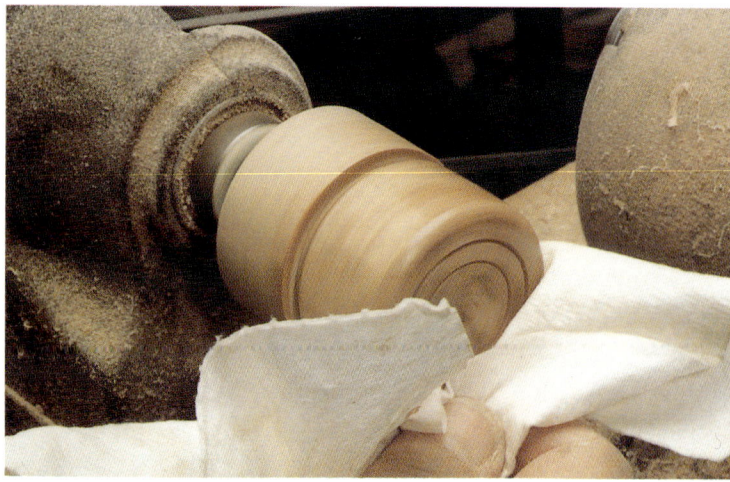

The sanding sealer is applied and friction dried as before.

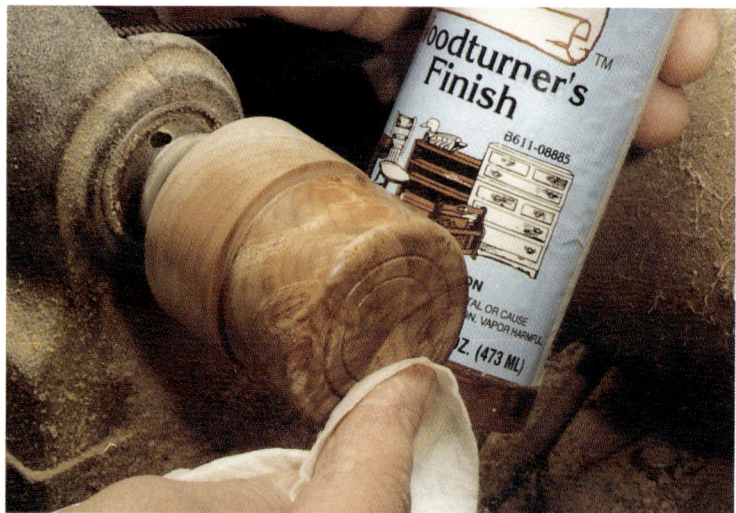

Woodturner's finish is applied to the bottom.

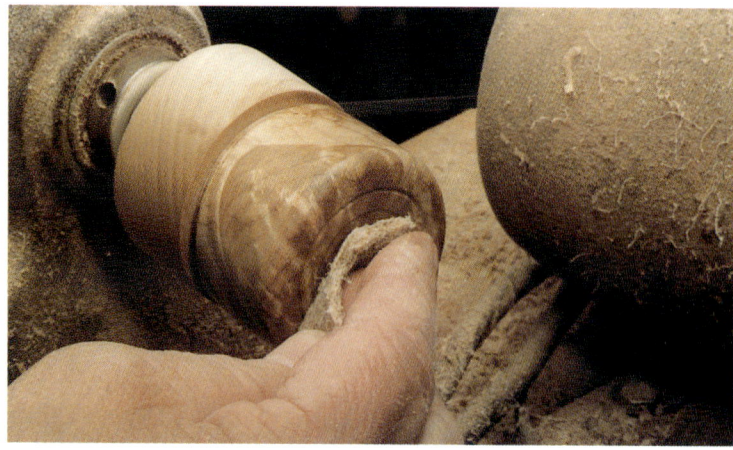

Wax is applied so that the finish on the base of the box matches the rest of the box.

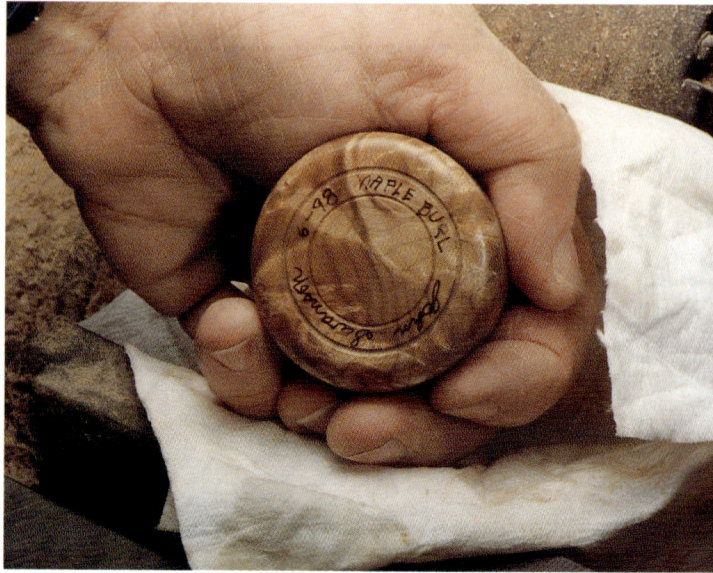

Sign and date your box as a finishing touch.

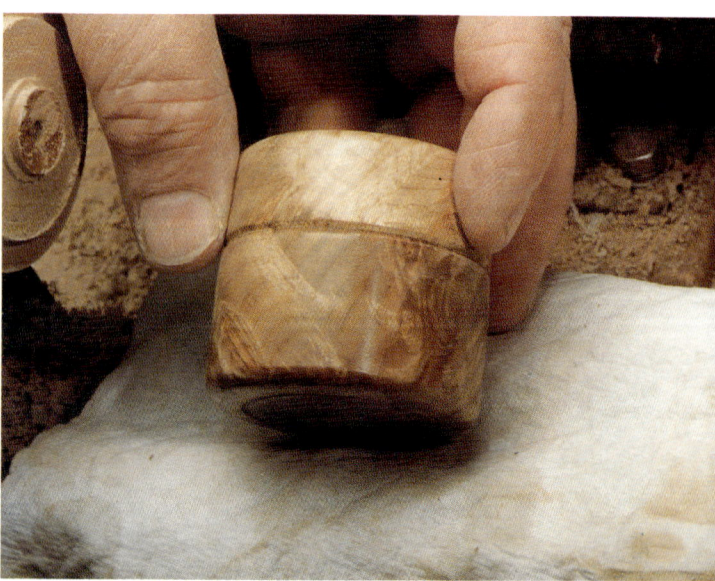

The finished box.

Gallery

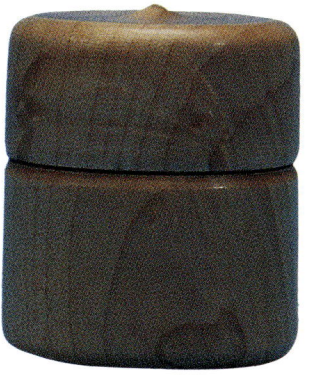

The completed first project.

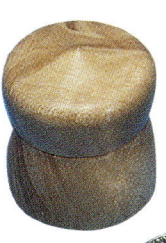

A very small maple burl box.

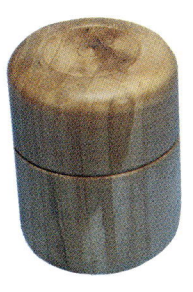

Figured western maple boxes.

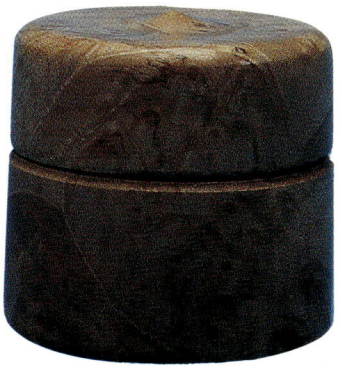

The second completed project.

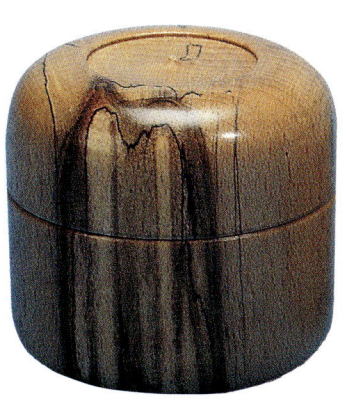
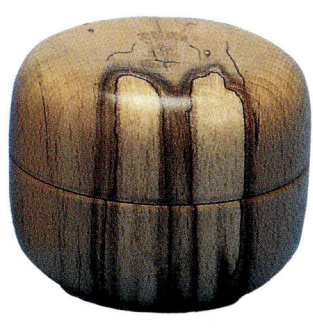

Spalted English beech.

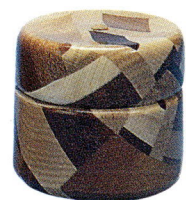

Busy block. Before and after. Not recommended for the beginners.

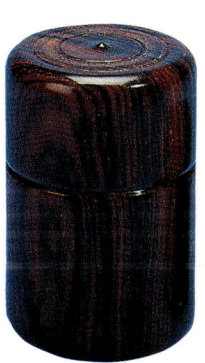
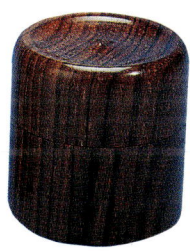

Cocobolo.

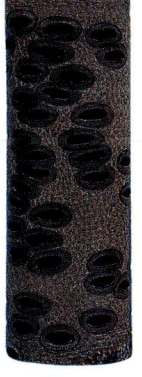
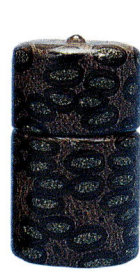

Banksia pod from Australia. Filled with brass shavings and thick CA glue.

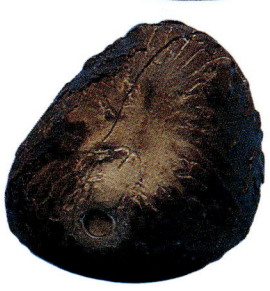
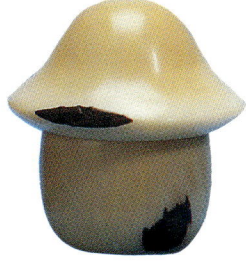

Tagua nuts from Brazil. The box is made from two Togua nuts.

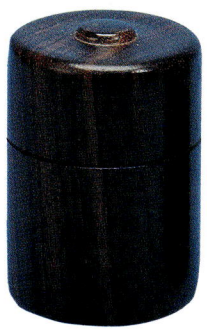
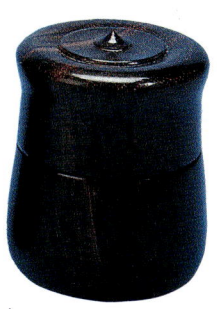

Rosewood.

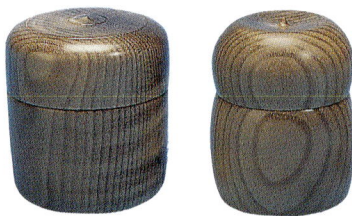
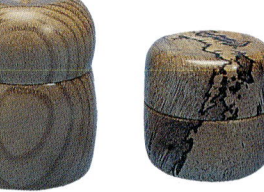

Plain, figured, and spalted myrtlewood.

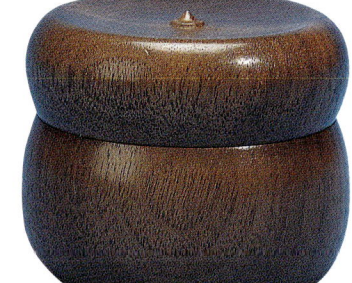

Walnut.

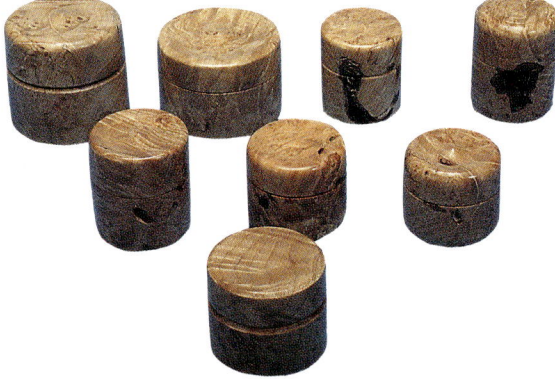

Western maple burl.

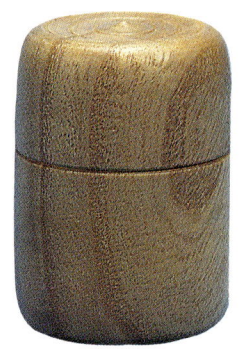

Hawthorne.

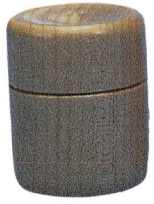
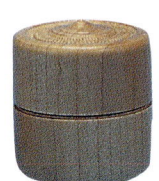
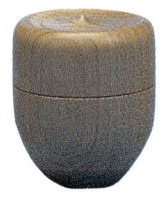
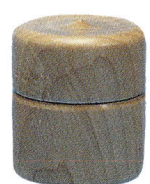
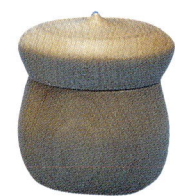

Eastern hard maple.

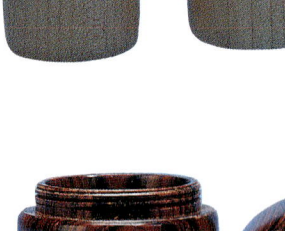
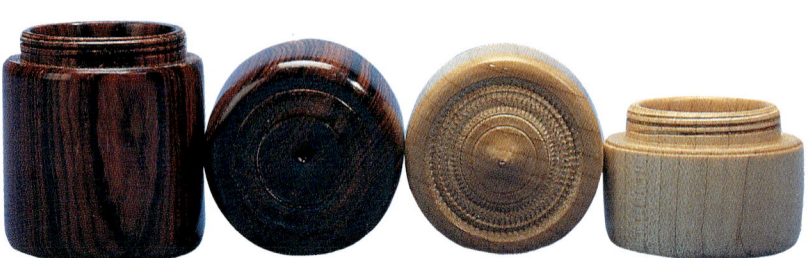

Boxes with chatter-work on the lids.

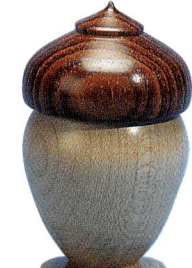

Maple bottom, cocobolo top.

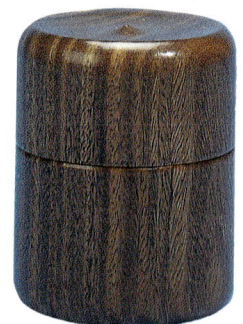

Vera wood.

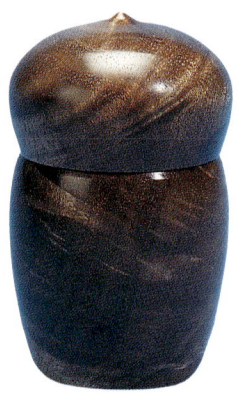

Claro walnut.

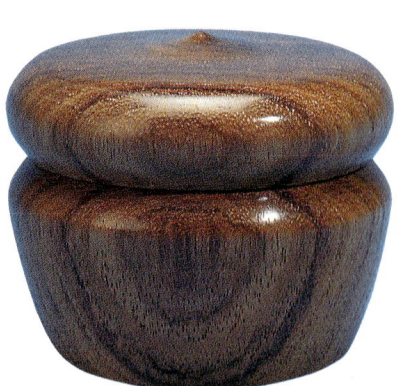

Palissander.

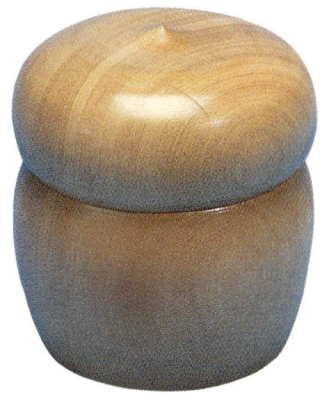

Madrone.

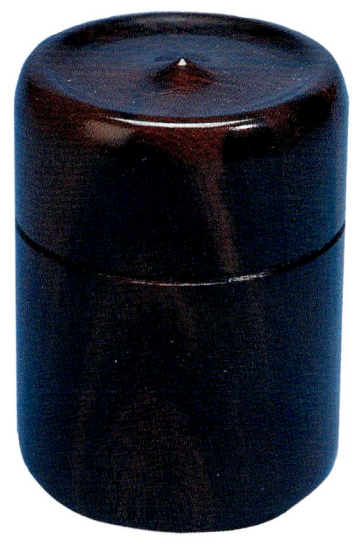

Desert ironwood.

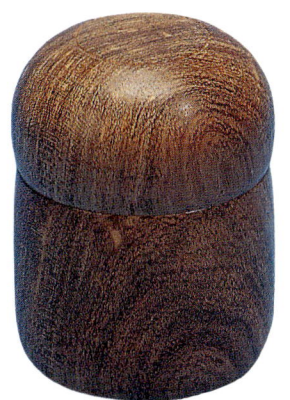

Mesquite.

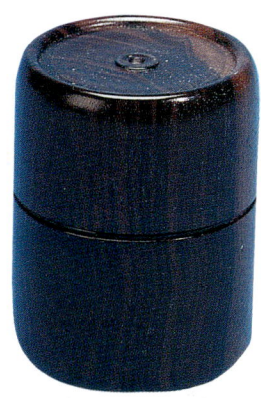

Zircote.

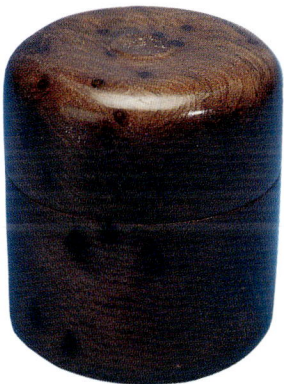

Redwood burl.

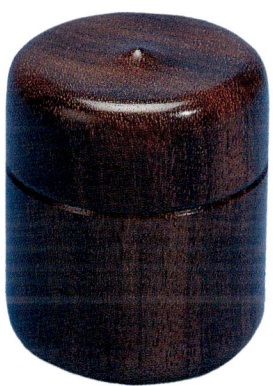

Granadillo.

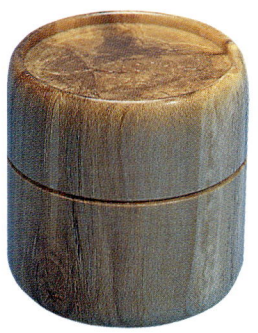

English birch.

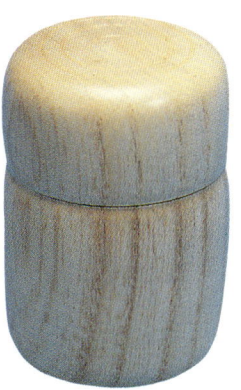

Oregon ash.

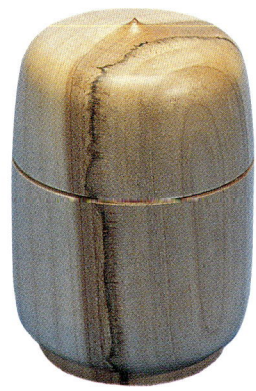

Western maple.

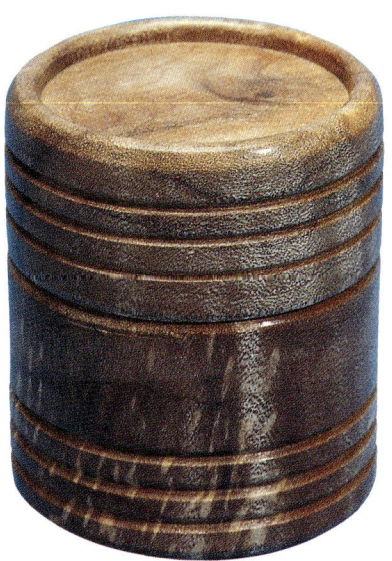

Spalted western maple.

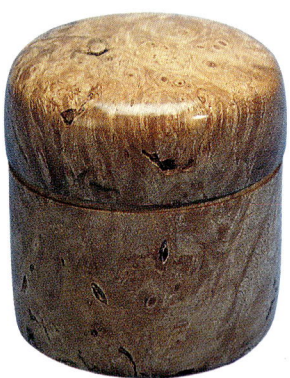

Western maple burl.

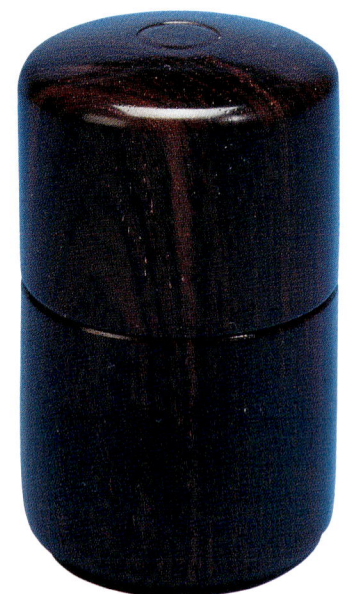

Cocobolo.

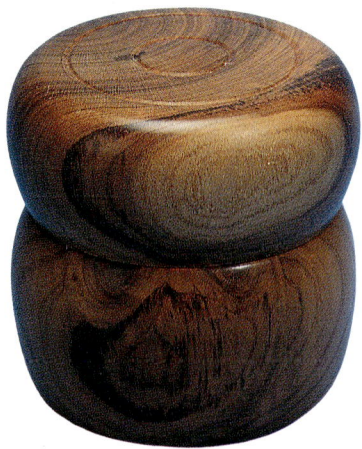

Apricot.

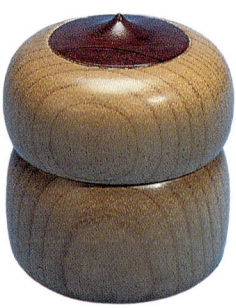

Myrtle wood with
purple heart inlay.